# THE INTERNATIONAL COMMITTEE OF THE RED CROSS AND ITS MANDATE TO PROTECT AND ASSIST

The purpose of this book is to consider the legality of the changing practice of the International Committee of the Red Cross (ICRC). It provides extensive legal analysis of the ICRC as an organisation, legal person, and humanitarian actor. It draws on the law of organisations, International Humanitarian Law, International Human Rights Law, and other relevant branches of international law in order to critically assess the mandate and practice of the ICRC on the ground. The book also draws on more abstract humancentric concepts, including sovereignty as responsibility and human security, in order to assess the development of the concept of humanity for the mandate and practice of the ICRC. Critically this book uses semistructured interviews with ICRC delegates to test the theoretical and doctrinal conclusions. The book provides a unique insight into the work of the ICRC. It also includes a case study of the work of the ICRC in the Democratic Republic of Congo.

Ultimately the book concludes that the ICRC is no longer restricted to the provision of humanitarian assistance on the battlefield. It is increasingly drawn into long-term and extremely complicated conflicts, in which, civilians, soldiers and non-State actors intermingle. In order to remain useful for the people on the ground, therefore, the ICRC is progressively developing its mandate. This book questions whether, on occasion, this could threaten its promise to remain neutral, impartial and independent. Finally, however, it should be said that this author finds that the work of the ICRC is unparalleled on the international stage and its humanitarian mandate is a vital component for those embroiled in the undertaking of and recovery from conflict.

**Volume 68 in the series Studies in International Law**

**Studies in International Law**

**Recent titles in this series**

Statelessness: The Enigma of the International Community
*William E Conklin*

The Reception of Asylum Seekers under International Law: Between Sovereignty and Equality
*Lieneke Slingenberg*

International Law and Child Soldiers
*Gus Waschefort*

The Contractual Nature of the Optional Clause
*Gunnar Törber*

Non-State Actors in International Law
*Edited by Math Noortmann, August Reinisch and Cedric Ryngaert*

The Rule of Law at the National and International Levels: Contestations and Deference
*Edited by Machiko Kanetake and André Nollkaemper*

Human Rights Obligations of Non-State Armed Groups
*Daragh Murray*

Security and International Law
*Edited by Mary E Footer, Julia Schmidt and Nigel D White*

Complicity and its Limits in the Law of International Responsibility
*Vladyslav Lanovoy*

Complicity in International Criminal Law
*Marina Aksenova*

Arctic Law and Governance: The Role of China and Finland
*Edited by Timo Koivurova, Qin Tianbao, Tapio Nykänen and Sébastien Duyck*

States, the Law and Access to Refugee Protection: Fortresses and Fairness
*Edited by Maria O'Sullivan and Dallal Stevens*

Revisiting the Concept of Defence in the Jus ad Bellum: The Dual Face of Defence
*Johanna Friman*

The International Legal Protection of Persons in Humanitarian Crises
*Dug Cubie*

The International Committee of the Red Cross and its Mandate to Protect and Assist: Law and Practice
*Christy Shucksmith*

**For a complete list of titles in this series, see www.bloomsburyprofessional.com/uk/series/studies-in-international-law**

# The International Committee of the Red Cross and its Mandate to Protect and Assist

## Law and Practice

Christy Shucksmith


•HART•
PUBLISHING
OXFORD AND PORTLAND, OREGON
2017

**Hart Publishing**
An imprint of Bloomsbury Publishing Plc

Hart Publishing Ltd
Kemp House
Chawley Park
Cumnor Hill
Oxford OX2 9PH
UK

Bloomsbury Publishing Plc
50 Bedford Square
London
WC1B 3DP
UK

**www.hartpub.co.uk**
**www.bloomsbury.com**

Published in North America (US and Canada) by
Hart Publishing
c/o International Specialized Book Services
920 NE 58th Avenue, Suite 300
Portland, OR 97213-3786
USA

**www.isbs.com**



First published 2017



**British Library Cataloguing-in-Publication Data**
A catalogue record for this book is available from the British Library.

ISBN: HB: 978-1-50990-817-2
ePDF: 978-1-50990-819-6
ePub: 978-1-50990-818-9

**Library of Congress Cataloging-in-Publication Data**

Names: Shucksmith, Christy, author.

Title: The International Committee of the Red Cross and its mandate to protect and assist : law and practice / Christy Shucksmith.

Description: Portland, Oregon : Hart Publishing, 2017. | Series: Studies in international law ; volume 68 | Includes bibliographical references and index. | Description based on print version record and CIP data provided by publisher; resource not viewed.

Identifiers: LCCN 2017013633 (print) | LCCN 2017015470 (ebook) | ISBN 9781509908189 (Epub) | ISBN 9781509908172 (hardback : alk. paper)

Subjects: LCSH: International Committee of the Red Cross. | Responsibility to protect (International law)

Classification: LCC KZ6469.I58 (ebook) | LCC KZ6469.I58 S48 2017 (print) | DDC 344.03/1772—dc23

LC record available at https://lccn.loc.gov/2017013633

Typeset by Compuscript Ltd, Shannon
Printed and bound in Great Britain by Lightning Source UK Ltd

# *Acknowledgements*

I would like to thank Professor Nigel White for his unwavering support throughout my time at the University of Nottingham, and previously, the University of Sheffield. I would also like to extend warm thanks to Sandesh Sivakumaran, my second supervisor, for his invaluable insights.

The Economic and Social Research Council (ESRC) funded my MA Sociolegal and Criminological Research and PhD. The ESRC Research Training and Support Grant funded my interviews at the ICRC headquarters in Geneva in April 2014. I was also supported by the College Research Fund at the University of Lincoln to undertake a second set of interviews in 2016. I was a Visiting Research Student at the Australian National University in September–October 2013, which was collectively funded by a University of Nottingham Graduate School Travel Prize and the Reuben-Lipman Travel Scholarship, School of Law. I would like to thank Dr Hitoshi Nasu and David Letts for their time and resources whilst I was in Canberra.

A great many thanks are owed to the participants in my interviews from the ICRC. Although they remain anonymous, I would like to recognise their invaluable insights and contributions, without which this book would not be possible.

I want to thank my family and fiancé who have always encouraged and supported me.

# Contents

*Acknowledgements* .......... v
*List of Abbreviations* .......... xi
*Table of Cases* .......... xv
*Introduction* .......... xvii

**1. The Governance of the International Red Cross and Red Crescent Movement** .......... 1
I. The Statutes of the IRCRCM .......... 2
II. The Governing Bodies of the IRCRCM .......... 3
A. The International Conference of the IRCRCM .......... 3
B. The Council of Delegates .......... 7
C. The Standing Commission of the IRCRCM .......... 8
III. The Components of the IRCRCM .......... 9
A. Red Cross and Red Crescent National Societies .......... 9
B. International Federation of the Red Cross .......... 10
C. International Committee of the Red Cross .......... 11
D. The Budget of the ICRC .......... 16
E. Increasing Cooperation within the Movement .......... 16
IV. Conclusion .......... 17

**2. The Legal Nature and International Legal Personality of the ICRC** .......... 19
I. Introduction .......... 19
II. What Kind of Organisation is the ICRC? .......... 21
A. Intergovernmental Organisations .......... 23
B. Private International Organisations .......... 29
C. Non-Governmental Organisations .......... 31
D. The ICRC as a Sui Generis Entity .......... 33
III. International Legal Personality .......... 34
A. The ICRC was Intended to be an International Legal Person .......... 41
B. The ICRC is in Fact an International Legal Person .......... 42
C. The Functions and Rights of the ICRC .......... 45
D. Conclusions on Personality .......... 50
IV. Conclusion .......... 54

**3. The ICRC and International Law in Armed Conflict and other Situations of Violence** .......... 57
I. Introduction .......... 57
II. The Normative and Legal Development of the Laws of War .......... 58
III. International Human Rights Law in Armed Conflict .......... 64
IV. Conclusion .......... 73

**4. Humanity as a Core Principle of the Red Cross and Red Crescent Movement** .......... 75
I. Introduction .......... 75
II. Humanity .......... 76
III. History of the Principle of Humanity .......... 78
IV. The IRCRCM Definition of Humanity .......... 80
V. Judicial Interpretations of Humanity .......... 81
VI. Neutrality and Independence .......... 84
VII. Conclusion .......... 88

**5. New Humanitarian Horizons for the ICRC** .......... 91
I. Introduction .......... 91
II. Sovereignty as Responsibility .......... 93
III. Human Security .......... 97
A. The Process of Defining Human Security .......... 98
IV. The Relationship between Human Security, International Human Rights Law and International Humanitarian Law .......... 107
V. Conclusion .......... 111

**6. Interviews with the ICRC** .......... 113
I. Introduction .......... 113
II. Reflections by Delegates on the Mandate .......... 114
III. Early Recovery .......... 122
A. Food, Health, Shelter and Water .......... 124
IV. Economic Security .......... 128
V. Local Ownership .......... 134
A. ICRC and National Societies .......... 139
VI. Prevention of Conflict .......... 141
VII. Conclusion .......... 143

**Case Study: Accounts of ICRC Delegates on the Democratic Republic of Congo** .......... 147
I. Introduction .......... 147
II. The Congo Wars in Brief: 1994–2016 .......... 149
III. The ICRC in the Democratic Republic of Congo .......... 155
A. Traditional Roles: Dissemination and Detention .......... 158

IV. ICRC and Health ........ 159
A. Sexual Violence and Psychosocial Support ........ 162
V. Food Security and Water ........ 164
VI. Economic Security ........ 166
VII. ICRC and the Congolese National Society ........ 171
VIII. Conclusion ........ 172

**Conclusion** ........ 175

**Appendix 1: Interview Guide 2016** ........ 185
**Appendix 2: Interview Guide 2014** ........ 191

*Bibliography* ........ 195
*Index* ........ 211

# *List of Abbreviations*

| | |
|---|---|
| **Additional Protocol I** | Protocol Additional to the Geneva Conventions of 12 August 1949, and relating to the Protection of Victims of International Armed Conflicts, (Protocol I), (adopted 8 June 1977, entered into force 7 December 1978) 1125 UNTS 3 |
| **Additional Protocol II** | Protocol Additional to the Geneva Conventions of 12 August 1949, and relating to the Protection of Victims of Non-International Armed Conflicts (Protocol II), (adopted 8 June 1977, entered into force 7 December 1978) 1125 UNTS 609 |
| **ALC** | Armée de Libération du Congo |
| **ANC** | Armée Nationale Congolaise |
| **ANT** | Armée Nationale Tchadienne (Chad National Army) |
| **CESCR** | Committee on Economic, Social and Cultural Rights |
| **CNDP** | National Congress for the Defence of the People |
| **DRC** | Democratic Republic of Congo |
| **ECOSOC** | Economic and Social Council |
| **ECOWAS** | Economic Community of West African States |
| **EU** | European Union |
| **FAA** | Angolan Armed Forces |
| **FAB** | Forces Armées Burundaises |
| **FAC** | Forces Armées Congolaises |
| **FARDC** | Forces Armées de la République Démocratique du Congo |
| **FDLR** | Democratic Forces for the Liberation of Rwanda |
| **Geneva Convention I** | Convention (I) for the Amelioration of the Condition of the Wounded and Sick in Armed Forces in the Field. Geneva (adopted 12 August 1949, entered into force 21 October 1950) 75 UNTS 31 |

| | |
|---|---|
| **Geneva Convention II** | Convention (II) for the Amelioration of the Condition of Wounded, Sick and Shipwrecked Members of Armed Forces at Sea. Geneva (adopted 12 August 1949, entered into force 21 October 1950) 75 UNTS 85 |
| **Geneva Convention III** | Convention (III) relative to the Treatment of Prisoners of War. Geneva (adopted 12 August 1949, entered into force 21 October 1950) 75 UNTS 135 |
| **Geneva Convention IV** | Convention (IV) relative to the Protection of Civilian Persons in Time of War. Geneva (adopted 12 August 1949, entered into force 21 October 1950) 75 UNTS 287 |
| **HDR** | Human Development Report |
| **ICC** | International Criminal Court |
| **ICCPR** | International Covenant on Civil and Political Rights (adopted 16 December 1966, entered into force 23 March 1976) 999 UNTS 171 |
| **ICESCR** | International Covenant on Economic Social and Cultural Rights (adopted 16 December 1966, entered into force 3 January 1976) 993 UNTS 3 |
| **ICISS** | International Commission on Intervention and State Sovereignty 2001 |
| **ICJ** | International Court of Justice |
| **ICRC** | International Committee of the Red Cross |
| **ICTY** | International Criminal Tribunal for the Former Yugoslavia |
| **IDP** | Internally Displaced Person |
| **IFRC** | International Federation of Red Cross and Red Crescent Societies |
| **IHL** | International Humanitarian Law |
| **IHRL** | International Human Rights Law |
| **ILC** | International Law Commission |
| **ILP** | International Legal Personality |
| **INTELSAT** | International Telecommunications Satellite Organisations |
| **IRCRCM** | International Red Cross and Red Crescent Movement |
| **IRRC** | International Review of the Red Cross |

| | |
|---|---|
| **MEI** | Microeconomic Initiative |
| **MLC** | Movement for the Liberation of Congo |
| **MONUC** | United Nations Organization Mission in the Democratic Republic of the Congo |
| **MONUSCO** | United Nations Organization Stabilization Mission in the Democratic Republic of the Congo |
| **NGO** | Non-Governmental Organisation |
| **NSA** | Non-State Actor |
| **OAU** | Organisation for African Union |
| **OECD** | Organisation for Economic Co-operation and Development |
| **OSCE** | Organization for Security and Co-operation in Europe |
| **PCIJ** | Permanent Court of International Justice |
| **RCD** | Rally for Congolese Dialogue |
| **RPF** | Rwandan Patriotic Front |
| **RtoP** | Responsibility to Protect |
| **TWAIL** | Third World Approaches to International Law |
| **UDHR** | Universal Declaration on Human Rights (adopted 10 December 1948 UNGA Res 217 A(III)) |
| **UN** | United Nations |
| **UN Charter** | United Nations, Charter of the United Nations, 24 October 1945, 1 UNTS XVI |
| **UNDP** | United Nations Development Programme |
| **UNESCO** | United Nations Educational, Scientific and Cultural Organization |
| **UNHCHR** | United Nations High Commissioner for Human Rights |
| **UNSCR** | United Nations Security Council Resolution |
| **UNTFHS** | United Nations Trust Fund for Human Security |
| **UPDF** | Uganda People's Defence Force |

# *Table of Cases*

Abella v Argentina, Case 11.137, Rep No 5/97, IAmCtHR OEA/Ser. L/V/II.95 Doc. 7 Rev (13 April 1998) ........ 83
Al-Skeini v Secretary of State for Defence [2007] UKHL 26 ........ 83
Application of the International Convention on the Elimination of all Forms of Racial Discrimination (Georgia v Russian Federation), Provisional Measures Order, ICJ Reports 2008 ........ 65
Case Concerning Armed Activities on the Territory of the Congo (DRC v Uganda), Judgment, ICJ Reports 2005 ........ 65, 83
Case Concerning Military and Paramilitary Activities in and against Nicaragua (Merits) [1986] ICJ Rep 14 ........ 81, 82
Case Concerning the Application of the Convention on the Prevention and Punishment of the Crime of Genocide (Bosnia and Herzegovina v Serbia and Montenegro) (Judgment) [2007] ICJ Rep 43 ........ 83
Case Concerning the Payments of Various Serbian Loans Issued in France (Judgment), 1929 PCIJ Series A No 20 ........ 19
Case of the SS Lotus, 1927 PCIJ (Ser A) No 10, 18 ........ 19
Certain Expenses of the United Nations (Article 17 paragraph 2 of the Charter), (Advisory Opinion) [1962] ICJ Rep 151 ........ 36
Corfu Channel Case (UK v Albania) (Merits) [1949] ICJ Rep 4, 22 ........ 81
Interpretation of the Agreement of 25 March 1951 between the WHO and the Egypt Case [1980] ICJ Rep 73 ........ 37
Isayeva v Russia App No 57950/00 (Judgment) (ECtHR 24 February 2005) ........ 83
La Grand (Germany v United States of America) (Judgment) [2001] ICJ Rep 466 ........ 21
Legal Consequences for States of the Continued Presence of South Africa in Namibia (South West Africa) notwithstanding Security Council Resolution 276 (1970) (Advisory Opinion) [1971] ICJ Rep 16 ........ 37
Legal Consequences of the Construction of a Wall in the Occupied Palestinian Territory, (Advisory Opinion) [2004] ICJ Rep 136 ........ 65, 83
Legality of the Threat or Use of Nuclear Weapons (Advisory Opinion) [1996] ICJ Rep 679 ........ 83
Legality of the Use by a State of Nuclear Weapons in Armed Conflict, (Advisory Opinion) [1996] ICJ Rep 226 ........ 37, 38, 65
Prosecutor v Furundžija (Judgment) ICTY IT-95-17/1-T (10 December 1998) ........ 83
Prosecutor v Kordic and Cerkez (Judgment/Trial Chamber) ICTY IT-95-14/2 (26 February 2001) ........ 83
Prosecutor v Martić (Review of the Indictment Pursuant to Rule 61) ICTY No IT-95-11-R61 (13 March 1996) ........ 83
Prosecutor v Simić et al (Decision on the Prosecution Motion under Rule 73 for a Rule Concerning the Testimony of a Witness), ICTY Trial Chamber 27 July 1999 ........ 34, 44, 45, 50

Prosecutor v Tadic (Appeals Chamber Decision on Defence Motion for Interlocutory Appeal on Jurisdiction) ICTY-1995-IT-49-I-AR72 (2 October 1995)..........73, 79, 83
Prosecutor v Tharcisse Muvunyi (Judgment and Sentence), ICTR-2000-55A-T (12 September 2006)..........45
Reparations for injuries suffered in the service of the United Nations, Advisory Opinion ICJ Reports, 1949, 174..........20, 35, 36, 37, 38, 40, 51, 176
South West Africa (Second Phase) ICJ Rep 1966 p 6..........37, 82

# *Introduction*

## I. THE DAY-TO-DAY IMPACT OF ARMED CONFLICT ON LOCAL PEOPLE AND COMMUNITIES

In armed conflicts today, individuals, villages, religious and other groups, within the same local community, take up arms to fight against each other. Conflicts increasingly continue for months, years, even decades, and have consequences that reach far beyond the battlefield. Protracted armed conflict tears the social fabric of communities and, until it can be repaired, feelings of resentment and fear continue to permeate the delicate balance between war and peace.[1] The term 'protracted armed conflict' refers to conflicts distinguishable by their *intractability* and *longevity*.[2] The International Committee of the Red Cross (ICRC) recently reported that 'situations in which the ICRC works may, strictly speaking, be more accurately described using phrases like *countries of chronic conflicts* or *long multiple conflicts*'.[3] The report includes the Democratic Republic of the Congo (DRC) in this definition. Recent and ongoing conflicts in, for example, the DRC, Syria and Ukraine have a myriad of different causes, from ethnic rivalries, to extremes of poverty and wealth, dictatorship and religious rifts.[4] The days of battlefield conflicts where soldiers, their weapons and equipment fought away from civilians are gone. The 'end' to the battle was traditionally signified physically on the battlefield or through a declaration of peace by the government of each warring state. The human effects of conflict are, today, more pronounced than ever, not least for civilians.

The birth of the Red Cross in 1863 was galvanised by the 'desire to bring assistance without discrimination to the wounded on the battlefield' and

[1] CT Call (ed), *Building States to Build Peace* (International Peace Institute, Boulder, CO, Lynne Rienner, 2008) 1.

[2] O Ramsbotham, 'The Analysis of Protracted Social Conflict: A Tribute to Edward Azar' (2005) 31(1) *Review of International Studies* 109–26.

[3] ICRC, 'Protracted Conflict and Humanitarian Action: Some Recent ICRC Experiences' (Geneva, ICRC, 2016) 10.

[4] The situations in the DRC, Ukraine and Syria are complex and continually evolving, reputable news sites such as Reuters provide up-to-date reports; for information on current armed conflicts see 'Global Peace Index 2016' (Institute for Economics and Peace) static.visionofhumanity.org/sites/default/files/GPI%202016%20Report_2.pdf: 'The index gauges global peace using three broad themes: the level of safety and security in society; the extent of domestic or international conflict; and the degree of militarization.'

'to prevent and alleviate human suffering wherever it may be found'.[5] Over time, the changing nature of conflict has forced the ICRC to adapt its protection and assistance roles to respond to the human needs on the ground. In the DRC, for example, which is the case study in this book, the ICRC currently promotes respect for international humanitarian law (IHL) in the treatment of civilians and detainees and helps those adversely affected by conflict and internal violence to survive and become self-sufficient. It also improves water supply and sanitation, strengthens healthcare for the wounded and sick, including victims of sexual violence, and reunites families.[6] The list of activities undertaken by the ICRC, publicised on its website, is ever growing and currently includes: healthcare in danger; economic security; water and habitat; family links; detention/helping detainees; protection of civilians; addressing sexual violence; building respect for the law; cooperation with national societies; enabling people with disabilities; forensic science and humanitarian assistance; humanitarian diplomacy; migration; landmine action; and working with the corporate sector.[7]

In non-international armed conflicts (NIACs), the people involved in the fighting also live amongst the civilian population. The sight of 'perpetrators' of violence walking the streets is not unusual, neighbours become threats and the 'danger' is within, rather than outside, the local community.[8] In a personal interview with a woman whose sons were disappeared in the town of Granada, Colombia, Romero wrote her story:

> I came from church and they killed a girl in the street. The killer said to me: 'pretend that nothing happened'. And I did exactly that: I walked over the corpse and I went home, with pain in my soul and immense fear, but I just walked away from that place.[9]

When conflicts occur within states experiences like these are not unusual; insecurity permeates every waking moment of people's daily lives and they live with the fear and possibility of conflict recurring.

Unfortunately, current international responses fail to adequately address insecurity at ground level, for people living through and after the conflict. The inability or unwillingness of the state to provide for basic human needs and take steps to build sustainable peace preclude

[5] A Durand, *The International Committee of the Red Cross: From Sarajevo to Hiroshima* (Geneva, ICRC, 1981) 55; See also R Coupland, 'Humanity: What Is it and How Does it Influence International Law?' (2001) 83 *IRRC* 969.

[6] 'The ICRC in DR Congo' (ICRC) www.icrc.org/eng/where-we-work/africa/congo-kinshasa/index.jsp.

[7] ICRC 'What We Do', https://www.icrc.org/en/what-we-do.

[8] GR Romero, 'Voices Around Us: Memory and Community Empowerment in Reconstruction Efforts in Colombia' (2012) 6 *International Journal of Transitional Justice* 1, 5.

[9] ibid.

the realisation of human security in the day-to-day lives of people on the ground. In fact, despite the proliferation of so-called peace-building mandates operationalised by the UN, states that do not return to conflict 'have suffered extremely high rates of "violent crime", with people forced to endure levels of insecurity exceeding those in many officially designated conflict zones'.[10] The physical effects of conflicts, such as the destruction of schools, hospitals, bridges and so on, force people to live without running water, mains electricity, access to basic social services, and supply of basic goods.[11] These consequences leave people unable to provide for their families and children. In these circumstances the desperate need for 'normality' saturates everyday life. In addition, weak or non-existent government institutions compound economic distress, a culture of impunity and a breakdown in the rule of law. Worryingly some estimates are that half of all 'post-conflict' countries return to war within five years.[12]

This book examines whether, and the extent to which, the ICRC is extending its work beyond the activities anticipated by the drafters of the Geneva Conventions I, II, III and IV 1949 and the Statutes of the International Red Cross and Red Crescent Movement (IRCRCM).[13] The IRCRCM Statutes state that the ICRC may undertake humanitarian initiative as a neutral intermediary[14] and, broadly speaking, provide the ICRC with a mandate to act in situations not amounting to armed conflict, that is, situations outside of the threshold for IHL. The ICRC Statutes are adopted at the International Conference of the Red Cross and Red Crescent, which takes place every four years, between state parties to the Geneva Conventions I, II, III and IV 1949 and components of the IRCRCM, including the ICRC, the International Federation of Red Cross and Red Crescent Societies (IFRC) and national societies. In addition, the 'right' to undertake

10 R Jenkins, *Peace Building: From Concept to Commission* (London, Routledge, 2013) 1.

11 R Paris, *At War's End: Building Peace after Civil Conflict* (Cambridge, Cambridge University Press, 2004) 3.

12 PA Collier and M Söderbom, Working Paper, Centre for the Study of African Economics (Department of Economics, Oxford University) WPS/2006-12, August 17 in T Call and EM Cousens, 'Ending Wars and Building Peace: International Responses to War Torn Societies' (2008) 9 *International Studies Perspectives* 1, 5.

13 Convention (I) for the Amelioration of the Condition of the Wounded and Sick in Armed Forces in the Field. Geneva (adopted 12 August 1949, entered into force 21 October 1950) Art 9 (Geneva Convention I); Convention (II) for the Amelioration of the Condition of Wounded, Sick and Shipwrecked Members of Armed Forces at Sea. Geneva (adopted 12 August 1949, entered into force 21 October 1950) Art 9 (Geneva Convention II); Convention (III) relative to the Treatment of Prisoners of War. Geneva (adopted 12 August 1949, entered into force 21 October 1950) Art 9 (Geneva Convention III); Convention (IV) relative to the Protection of Civilian Persons in Time of War. Geneva (adopted 12 August 1949, entered into force 21 October 1950) Art 10 (Geneva Convention IV); Statutes of the ICRC, 3 October 2013 (the present Statutes replace the Statutes of the International Committee of the Red Cross of 21 June 1973, revised on 20 July 1998 and 8 May 2003) (Statutes of the ICRC) Art 4.

14 IRCRCM Statutes, Art 5(3).

its mandate in a given state is provided for in Headquarters Agreements, which the ICRC negotiates and agrees on an individual and confidential basis with each host state.[15] The process of adopting the Headquarters Agreements and their content is discussed in chapters 1 and 2.

In addition to its mandate to act in certain circumstances and undertake specific humanitarian activities, the ICRC is guided by the Fundamental Principles of the IRCRCM, which include humanity, impartiality, neutrality, independence, voluntary service, unity and universality. Humanity and impartiality form the 'core' of the ICRC, that is, they aim to bring humanity to those affected by armed conflict and they do so for anyone who needs help. The principles of neutrality and independence are 'tools' to secure host state consent to their presence and work.

This research focuses on the ICRC, as a unique international actor with its own history, organisational structure and legal framework. The ICRC has a mandate to provide protection and assistance to victims of armed conflict. Protection refers to its work of visiting people deprived of their liberty; and work on behalf of civilian victims and the restoration of family links during and after conflict. Assistance, on the other hand, refers to the provision of humanitarian aid to 'various categories' of victims. The ICRC has undertaken increasing roles within states and the protracted nature of many current armed conflicts has necessitated the development of activities and projects that address the ongoing needs of civilians and those involved in conflicts. This means, for example, that, instead of the ICRC providing food parcels, the ICRC is now facilitating farming projects,[16] so that food production within a given community is sustainable, both during and after conflict.[17] The specifics of such projects will be examined in chapter 6 and the case study. They are by no means indicative of projects being undertaken in every situation in which the ICRC has a presence but are, nevertheless, specific examples of the changes in the work of the ICRC since the drafting of the Geneva Conventions I, II, III and IV 1949.

It follows from the introductory remarks that the primary or 'meta' research question asks: to what extent have the protection and assistance activities of the ICRC expanded beyond those provided for in the mandate

[15] eg 'Agreement between the International Committee of the Red Cross and the Swiss Federal Council to Determine the Legal Status of the Committee in Switzerland' (1993) 293 IRRC 152, Arts 1, 3, 4 and 5 (Headquarters Agreement 1993).

[16] 'Central African Republic: ICRC Boosts Farming in West of Country' (14 June 2014) News Release.14/103 https://www.icrc.org/eng/resources/documents/news-release/2014/06-14-central-african-republic-farming-west.htm; SC Ocampo, 'Relinking with ICRC at Ground Level', *The Phillipine Star*, 1 June 2013, www.philstar.com/opinion/2013/06/01/948687/relinking-icrc; 'How the Red Cross and Somali Red Crescent are Fighting Famine' (25 July 2011) blogs.redcross.org.uk/emergencies/2011/07/red-cross-somalia-red-crescent-famine/.

[17] SR Ratner, 'Law Promotion Beyond Law Talk: The Red Cross, Persuasion, and the Laws of War' (2011) 22(2) *European Journal of International Law* 459, 460.

of the ICRC, contained in the Geneva Conventions I, II, III and IV 1949 and the IRCRCM Statutes?

This opens up a number of sub-questions that ask: is there a disjunction between the legal mandate that the ICRC has and the way that it operates in practice? Is the ICRC an organisation with international legal personality (ILP)? To what extent have the developments in IHL and international human rights law (IHRL), since the drafting of the Geneva Conventions I, II, III and IV 1949, affected the ICRC and its place within general international law? To what extent has the definition of humanity developed beyond a recognised principle behind IHL? In particular, have significant developments in the latter part of the twentieth century, including sovereignty as responsibility, human security and responsibility to protect (RtoP) informed the mandate and practice of the ICRC? Is the ICRC's reputation for neutrality and independence, or will it become, compromised if the ICRC continues to develop its activities? And, if so, is it possible that states will choose to deny access to the ICRC.

## II. METHODOLOGY

This research presents an objective legal analysis of the ICRC as an organisation and an international legal person. It also makes an original academic contribution to the understanding of its mandate and current practice in armed conflicts and other situations of violence. This includes the post-conflict or recovery phase. This book deploys a combination of research methods, including doctrinal, theoretical and empirical methods, to answer the research questions above. The empirical methods, specifically, are interviews with ICRC delegates who currently work at the Geneva-based headquarters but who have experience in the field. The recruitment, interviewing and analysis methodology is outlined later in the methodology.

The Geneva Conventions I, II, III and IV 1949 and the IRCRCM Statutes should be understood as living instruments, designed to allow the ICRC to respond to the humanitarian needs on the ground in different situations. Indeed, the adoption of Additional Protocols I and II 1977 and the publication of the 'ICRC Study on Customary IHL' is evidence of the necessity of interpreting and developing the law in relation to the needs on the ground.[18] To this end, this research also considers how the law works in practice. If the ICRC was caught in the vision of armed conflict and the idea of protection and assistance as defined in 1949 there would

[18] J-M Henckaerts and L Doswald-Beck, *Customary International Humanitarian Law*, vol 1: *Rules* (Cambridge, Cambridge University Press, 2005).

be many people living in insecurity, without their basic human needs being met, the world over. The extent to which the ICRC can expand its powers before it is usurping its mandate to satisfy humanitarian needs is questioned throughout this book.

This research examines what the 'law in context' or 'law in action' looks like.[19] It uses qualitative interviews with ICRC headquarters delegates to discover the 'gap' between the law and actual practice on the ground. Qualitative research 'is a situated activity that locates the observer in the world… qualitative researchers study things in their natural settings, attempting to make sense of, or interpret, phenomena in terms of the meanings people bring to them'.[20] The interviews not only add a unique insight to the book but also provide context and real-life experiences to the doctrinal and theoretical research earlier in the book. Critically this research employed interviewing to gain insight into a somewhat opaque organisation. Indeed, there are very few academics with personal access to the ICRC, and able to analyse the organisation's activities from an external perspective.[21]

## A. The Interview Method

The study design, including the sampling strategy, choice of elite interviewing, recruitment strategy, interview schedule and procedure, ethical consideration and analytic process, was created to generate data concerning the expansion of the ICRC mandate. The interviews were also utilised to gather data on the work of the ICRC in the DRC. According to Silverman: '[O]ne of the strengths of qualitative research is its ability to access directly what happens in the world, ie to examine what people actually do in real life rather than asking them to comment on it.'[22] In a similar vein, Byrne stated that: '[Q]ualitative interviewing is particularly useful as a research method for accessing individual's attitudes and values—things that cannot necessarily be observed or accommodated in a formal

[19] M Salter and J Mason, *Writing Law Dissertations: An Introduction and Guide to the Conduct of Legal Research* (London, Longman, 2007) 119, 150–53.

[20] NK Denzin and YS Lincoln, *Handbook of Qualitative Research* (Thousand Oaks, CA, Sage, 2005) 1–32 in S Sarantakos, *Social Research* (Basingstoke, Palgrave Macmillan, 2013) 37.

[21] One of the best-known authors on the ICRC is David Forsythe. See DP Forsythe, *The Humanitarians: The International Committee of the Red Cross* (Cambridge, Cambridge University Press, 2005); DP Forsythe and BAJ Rieffer-Flanagan, *The International Committee of the Red Cross—A Neutral Humanitarian Actor* (London, Routledge, 2007).

[22] D Silverman, *Interpreting Qualitative Data: Methods for Analysing Talk, Text and Interaction*, 3rd edn (London, Sage, 2006) 113.

questionnaire.'[23] Interviews were therefore an appropriate method to discover to what extent the activities of the ICRC have expanded beyond those provided for in the Geneva Conventions I, II, III and IV 1949 and the Statutes of the ICRC. Qualitative research, such as interviewing, is a research strategy that usually emphasises words rather than quantification in the collection and analysis of data.[24] The general distinction in qualitative research, as regards the data the researcher wishes to collect, is between seeking to find out what people know, what they do and what they think or feel.[25] The interviews were used to find out what ICRC delegates knew and what they do as part of ICRC activities.

The interviews are a supplementary evidence base for the arguments made as regards the expansion of the ICRC mandate and the activities of the ICRC on the ground. The interviews were designed to elucidate accounts of how the ICRC delegates interpret the mandate and to establish the types of projects that are currently being undertaken, in terms of the roles described under the mandate and specifically in the DRC. The data collected during the interviews was used to provide context and 'real life' accounts of the work of the ICRC. The interviewees were long-standing ICRC delegates with experience in the Geneva headquarters and the field. The interviewees have worked for the ICRC for between five and twenty-five years. They include national head of mission staff, programme coordinators and legal advisors.

The study design, described below, was created to test the theoretical and legal conclusions drawn during the undertaking of the book. The data collected is intended to allow analysis of the expansion of the ICRC mandate from the Geneva Conventions I, II, III and IV 1949, the ICRC Statutes and the Headquarters Agreements. It also provides first-hand accounts of projects on the ground, in particular in the DRC. The intention is not to provide data that can be generalised or extrapolated to indicate broader trends in humanitarianism or even the ICRC as a whole. It is designed as a mechanism to 'bring to life' the theoretical and legal analysis provided in the book. It is important to provide context to analysis as the book concerns 'humanity', humanitarianism and human security, all of which have a focus on the plight of human beings in vulnerable situations, including armed conflict, situations of violence and other fraught situations. To this end, it is important to consider the work on the ground undertaken by the ICRC to see how its delegates understand and interpret their role in terms of the plight of these populations.

[23] B Byrne, 'Qualitative Interviewing' in C Seale (ed), *Researching Society and Culture*, 2nd edn (London, Sage, 2004) 182.

[24] A Bryman, *Social Research Methods*, 3rd edn (Oxford, Oxford University Press, 2012) 366.

[25] C Robson, *Real World Research: A Resource for Social Scientists and Practitioner-Researchers* (Oxford, Blackwell, 1993) 228.

The research used snowball sampling in 2014 and again in 2016. It was necessary for participation in the research to be voluntary. In addition, the participants must be able to withdraw and to review the interview material. The ICRC is an inherently confidential organisation and therefore my contacts and interviewees remained anonymous in view of the personal and professional risks in providing information. Numbers in the footnotes to this book, eg INTERVIEW 001, references the information and quotations taken from interviews. The interview guide is included in the Appendix to this book.[26]

The final aspect of the methodology which must be explained is the case study of the DRC. This book uses a single case study of the work of the ICRC in the DRC. 'A case study is an empirical inquiry that investigates a contemporary phenomenon in depth and within its real life context, especially when the boundaries between phenomenon and context are not clearly evident.'[27] Overall the case study shows how the ICRC has broadened its approach to its mandate and what its practice includes nowadays. It therefore contributes to answering the 'meta' research question.

## III. BOOK STRUCTURE

Chapter 1 of this book reflects on the ICRC within the structure of the IRCRCM. It describes the IRCRCM and the relationship between the three components of the movement, including the ICRC, the International Federation of the Red Cross and Red Crescent and the national societies. It is significant to the overall book that the ICRC be understood both as a component of the IRCRCM and an individual entity.

Chapter 2 considers the specific mandate of the ICRC, in particular, its protection and assistance roles, provided for in the Geneva Conventions I, II, III and IV 1949, Additional Protocols 1977, the ICRC Statutes and the IRCRCM Statutes. It also determines whether the ICRC is an international legal person, with rights and duties on the international stage. It considers the applicability of the circumstances identified in the *Reparation for Injuries* Advisory Opinion, which led to an International Court of Justice (ICJ) determination that the UN was an organisation with ILP.[28] This author embarked on this study as existing literature on the ICRC describes the type of organisation that the ICRC is in a myriad of different ways.

[26] Interview guides are on file with the author.

[27] RK Yin, *Case Study Research: Design and Methods*, 4th edn (Sage, London 2009) 18.

[28] *Reparation for Injuries Suffered in the Service of the United Nations* (Advisory Opinion) [1949] ICJ Rep 174, 178–79.

Chapter 3 investigates the development of the laws of war and peace. This chapter argues that the ICRC institutionalised the binary distinction between the laws of war and peace by endeavouring to develop the laws of war following the cessation of hostilities at the end of the Second World War. Chapter 3 also considers the work of the UN during this time, which focused on the *jus ad bellum* and latterly IHRL. The changing nature of conflict necessitated the development of the Human Rights in Armed Conflict agenda of the General Assembly. At a similar time, the ICRC was working on the development of Additional Protocols I and II, which better reflected the types of armed conflicts being fought around the world after the Second World War, in part, by recognising the increasing number of NIACs. Later in the twentieth century international criminal courts adjudicated on this transformation in the nature of armed conflict, to find that both IHL and IHRL apply during armed conflict. The analysis in this chapter informs later analysis in the book, in particular human security research, because it shows the multiplicity of legal frameworks applicable during modern armed conflicts. This chapter leads into later analysis, which considers the applicability, and the relevance, of IHRL to the protection and assistance work of the ICRC.

Chapters 4 and 5 of the book consider the principles of humanity and its developments in the international legal order and focus on sovereignty as responsibility and human security. This book will show that human security is synonymous with the sovereignty as responsibility paradigm, which Kofi Annan thrust onto the international stage during his time as Secretary-General of the UN. Human security, if properly realised, has the potential to reach people on the ground, as a more comprehensive and long-term approach to humanitarian protection and assistance. It considers whether the ICRC, in its current interpretation of its mandate to protect and assist, is actually progressively realising sustainable human security for individuals and communities recovering from conflict. Has the principle of humanity, as it has moved beyond the battlefield, pushed the ICRC to seek longer-term solutions to humanitarian needs? Is human security a viable approach to such?

Chapter 6 considers ICRC activities in states and communities. It utilises data from semi-structured interviews conducted with ICRC delegates in 2014 and 2016. It considers whether, in terms of human security, as a humanitarian actor, the ICRC is well placed to provide human security on the ground. The crux of the analysis is that the ICRC did not actually foresee the human security agenda; in fact, the interviews provided context to this analysis and identified the gap between the law and practice of the ICRC. It also identifies the risks to the ICRC in being affiliated with security discourse and practice. It is argued, in particular, that states may be unwilling to consent to ICRC presence if it is no longer perceived as being a neutral and independent humanitarian organisation.

The final part of the book is a case study on the DRC, which reflects upon the conclusions drawn in the preceding chapters, and shows how the ICRC works in practice today. Since 1978 the ICRC has had a permanent mission in the DRC, which aims to promote respect for IHL amongst warring factions and also provides relief to civilians affected by the armed conflict.[29] The case study draws particular attention to the controversial steps of the ICRC away from the Geneva Conventions I, II, III and IV 1949 taken in the name of economic security. The case study considers the positive impact of the ICRC in terms of human security in the DRC. It builds on existing academic literature to examine the impact, or lack thereof, of the sovereignty as responsibility paradigm in the DRC. It contextualises the analysis through incorporation of interview findings. Many of the delegates interviewed at the ICRC headquarters in Geneva have worked in the DRC and were able to provide first-hand accounts of projects and events on the ground in the DRC. The case study also, therefore, considers the local implications of the work of the ICRC in the DRC.

[29] 'The ICRC in DR Congo' (ICRC) www.icrc.org/eng/where-we-work/africa/congo-kinshasa/index.jsp.

# 1

# *The Governance of the International Red Cross and Red Crescent Movement*

HENRY DUNANT ONCE stated: 'I dream of a Red Cross and Red Crescent Movement that has global moral authority and can call the attention of the world to humanitarian issues of concern, a Movement which independently chooses which issues to focus on.'[1] The Seville Agreement of 1997 states that the mission of the IRCRCM is:

> To prevent or alleviate human suffering wherever it may be found, to protect life and health, to ensure respect for human dignity (in particular during times of armed conflict and other emergencies), to work for the prevention of disease and the promotion of health and social welfare, to encourage voluntary service and a constant readiness to help and, finally, to foster a universal sense of solidarity towards all those in need of the Movement's protection and assistance.[2]

This chapter presents a holistic overview of the legal frameworks and governance structures at work within the Movement. In essence, it provides context to the analysis of the mandate of the ICRC, which is the focus of this book. To this end, the humanitarian mission, mandated to the ICRC, is to be carried out by the components of the IRCRCM, including the ICRC, the International Federation of the Red Cross (IFRC) and the 190 national societies.[3] In addition to the three constituent components of the IRCRCM, there are also three governing bodies: the International Conference of the Red Cross and Red Crescent,[4] the Council of Delegates of the

[1] Standing Commission of the Red Cross and Red Crescent, standcom.ch/components-of-the-movement/.

[2] Council of Delegates (ICRC), 'Agreement on the Organization of the International Activities of the Components of the International Red Cross and Red Crescent Movement—The Seville Agreement' (Council of Delegates, ICRC, 25–27 November 1997) www.icrc.org/eng/resources/documents/misc/57jp4y.htm, preamble (Seville Agreement).

[3] IFRC, 'National Societies', www.ifrc.org/en/who-we-are/the-movement/national-societies/.

[4] Statutes of the International Red Cross and Red Crescent Movement 1986 (adopted by the 25th International Conference of the Red Cross at Geneva in 1986 and amended in 1995 by Resolution 7 of the 26th International Conference of the Red Cross and Red Crescent at Geneva and 2006 by Resolution 1 of the 29th International Conference of the Red Cross and

IRCRCM[5] and the Standing Commission of the Red Cross and Red Crescent.[6] This chapter takes each component in turn and looks at its governance structure, authority and powers within the organisation and states. Each component of the IRCRCM has its own legal identity, functions and rules, united by seven fundamental principles, namely humanity, impartiality, neutrality, independence, voluntary service, unity and universality. Finally, the chapter reflects on the resolution entitled 'Strengthening Movement Coordination and Cooperation (SMCC): Optimizing the Movement's Humanitarian Response' which was adopted by the Council of Delegates on 7 December 2015.

## I. THE STATUTES OF THE IRCRCM

The IRCRCM Statutes confer roles upon the ICRC, as do the Statutes of the ICRC.[7] The founding conference of the ICRC in 1863 adopted a resolution outlining the intended purpose of the national committees of the Red Cross.[8] In 1928 the Thirteenth International Conference of the Red Cross at The Hague adopted a draft set of Statutes.[9] The Statutes were seen to provide defined powers to the Red Cross statutory bodies.[10] It was not until 1982 that full consideration was given to the Statutes and steps were taken to review and revise them.[11] The 1986 Statutes of the IRCRCM provide more comprehensive details of the powers and tasks of the components of the IRCRCM, including the ICRC.[12]

The legal nature of the Statutes is complicated, as 'unlike other organizations, the Movement's constitutive document (the Statutes of the Movement) is not a treaty with parties. It is a document adopted by the International Conference in a decision-making process involving States

Red Crescent at Geneva) Arts 8–11 (IRCRCM Statutes); See also Rules of Procedure of the International Red Cross and Red Crescent Movement (adopted by the 25th International Conference of the Red Cross at Geneva in October 1986 and amended by the 26th International Conference of the Red Cross and Red Crescent at Geneva in December 1995) Arts 4–22 (IRCRCM Rules of Procedure).

[5] IRCRCM Statutes, Arts 12–15.

[6] IRCRCM Statutes, Arts 16–19.

[7] See n 4.

[8] Resolutions of the Geneva International Conference. Geneva, 26–29 October 1863.

[9] These statutes were revised by the Eighteenth International Conference (Toronto, July–August 1952), but their basic tenor remained unchanged.

[10] F Bugnion, 'Red Cross Law' (1995) 308 *IRRC* 491, 497.

[11] ibid.

[12] The Statutes of the International Red Cross and Red Crescent Movement were adopted by consensus at the Twenty-fifth International Conference of the Red Cross, meeting in Geneva, October 1986.

and National Societies, the ICRC and the International Federation'.[13] However,

> the fact that the Statutes were not adopted as a treaty does not mean that States are not bound by them: governments are free to give their consent in any way they choose. Although the Statutes were not adopted in the form of an international treaty, they nevertheless constitute an international instrument, which, by its nature, binds the States.[14]

The ICRC is thus entitled to insist on the recognition by the states party to the Geneva Conventions of the powers it has been granted by the movement's Statutes. When states sign up to the Geneva Conventions, attend the International Conference and adopt resolutions and Headquarters Agreements, they facilitate the presence and work of the ICRC.

## II. THE GOVERNING BODIES OF THE IRCRCM

### A. The International Conference of the IRCRCM

The importance of the International Conference as a humanitarian forum cannot be understated as it brings together all state parties and components of the movement every four years. The ICRC, IFRC and 190 national societies attend the International Conference. Other attendees include: all 194 state parties to the Geneva Conventions I, II, III and IV 1949; observers from other humanitarian organisations; the UN system; and national societies in formation or awaiting recognition. The Conference ensures Red Cross/Red Crescent unity of effort and respect for the Fundamental Principles and is seen as a unique global opportunity to bring everyone together, as 'the basic concept of the International Conference—namely, a meeting between State representatives and representatives of relevant private organisations to consider and decide upon practical matters of mutual humanitarian concern—is at the origin of the International Red Cross and Red Crescent Movement'.[15] It is essential to the functioning of the movement that the International Conference continues to harmonise the

[13] D Casalin and C Lamb, 'Participation of States in the International Conference of the Red Cross and Red Crescent and Assemblies of other International Organisations' (2009) 91 *IRRC* 733, 752.

[14] R Perruchoud, *Les Résolutions des Conférences Internationales de la Croix-Rouge* (Henry Dunant Institute, Geneva, 1979) 107–08; See also A-R Werner, *La Croix-Rouge et Les Conventions de Genève* (Geneva, Georg & Cie, 1943) 79 in Bugnion (n 10) 501.

[15] M Meyer, 'The Importance of the International Conference of the Red Cross and Red Crescent to National Societies: Fundamental in theory and practice' (2009) 91 *IRRC* 713, 714–15.

national societies and governments. This equal footing between states and national societies is unique on the international stage. Indeed, Casalin and Lamb have stated that: '[T]he origins of the International Conference, and its capacity to adopt decisions that are binding on both National Red Cross and Red Crescent Societies and on governments in their dealings with National Societies as their auxiliary partners, give rise to special considerations concerning state participation.'[16]

Article 8 of the IRCRCM Statutes states that:

> The International Conference is the supreme deliberative body for the Movement. At the International Conference, representatives of the components of the Movement meet with representatives of the States Parties to the Geneva Conventions, the latter *in exercise of their responsibilities under those Conventions and in support of the overall work of the Movement* in terms of Article 2. Together they examine and decide upon humanitarian matters of common interest and any other related matter.[17]

Under Article 9(2) each delegation has one vote, which ensures parity between states and components of the movement. Article 11(7) of the Statutes of the Movement states that the Conference 'shall endeavour to adopt its resolutions by consensus'. The functions of the International Conference are contained in Article 10 of the Statutes of the Movement.[18]

[16] Casalin and Lamb (n 13) 733.

[17] Emphasis added.

[18] The International Conference contributes to the unity of the Movement and to the achievement of its mission in full respect of the Fundamental Principles.

1. The International Conference contributes to the respect for and development of international humanitarian law and other international conventions of particular interest to the Movement.
2. The International Conference shall have the sole competence:
   *a)* to amend the present Statutes and the Rules of Procedure of the International Red Cross and Red Crescent Movement (hereinafter called "Rules of Procedure");
   *b)* to take, at the request of any of its members, the final decision on any difference of opinion as to the interpretation and application of these Statutes and Rules;
   *c)* to decide on any question, referred to in Article 18, paragraph 2 *b)*, which may be submitted to it by the Standing Commission, the International Committee or the Federation.
3. The International Conference shall elect in a personal capacity those members of the Standing Commission mentioned in Article 17, para 1 *a)* of the present Statutes, taking into account personal qualities and the principle of fair geographical distribution.
4. Within the limits of the present Statutes and of the Rules of Procedure, the International Conference shall adopt its decisions, recommendations or declarations in the form of resolutions.
5. The International Conference may assign mandates to the International Committee and to the Federation within the limits of their statutes and of the present Statutes.

The Conference can also be called at other times to deal with issues faced by the movement.

The agenda for the International Conference is put together by the Presidency of the ICRC which receives submissions from ambassadors of states, the ICRC, the IFRC and individual national societies. The submissions contribute to a 'Concept Note'. The opening statement of the concept note from the 32nd International Conference states that:

> We are the International Red Cross and Red Crescent Movement. We are a global humanitarian network, which helps people prepare for, deal with and recover from crisis. Whether you are facing natural or man-made disasters, armed conflict or health and social care issues, Red Cross and Red Crescent volunteers and staff are there to help, without adverse discrimination. Guided by our Fundamental Principles, we mobilise the power of humanity to save lives and relieve suffering.[19]

This statement shows the evolution of the ICRC from a humanitarian organisation strictly concerned with the guardianship of IHL during armed conflict to one with the willingness and ability to intervene in 'crisis', 'disasters' and 'health and social care issues'. Thus expanding its mandate, but not without limits. We know from Article 9(6) of the Statutes of the IRCRCM that the 'the International Conference may assign mandates to the International Committee and to the Federation within the limits of their statutes and of the present Statutes'. Any development of the mandate of the ICRC is therefore restricted by their statutes and, although the Statutes of the movement may be updated, they have not been changed for the past thirty years.[20] The changes in the roles of the ICRC on the ground therefore must be mandated in a more nuanced manner than simply changing the constituent document; we shall return to this theory in chapter 2, when the book looks at the autonomy and personality of the ICRC.

### *(i) What Authority Do the Decisions of the International Conference Have?*

Under Article 10(5) of the IRCRCM Statutes 'the International Conference shall adopt its decisions, recommendations or declarations in the form of resolutions'. Since part of the role of the International Conference is to set the agenda for the ICRC (to which state parties will consent), it is important

> 6. The International Conference may enact, when necessary and by a two-thirds majority of its members present and voting, regulations relating to matters such as procedure and the award of medals.
> 7. The International Conference may establish for the duration of the Conference subsidiary bodies in accordance with the Rules of Procedure.

[19] rcrcconference.org.

[20] IRCRCM Statutes, Art 9(3)(a).

to consider the authority of such decisions. Bugnion has argued that: '[A]mong the texts which must be considered as mandatory are resolutions concerning internal regulations, such as the Rules of Procedure of the International Red Cross and Red Crescent Movement, resolutions concerning the establishment of subsidiary bodies and the rules governing the various Funds and Medals.'[21] In addition, Bugnion has stated that: '[T]hroughout its history the ICRC has relied on resolutions of International Conferences for support, in particular those which have granted it mandates or acknowledged its authority in particular fields.'[22] Indeed Article 10(6) of the Statutes allows the Conference to assign mandates to the ICRC and to the Federation. In addition, Article 5(2)(h) of the ICRC Statutes states that the ICRC *shall* carry out mandates entrusted to it by the International Conference.[23] It is clear, therefore, that the decisions of the International Conference are binding on the ICRC. During the International Conference the ICRC may propose a future mandate, such as Health Care in Danger.[24] When these conditions are met, the mandate is then binding on the ICRC.[25] For the ICRC, therefore, the Conference postulates a two-part role: the ICRC may be given a project, such as Health Care in Danger, but the ICRC can also use the Conference as an opportunity to gain leverage for a particular topic that it is concerned with, as the Conference can garner support for such, or at least raise the profile of the cause.

The Council of Delegates reports on specific issues, 'appeals' to states, and 'calls upon' members of the movement to reach for certain outcomes; for example, the 31st International Conference 'Resolution 1: Working Towards the Elimination of Nuclear Weapons' states that the Council of delegates, under paragraph 3:

> *Appeals* to all States: to ensure that nuclear weapons are never again used, regardless of their views on the legality of such weapons; to pursue in good faith and conclude with urgency and determination negotiations to prohibit the use of and completely eliminate nuclear weapons through a legally binding international agreement, based on existing commitments and international obligations.

[21] Perruchoud (n 14) 110–29.

[22] Bugnion (n 10) 518 states that: '[I]n this respect, particular reference should be made to Resolution IV/3 of the Berlin Conference (1869) concerning the creation of an information agency; Resolution VI of the Washington Conference (1912) concerning assistance to prisoners of war, and Resolution XIV of the Geneva Conference (1921) concerning the work of the Red Cross in the event of civil war.'

[23] Emphasis added.

[24] 31st Conference of the International Red Cross and Red Crescent Movement, 'Resolution 5—Health Care in Danger: Respecting and Protecting Health Care' (Geneva, Switzerland, 28 November–1 December 2011) www.icrc.org/eng/resources/documents/resolution/31-international-conference-resolution-5-2011.htm; Health Care in Danger website https://www.icrc.org/eng/what-we-do/safeguarding-health-care/solution/2013-04-26-hcid-health-care-in-danger-project.htm.

[25] Perruchoud (n 14) 144–63.

Under paragraph 4 it '*calls on* all components of the Movement, utilizing the framework of humanitarian diplomacy'. To this end, the International Conference guides the objectives of state parties to the Geneva Conventions I, II, III and IV 1949 and the bodies of the IRCRCM. The resolutions are not legally binding, and do not resemble UN Security Council resolutions, but indicate a willingness of states to be bound by and facilitate the upcoming work of the ICRC. In addition, through individual Headquarters Agreements, states have consented to the presence and work of the ICRC within their territories.

By example, the ICRC is responsible for the recognition of new national societies.[26] The role of the International Conference in this process was significant in the case of the Israeli national society and the Palestinian Red Cross.[27] Moreover, sometimes the resolutions adopted at the Conference can create mandates, which conjoin the ICRC and states. The ICRC and Switzerland, for example, undertook a study on compliance, which lasted for four years.[28] The International Conference is an opportunity for the ICRC, alongside the states party to the Geneva Conventions I, II, III and IV 1949, to progress the protection and assistance work of the ICRC. Overall, the legal framework and practice of the ICRC shows the adaptation of its work on the international stage. This can be through large-scale projects, such as Health Care in Danger, which are a response to general trends in humanitarian assistance and protection, or a response to specific situations through the adoption of memoranda of understanding. This is critical in terms of the ICRC remaining relevant and useful for people on the ground who are affected by armed conflict and other situations of violence.

## B. The Council of Delegates

The Conference is preceded by the Council of Delegates, comprising all components of the movement, which adopts the provisional agenda of the Conference and proposes the Conference officers for election. The Council

[26] IRCRCM Statutes, Art 4.

[27] 31st International Conference of the Red Cross and Red Crescent, 'Resolution 5: Implementation of the Memorandum of Understanding and Agreement on Operational Arrangements, dated 28 November 2005, between the Palestine Red Crescent Society and the Magen David Adom in Israel' www.rcrcconference.org/images_upl/files/Blue%20Book%2031st%20IC_ENG.pdf; See also 31st International Conference of the Red Cross and Red Crescent, 'Explanatory Note to the Memorandum of Understanding and the Agreement on Operational Arrangements' (18 November 2011) https://www.icrc.org/eng/resources/documents/red-cross-crescent-movement/31st-international-conference/31-international-conference-mou.html.

[28] 31st International Conference of the Red Cross and Red Crescent, 'Strengthening Legal Protection for Victims of Armed Conflicts' (Geneva, Switzerland, 28 November–1 December 2011) Resolution 31IC/11/5.1.1, Part 2.

of Delegates debates and decides on 'global strategic issues, and matters that concern the Movement as a whole'.[29] In the Council of Delegates each national society, the ICRC and the IFRC maintains its independent legal status and has one vote. However, decisions are normally by consensus.[30]

## C. The Standing Commission of the IRCRCM

The final governing body of the IRCRCM is the nine-member Standing Commission.[31] It organises the International Conferences and the Council of Delegates, and is the 'trustee' of the International Conference. It is the highest deliberative body and all components of the ICRC are represented. In addition to its responsibilities regarding arrangements for International Conferences and meetings of the Council, the Standing Commission shall:

> Promote harmony in the work of the Movement and, in this connection, coordination among its components; encourage and further the implementation of resolutions of the International Conference; examine, with these objects in view, matters which concern the Movement as a whole.[32]

The functions of the Standing Commissions are defined in Article 18 of the Statutes of the Movement and have been further developed in Council of Delegates and International Conference resolutions.[33] The Standing

[29] IRCRCM Statutes (s III 'Statutory Bodies') Arts 12–15; IRCRCM Rules of Procedure, Arts 23–28.

[30] The International Conference, the Standing Commission, the ICRC and the Federation or National Societies can refer issues to the Council. The Council cannot, however, give an opinion, pass a resolution or make a decision in conflict with decisions already taken by an International Conference.

[31] IRCRCM Statutes (s III 'Statutory Bodies') Arts 16–19; IRCRCM Rules of Procedure, Arts 29–31. The Standing Commission comprises nine members: five from different National Societies (each elected in a personal capacity by the International Conference and holding office until the close of the following International Conference), two representatives of the ICRC and two representatives of the International Federation. The Standing Commission elects a Chairman and a Vice-Chairman from among its members. Its functions have been further developed in Council of Delegates and International Conference resolutions.

[32] Standing Commission, www.standcom.ch (accessed 6 January 2015).

[33] In addition to the set statutory tasks, its main additional functions in recent years can briefly be summarised as follows: to encourage the implementation of the resolutions of the International Conference and the Council of Delegates (Art 18, CoD Resolution 3/95, 27th and 28th IC Resolutions 1/99and 1/03); to ensure promotion of the strategy for the movement and monitor, evaluate and analyse progress made in its implementation by all components (CoD Resolutions 3/01 and 7/03); to continue to give high priority to securing a comprehensive and lasting solution to the question of the emblem (CoD Resolutions 3/95, 2/97, 2/99, 6/01, 5/03 and International Conference Resolutions 3/99 and 3/03); to contribute to the development of effective international relief operations (CoD Resolutions 2/03, 5/99); to monitor the implementation of the Seville Agreement and to analyse challenges in the implementation of it and develop ways to enhance and strengthen cooperation within the framework of the Agreement (CoD Resolution 8/03).

Commission works with the ICRC, IFRC and National Societies, to provide strategic guidance in matters that concern the movement as a whole. Critically, the Standing Commission is not operational, rather, it 'prepares Movement-wide policies such as the Strategy for the Movement, which aim at harmonious coordination and cohesion in action, building on the strengths and specific mandates of each component'. It is the responsibility of the ICRC, the IFRC and national societies to implement its decisions.

In preparing various issues, the Commission emphasises the importance of the participation of and consultation with the national societies in order to stay in touch with their realities and with external developments when positioning the movement to best serve victims and other beneficiaries. For this purpose, there were four different ad hoc working groups in action until the end of 2005, established by the Commission as advisory bodies on the emblem, the Seville Agreement, the Strategy for the Movement and for planning of the Statutory Meetings. The groups involved members, appointed ad personam, from some thirty national societies representing all geographical regions. As of January 2006, two working groups are continuing in their function.[34]

Overall, new agreements and rules of procedure show that the IRCRCM and its constituent parts continue to develop in response to changing humanitarian needs on the ground. Nevertheless, its internal rules and structures preclude arbitrary developments and, as with organisations much more familiar to textbooks on international institutional law, the IRCRCM has its own system of checks and balances, as described above. This institutional structure and the Statutes of the IRCRCM, the Statutes of the ICRC and the Statutes of the IFRC are borne in mind throughout this book.

## III. THE COMPONENTS OF THE IRCRCM

### A. Red Cross and Red Crescent National Societies

Bugnion has stated that:

> [I]n order to preserve the bonds of solidarity that united them across national borders, the Red Cross Societies were to meet regularly, as laid down by Article 9 of the 1863 resolutions: 'The Committees and Sections of different countries may meet in international assemblies to communicate the results of their experience and to agree on measures to be taken in the interest of the work.'[35]

[34] Standing Commission of the Red Cross and Red Crescent, 'About the Commission', standcom.ch/about-the-commission/.

[35] Bugnion, (n 10).

Today, national societies, such as the British Red Cross and the Red Cross of the DRC,[36] provide a range of services, depending on the humanitarian needs of the population they serve. The British Red Cross, for example, provides first aid training, health and social care, and refugee services.[37] The Red Cross of the DRC, on the other hand, must respond to conflict-related humanitarian needs, the need for capacity building, and forced migration.[38]

In order to participate in the IRCRCM, national societies must first be recognised by the ICRC and then admitted by the International Federation. Article 4 of the IRCRCM Statutes provides ten conditions for recognition as a national society, including Article 4(1), which states that national societies be constituted on the territory of an independent state where the 'Geneva Convention for the Amelioration of the Condition of the Wounded and Sick in Armed Forces in the Field' is in force. In addition, under Article 4(3) a national society must be duly recognised by the legal government of its country on the basis of the Geneva Conventions I, II, III and IV 1949 and of the national legislation as a voluntary aid society, auxiliary to the public authorities in the humanitarian field.

## B. International Federation of the Red Cross

The IFRC inspires, facilitates and promotes all humanitarian activities carried out by its member national societies on behalf of the most vulnerable people. The IFRC has its own constitution.[39] It was established in 1919 and is made up of national societies. Article 6(1) of the IRCRCM Statutes states that: '[T]he International Federation of Red Cross and Red Crescent Societies comprises the National Red Cross and Red Crescent Societies. It acts under its own Constitution with all rights and obligations of a corporate body with a legal personality.' It is an 'independent humanitarian organization which is not governmental, political, racial or sectarian in character'.[40] Moreover, the 'general object of the Federation is to inspire, encourage, facilitate and promote at all times all forms of humanitarian activities by the National Societies, with a view to preventing and alleviating

[36] IFRC, 'Democratic Republic of Congo', www.ifrc.org/en/news-and-media/news-stories/africa/congo-democratic-republic-of/.

[37] British Red Cross, www.redcross.org.uk/.

[38] IFRC, 'Democratic Republic of Congo', www.ifrc.org/en/news-and-media/news-stories/africa/congo-democratic-republic-of/.

[39] IFRC, 'Constitution: Revised and Adopted by the 16th Session of the General Assembly' (IFRC, Geneva, Switzerland, 20–22 November 2007) www.ifrc.org/Global/Governance/Statutory/Constitution_revised-en.pdf.

[40] IRCRCM Statutes, Art 6(2).

human suffering and thereby contributing to the maintenance and the promotion of peace in the world'.[41] Under Article 6(4) IRCRCM Statutes its functions include:

> *a)* to act as the permanent body of liaison, coordination and study between the National Societies and to give them any assistance they might request; *b)* to encourage and promote in every country the establishment and development of an independent and duly recognized National Society; *c)* to bring relief by all available means to all disaster victims; *d)* to assist the National Societies in their disaster relief preparedness, in the organization of their relief actions and in the relief operations themselves; *e)* to organize, coordinate and direct international relief actions in accordance with the Principles and Rules adopted by the International Conference; *f)* to encourage and coordinate the participation of the National Societies in activities for safeguarding public health and the promotion of social welfare in cooperation with their appropriate national authorities; *g)* to encourage and coordinate between National Societies the exchange of ideas for the education of children and young people in humanitarian ideals and for the development of friendly relations between young people of all countries; *h)* to assist National Societies to recruit members from the population as a whole and inculcate the principles and ideals of the Movement; *i)* to bring help to victims of armed conflicts in accordance with the agreements concluded with the International Committee; *j)* to assist the International Committee in the promotion and development of international humanitarian law and collaborate with it in the dissemination of this law and of the Fundamental Principles of the Movement among the National Societies; *k)* to be the official representative of the member Societies in the international field, *inter alia* for dealing with decisions and recommendations adopted by its Assembly and to be the guardian of their integrity and the protector of their interests; *l)* to carry out the mandates entrusted to it by the International Conference.

Finally, 'in each country the Federation shall act through or in agreement with the National Society and in conformity with the laws of that country'.

## C. International Committee of the Red Cross

The ICRC defines itself as 'an independent, neutral and impartial humanitarian organisation whose mission is to protect the lives and dignity of victims of armed conflict and other situations of violence and to provide them with assistance'.[42] This book examines the ICRC as an entity, how it functions, and the contexts in which it functions. In 2012, Peter Maurer, President of the ICRC, stated that: '[T]he motivation behind our work has

[41] IRCRCM Statutes, Art 6(3).

[42] 'The ICRC's Mandate and Mission' (ICRC, 29 October 2010) www.icrc.org/eng/who-we-are/mandate/overview-icrc-mandate-mission.htm.

not changed since the final pages of Henry Dunant's ground breaking book "A Memory of Solferino".[43] What changes, however, is how the organization adapts its response to different patterns of conflict and different contexts.'[44] Maurer went on to state that: '[T]he working method of the ICRC is to be close to victims, root action in response to needs rather than political agendas, to contextualise the humanitarian response and reunite assistance, protection and prevention.'[45]

The governance of the ICRC, as we see it today, is a tried and tested infrastructure which has its headquarters in Geneva and field operations across the world. The relationships between the governing bodies, delegations, staff, volunteers and the communities that they serve are ever evolving but the operations, broadly speaking, sit within the same organisational structure.

The activities that can be undertaken by the ICRC are defined in Common Article 3, Article 9 of the Geneva Conventions I, II and III 1949 and Article 10 of the Geneva Convention IV 1949. Under Common Article 3(2) of Geneva Conventions I, II, III and IV 1949 'an impartial humanitarian body, such as the International Committee of the Red Cross, may *offer its services* to the Parties to the conflict'.[46] In addition, Article 18 of Additional Protocol II contains specific roles for relief societies and relief actions.[47] In non-international armed conflicts, therefore, the ICRC enjoys a right of humanitarian initiative recognised by the international community and enshrined in Article 3 common to the four Geneva Conventions.

Articles 9, 9, 9 and 10 of the Geneva Conventions I, II, III and IV 1949, respectively, which concern international armed conflicts, state that:

> The provisions of the present Convention constitute no obstacle to the humanitarian activities which the International Committee of the Red Cross or any other impartial humanitarian organisation may, subject to the consent of the Parties to the conflict concerned, undertake for the protection of wounded and sick, medical personnel and chaplains, and for their relief.

[43] H Dunant, *A Memory of Solferino* (Geneva, ICRC, 1986).

[44] 'Interview with Peter Maurer' (2012) 94 (888) *IRRC* 1, 2.

[45] ibid 3.

[46] Emphasis added.

[47] AP II Art 18 on relief societies and relief actions states that: '1. Relief societies located in the territory of the High Contracting Party, such as Red Cross (Red Crescent, Red Lion and Sun) organizations, may offer their services for the performance of their traditional functions in relation to the victims of the armed conflict. The civilian population may, even on its own initiative, offer to collect and care for the wounded, sick and shipwrecked. 2. If the civilian population is suffering undue hardship owing to a lack of the supplies essential for its survival, such as foodstuffs and medical supplies, relief actions for the civilian population which are of an exclusively humanitarian and impartial nature and which are conducted without any adverse distinction shall be undertaken subject to the consent of the High Contracting Party concerned.'

Finally, in the event of internal disturbances and tensions, and in any other situation that warrants humanitarian action, the ICRC also enjoys a right of initiative, which is recognised in the IRCRCM Statutes. Thus, wherever international humanitarian law does not apply, the ICRC may offer its services to governments without that offer constituting interference in the internal affairs of the state concerned. In this regard, it is important to remember that by signing up to the statutes of the IRCRCM they become binding on every member of the movement.

In addition to the IRCRCM Statutes, the ICRC also has its own Statutes.[48] The ICRC Statutes, like the ICRC itself, have a hybrid nature:

(i) The ICRC is a private association under Swiss domestic law, within the meaning of Article 60 of the Swiss Civil Code.[49] From this perspective, the ICRC Statutes are like the statutes of any private association under Swiss law and are registered in the Geneva Register of Commerce.[50]

(ii) The ICRC has also a status that is equivalent to that of an international organisation and it has the international legal personality in the exercise of its functions, which enables it to collaborate with states in the fulfilment of its mandate.[51]

The significance of its hybrid nature is returned to in chapter 2 of this book.

### *(i) Governance in the ICRC*

The ICRC is made up of a number of governing bodies, including the Assembly; the Assembly Council; the Office of the President; the Directorate; the Internal Audit Unit; and the Data Protection Independent Control Commission (Data Protection Commission).[52] This section provides a brief overview of each body.

[48] ICRC Statutes, 3 October 2013 (the present Statutes replace the Statutes of the International Committee of the Red Cross of 21 June 1973, revised on 20 July 1998 and 8 May 2003).

[49] The first Statutes of the ICRC of November 1915 identify the ICRC, in legal terms, as an association governed by the Swiss Civil Code. See ICRC Archives B CR 92/1, 1–100, ICRC Statutes, 15 November 1915, in D Palmieri 'An Institution Standing the Test of Time? A Review of 150 Years of the History of the International Committee of the Red Cross' (2012) 94 *IRRC* 1273, 1278.

[50] Registre du Commerce, 'Fondation pour le Comité International de la Croix Rouge', rc.ge.ch/ecohrcmatic/.

[51] As described above.

[52] Internal Regulations of the ICRC (in force from 1 January 2016) Art 10; ICRC Statutes, Art 8.

### (a) The Assembly[53]

Article 9 of the ICRC Statutes states that:

> [T]he Assembly is the ICRC's supreme governing body. It is in charge of oversight of the organization and ensures that it carries out its mission. It defines the ICRC's institutional strategy, formulates policy and approves the budget and accounts. … [T]he Assembly shall be composed of the members of the ICRC. It shall be collegial in character.[54]

The Assembly is comprised of between fifteen and twenty-five co-opted Swiss nationals. They are appointed for a four-year term of office, which can be renewed twice, with an age limit of 72 years. Its president and vice-president are the president and vice-president of the ICRC. It also appoints key management officials, including the director-general, the directors and the head of the Internal Audit Unit. Finally, the Assembly sets out the framework for cooperation and working relationships with the other components of the IRCRCM and recognises new national societies which fulfil the requisite conditions.

### (b) The Assembly Council

The Assembly Council is a subsidiary body of the Assembly. It ensures the smooth functioning of the ICRC, in particular as regards human resources and financial management—for example, it approves budget extensions. It prepares the Assembly's discussions on financial matters, particularly those requiring the Assembly's approval with regard to changes in the financial reserves, ICRC funds and foundations, and budgets. It also helps identify potential candidates for Directorate positions. The Assembly Council may carry out any of the Assembly's duties in situations requiring an urgent decision.[55]

### (c) The Office of the President

The Office of the President is made up of a president and a vice-president.[56] The president represents the ICRC on the international scene, bears primary responsibility for the ICRC's external relations and conducts ICRC humanitarian diplomacy in close cooperation with the Office of the

[53] https://www.icrc.org/en/the-assembly.

[54] Art 13 outlines the Assembly Responsibilities and Tasks; See also Arts 11–16 Internal Regulations of the International Committee of the Red Cross, adopted on 19 November 2015 and came into force on 1 January 2016, https://www.icrc.org/en/document/internal-regulations-international-committee-red-cross.

[55] See IRCRCM Statutes, Art 10; Internal Regulations, Arts 21–25.

[56] ICRC Statutes, Art 11; Internal Regulations, Arts 26–29.

Director-General. He also attends to the internal cohesion, smooth running and development of the organisation. At the time of writing, the Office of the President is made up of the president, Peter Maurer, who succeeded Jakob Kellenberger on 1 July 2012, and the vice-president, Christine Beerli, who succeeded Jacques Forster on 1 January 2008.[57]

The president represents the ICRC and assumes primary responsibility for its relations with outside bodies, in particular through humanitarian diplomacy. As chair of the Assembly and the Assembly Council, the president ensures that the responsibilities assigned to these two bodies remain under their control and closely monitors the running of the ICRC. Whilst the president is responsible for developing the institutional strategy and proposing it to the Assembly, the vice-president assists the president in carrying out his duties and substitutes for the president when he is absent or unable to carry out his duties or at his request. She is also responsible for the cohesion, smooth running and development of governance and oversight mechanisms.

### (d) The Directorate

The Directorate is the ICRC's executive body. It directs the administration, which comprises all ICRC staff, except for the Internal Audit Unit. It is responsible for running the administration and ensuring the ICRC's operational effectiveness. The Directorate comprises the director-general and between three and seven directors and is chaired by the director-general.[58] The members of the ICRC Directorate are appointed by the Assembly for four-year terms.

### (e) The Internal Audit Unit

Lastly, the Internal Audit Unit assesses, independently of senior management, the extent to which the ICRC is in control of its activities. It proceeds through internal operational and financial audits. The Internal Audit Unit's work covers the entire ICRC, both field and headquarters. Its aim is to assess, on an independent basis, the organisation's performance and the pertinence of the means deployed in relation to the ICRC's strategy. It reports directly to the Assembly. Finally, in the area of finance, the role of the Internal Audit Unit complements that of the external auditing firm.[59]

[57] See ICRC President and Vice-President Re-elected (ICRC) https://www.icrc.org/en/document/icrc-president-and-vice-president-re-elected.

[58] ICRC Statutes, Art 12.

[59] ICRC Statutes, Art 14 Internal Audit Unit.

## D. The Budget of the ICRC

The principal assets of the ICRC are the contributions of governments and national societies, as well as funds from private sources and its income from securities.[60] 'There is no assessed payment system to fund the activities of the ICRC.'[61] The Internal Audit Unit (internally) and auditing firms (externally) oversee the assets and funds. If the ICRC is ever dissolved, the assets at its disposal will be awarded in their entirety to one or more tax-exempt organisations pursuing humanitarian goals. The ICRC Statutes stipulate that: '[U]nder no circumstances may such assets be returned to the ICRC's donors, individual founders, or members, nor used in whole or in part for their profit in any manner whatsoever.'[62]

> During the last 20 years, annual spending has not dropped below 600 million Swiss Francs. Moreover, since 2007, annual spending has been well over a billion francs. This surge, of course, has been accompanied by a considerable and constant increase in ICRC activities and, in turn, in the number of beneficiaries of its actions.[63]

## E. Increasing Cooperation within the Movement

Article 7 of the Statutes of the Movement states that:

> [T]he components of the Movement shall cooperate with each other in accordance with their respective statutes and with Articles 1, 3, 5 and 6 of the present Statutes. In particular the International Committee and the Federation shall maintain frequent regular contact with each other at all appropriate levels so as to coordinate their activities in the best interest of those who require their protection and assistance.[64]

In addition, 'cooperation between the components of the Movement on a regional basis shall be undertaken in the spirit of their common mission and the Fundamental Principles, within the limits of their respective statutes'. Finally,

> [T]he components of the Movement, while maintaining their independence and identity, cooperate whenever necessary with other organizations which are

[60] ICRC Statutes, Art 16 Assets and Financial Oversight.

[61] DP Forsythe and B Rieffer-Flanagan, *The International Committee of the Red Cross: A Neutral Humanitarian Actor* (London, Routledge, 2007) 33.

[62] ICRC Statutes, Art 16(4).

[63] Palmieri (n 49) 1293–94.

[64] Art 7 states: 'Within the framework of the present Statutes and their respective statutes, the International Committee and the Federation shall conclude with each other any agreements required to harmonize the conduct of their respective activities. Should, for any reason, such agreements not exist, Art 5, para 4 *b)* and Art 6, para 4 *i)* shall not apply and the International Committee and the Federation shall refer to the other provisions of the present Statutes to settle matters relative to their respective fields of activities.'

> active in the humanitarian field, provided such organizations are pursuing a purpose similar to that of the Movement and are prepared to respect the adherence by the components to the Fundamental Principles.

The Seville Agreement between the members of the IRCRCM was adopted in 1997 and sought to create a 'profound change' between the members of the IRCRCM. It sought to foster a 'stronger sense of identity, of solidarity, of mutual trust and of shared responsibility'.[65] The ICRC is a constituent component of the IRCRCM. The requirement that the ICRC maintain 'close contact' with the national societies and the IFRC is described in Article 5 of the ICRC Statutes. In addition, Article 2 of the ICRC Statutes states that 'as an association governed by Article 60 and following of the Swiss Civil Code, the ICRC has legal personality'.

In December 2015 the Council of Delegates of the IRCRCM adopted a resolution entitled 'Strengthening Movement Coordination and Cooperation (SMCC): Optimizing the Movement's Humanitarian Response'.[66] The accompanying Plan of Action 2016–17 'aims to ensure that through implementing the actions the Movement is "fit for purpose" to provide predictable, coherent and effective humanitarian response in a changing humanitarian landscape'. The ability of the movement to fulfil these objectives is reflected on throughout this book.

## IV. CONCLUSION

This chapter has provided a concise overview of the IRCRCM, its legal framework and governance structures. Recall that the ICRC sprung from the mind of Henry Dunant, when in 1859 he witnessed the horrors of the aftermath of the Battle of Solferino. Soldiers were wounded, and without water and medical supplies. Dunant envisaged the establishment of national societies of volunteers who would come to the aid of wounded soldiers in armed conflicts. By 1863 the ICRC was established and for the past 150 years or so this unique humanitarian organisation has continued to respond to the plight of those in and affected by armed conflict.

The IRCRCM is composed of the ICRC, the IFRC and 190 national societies. This chapter has described the structure of the ICRC, within the IRCRCM, in order to introduce the organisation and its mandated roles on the international stage and within states. The focus of the ICRC is the provision of protection and assistance to victims of armed conflict, within the parameters of activities that adhere to the seven fundamental

[65] Seville Agreement (n 2).

[66] Council of Delegates of the IRCRCM, 'Strengthening Movement Coordination and Cooperation (SMCC): Optimizing the Movement's Humanitarian Response' (7 December 2015) CD/15/R1.

principles. This chapter provides the basis of analysis throughout this book. The question of what type of organisation it is, in terms of international institutional law, will be answered in chapter 2. Whether the ICRC is a subject of international law, capable of bearing rights and obligations under international law, is also a matter for chapter 2. The analysis will draw on the considerations in this chapter of the structure of the ICRC, its humanitarian assistance and initiative rights, and its reputation for being an impartial and neutral organisation.

# 2

# *The Legal Nature and International Legal Personality of the ICRC*

## I. INTRODUCTION

HISTORICALLY ONLY STATES were considered to possess ILP, which made them subjects of international law and allowed them to exercise sovereign power.[1] One consequence of the proliferation of actors on the international stage has resulted in organisations also being identified as 'subjects' of international law. 'If [intergovernmental organisations], meeting certain criteria, have personality automatically they are subjects of international law just as States are and, furthermore, they are distinct in legal terms from their members.'[2] The first international organisations were intergovernmental conferences for cooperation among sovereign states,[3] but increasingly emphasis was placed on an international organisations' 'separate will' and, ultimately, ILP.[4] The significance of ILP is that states and organisations with personality can act as a distinct personality, manifest itself on the international stage, and enter

[1] A Meijknecht, *Towards International Legal Personality: The Position of Minorities and Indigenous Peoples in International Law* (London, Intersentia, 2001) 26; *Case of the SS Lotus*, 1927 PCIJ (Ser A) No 10, 18; See also *Case Concerning the Payments of Various Serbian Loans Issued in France* (Judgment), 1929 PCIJ Series A No 20 at 41, which principally adhered to the states-only concept of ILP.

[2] ND White, *The Law of International Organisations*, 3rd edn (Manchester, Manchester University Press, 2017) 113–14.

[3] P Sands QC and P Klein, *Bowett's Law of International Institutions*, 6th edn (London, Sweet & Maxwell, 2009) 469.

[4] P Reuter, *International Institutions* (London, George Allen & Unwin, 1958) 195 (trans JM Chapman from the French *Institutions Internationales* (Paris, Presses Universitaires de France, 1955); DJ Bedermann, 'The Souls of International Organizations: Legal Personality and the Lighthouse at Cape Spartel' (1996) 36 *Virginia Journal of International Law* 275, 371–74; D Kennedy, 'The Move to Institutions' (1987) 8 *Cardozo Law Review* 840, 841–42; ND White, *The Law of International Organisations* (Manchester, Manchester University Press, 2005) 1–2; C Brölmann, *The Institutional Veil in Public International Law: International Organisations and the Law of Treaties* (Oxford, Hart Publishing, 2007) 66; I Brownlie, *Principles of Public International Law*, 7th edn (Oxford, Oxford University Press, 2008) 676–79; J Klabbers, *An Introduction to International Institutional Law*, 2nd edn (Cambridge, Cambridge University Press, 2009) 11–12.

into relationships with other subjects of international law,[5] rather than just providing a forum for member states to pursue their own interests.[6]

The question of the ILP of the UN was answered in the *Reparation for Injuries Advisory Opinion* at the ICJ. The ICJ determined the ability of an organisation to have legal personality:

> In the opinion of the Court, the Organization was *intended* to exercise and enjoy, and is *in fact* exercising and enjoying functions and rights which can only be explained on the basis of the possession of a large measure of international personality and the capacity to operate upon an international plane.[7]

Determination of ILP can therefore be subject to two concurrent tests. The first question is whether the organisation has ILP because it has to—that is, the state signatories to the UN Charter, for example, intended it to act autonomously. The second question is whether the UN acts in specific capacities that show that it is exercising its own personality; for the UN, the ICJ considered making claims, negotiating treaties, and the possession of privileges and immunities to be exercises in personality. When applied to the ICRC, therefore, we can approach ILP from two perspectives: was it intended for the ICRC to be an ILP? And is there evidence of the ICRC exercising ILP? The second question has two areas of analysis: firstly, by analogy to the UN; and secondly, by examining the ICRC's own exercise of its duties and powers on the international stage. The limit of this approach to determining ILP is that the ICRC itself does not have member states, which the UN does, but it takes its mandate to provide humanitarian protection and assistance from the Geneva Conventions to which states are party and its Assembly sets the agenda at the International Conference, which states agree to. This chapter, therefore, looks at the ICRC from the perspective of intention and its exercise of functions and rights to come to a reasoned conclusion that the ICRC does, in fact, possess ILP. ILP distinguishes the UN from, for example, the G20. In terms of the ICRC, it means that the delegates in Geneva and the field can act autonomously to implement the mandate. The decisions made in Geneva do not need authorisation by all state parties to the Geneva Conventions or IRCRCM Statutes, or even majority vote. The ICRC president and staff can negotiate new Headquarters Agreements and authorise new humanitarian protection and assistance missions. The ICRC can act distinct from

[5] C Barbara, 'International Legal Personality: Panacea or Pandemonium? Theorizing about the Individual and the State in the Era of Globalization' (2008) 20(1) *Sri Lanka Journal of International Law* 243, 245.

[6] RA Wessel, 'Revisiting the International Legal Status of the EU' (2000) 5 *European Foreign Affairs Review* 507, 515.

[7] *Reparations for Injuries Suffered in the Service of the United Nations*, Advisory Opinion ICJ Reports, 1949, 174, 179 (emphasis added).

states, and the individuals that work there interpret and implement its mandate from Geneva.

This chapter shows that the ICRC must, accordingly, possess ILP to be recognised as an autonomous entity and participate meaningfully in legal life. Entities currently recognised as having ILP include independent states; internationalised territories, such as the Free City of Danzig; UN Missions established by the UN Security Council to administer territories in transition to self-government, such as East Timor and Kosovo; intergovernmental organisations such as the UN; in limited circumstances individuals;[8] de facto regimes such as Taiwan, and insurgents and belligerents; and national liberation movements such as the Palestine Liberation Organization. The international community has also opened up for the possibility for sui generis entities to possess ILP, entities such as the Holy See and the Sovereign Order of Malta.[9] Other candidates for ILP are NGOs, multinational corporations and indigenous peoples.[10] The ICRC may well have some capacities in common with other ILPs, such as the UN, but it also, by virtue of its ability to interpret its own mandate, has powers that are unique to it as a humanitarian entity. In order, therefore, to critically assess its status on the international stage, this chapter begins by considering what kind of organisation the ICRC is.

## II. WHAT KIND OF ORGANISATION IS THE ICRC?

Before assessing whether the ICRC has ILP, it will prove necessary to examine the organisation, to look at its governance structure and the type of organisation that it can be defined as. Principally, the ICRC is a legal person under the Swiss Civil Code and has its headquarters in Geneva. Article 60(1) of the Swiss Civil Code concerns the formation of associations and states that: '[A]ssociations with a political, religious, scientific, cultural, charitable, social or other non-commercial purpose acquire legal personality as soon as their intention to exist as a corporate body is apparent from their articles of association.'[11] Under the Swiss Civil Code an association must equip itself with organs provided for in the law and in the statutes, namely: a General Assembly (comprising all members of

[8] *La Grand (Germany v United States of America)* (Judgment) [2001] ICJ Rep 466.

[9] C Bisaz, *The Concept of Group Rights in International Law: Groups as Contested Right-Holders, Subjects and Legal Persons* (Leiden, Martinus Nijhoff, 2012) 37; I Rossi, *Legal Status of Non-Governmental Organizations in International Law* (Cambridge, Intersentia, 2010) 36.

[10] A Kaczorowska, *Public International Law* (London, Taylor & Francis, 2010) 176.

[11] Swiss Civil Code of 10 December 1907 (status as of 1 July 2014). The statutes must be in writing and adopted by a constitutive General Assembly. They should be concise, precise and clear. Details not formally related to the statutes may be set out in rules of procedure or other ad hoc document. The statutes do not need to be authenticated before a notary.

the association); a Committee (comprising at least a president, a secretary and a treasurer) and an auditor. Only the General Assembly has the authority to amend the Statutes, but an elected committee may amend the rules of procedure.[12] The Swiss Civil Code determines that as soon as the statutes have been adopted by the General Assembly, the association has legal personality and may exercise its legal rights. The ICRC fulfils these requirements, as the statutory bodies of the ICRC include the Assembly, Assembly Council, Presidency, Directorate and Internal Audit. Articles 9–14 of the ICRC Statutes describe the roles of each statutory body.

By proclaiming itself 'international', in its title, the ICRC exposed itself to criticism because at the time its members were from only one small Swiss canton, Geneva.[13] The ICRC was never, however, 'just' a Swiss organisation as it has capacity to enter into agreements with states; it is the 'guardian' of IHL; it has observer status at the UN General Assembly, and it has a global presence and mandate in matters of humanitarian protection and assistance. Consequently, anyone who looks closely at the ICRC as an organisation would struggle to confine it to just one definition, namely that of a Swiss organisation.

Bugnion has argued that:

> [F]rom the outset, the Red Cross differed from other charitable organizations that flourished during the second half of the nineteenth century in two basic respects: the permanent nature and the international aspirations of the institutions set up on the basis of the resolutions adopted at the Geneva Conference of October 1863 which gave birth to the Red Cross.[14]

This author is in agreement with Bugnion on that point. The ICRC is different from an NGO given its organisational structure and the involvement of states. Arguably, it has the 'best of all worlds': it has the support of states and enters into Headquarters Agreements with them; it has the local contacts and support that NGOs are often privy to, and, yet, it remains humanitarian to its core. Furthermore, the people who work in the ICRC are staunch advocates of the fundamental principles, often to the frustration of other organisations who might be working in the same conflict-affected area. How, then, should we characterise the ICRC as an organisation? Is it intergovernmental, private or an NGO? This chapter examines each type of organisation before drawing a conclusion as to the status of the ICRC.

[12] Rule 32 Rules of Procedure of the IRCRCM (adopted by the 25th International Conference of the Red Cross at Geneva in October 1986 and amended by the 26th International Conference of the Red Cross and Red Crescent at Geneva in December 1995).

[13] D Palmieri, 'An Institution Standing the Test of Time? A Review of 150 Years of the History of the International Committee of the Red Cross' (2012) 94 *IRRC* 1273, 1275.

[14] F Bugnion, 'Red Cross Law' (1995) 308 *IRRC* 491, 492–93.

## A. Intergovernmental Organisations

We know that the ICRC was conceived of in 1859 and has grown from the Committee of Five to the organisation it is today. It has therefore developed alongside a number of other organisations, including the League of Nations and the UN. The ICRC has continued to provide humanitarian protection and assistance whilst other organisations have come and gone. Its sustainability could be, in part, due to its principles, which set it apart from other more politicised or economically focused organisations.

The landscape of the international stage began to change when states became more closely connected in trade, politics and relations. It was necessary to establish ad hoc international conferences to bring states to one table to enter into agreements or make decisions that affected more than one state. The Concert of Europe, for example, was the 'international system within which European governments formulated and conducted policy'; it was established to deal with 'balance-of-power' politics.[15] In time these ad hoc conferences became the building blocks for international organisations to which states ceded elements of sovereign power.[16] The era following the Second World War saw the greatest proliferation of intergovernmental organisations, as, in some instances, they were seen as entities that could guarantee the 'salvation of mankind'.[17] In this period, states needed to coexist and work together to make decisions.[18] States were still the dominant actors on the international stage and their interests guided the development of international law. It was, in fact, the dependence on the consent of the state and the importance of state sovereignty that led to calls for a greater institutionalisation of the system in order to ensure the development of a stronger notion of the rule of law. Nevertheless, it should be recognised that even Grotius saw 'an intimate connexion between the rejection of ideas of "reason of State" and the affirmation of the legal and moral unity of mankind'.[19] The institutional landscape continued to evolve during the latter half of the twentieth century and the

[15] RB Elrod, 'The Concert of Europe: A Fresh Look at the International System' (1970) 28(2) *World Politics* 159, 160–62.

[16] I Brownlie, *Principles of Public International Law*, 7th edn (Oxford, Oxford University Press, 2008) ch 31; R Collins and ND White, 'International Organizations and the Idea of Autonomy, Introduction and Overview' in R Collins and ND White, *International Organisations and the Idea of Autonomy: Institutional Independence in the International Legal Order* (London, Routledge, 2011) ch 1.

[17] J Klabbers, *Organisations: The Library of Essays in International Law* (Aldershot, Ashgate/Dartmouth, 2005) 164.

[18] P Jessup, *A Modern Law of Nations* (New York, Macmillan, 1948) 17.

[19] H Lauterpacht, 'The Grotian Tradition in International Law' (1946) 23 *British Yearbook of International Law* 31 in RG Teitel, *Humanity's Law* (Oxford, Oxford University Press, 2011) 23–24.

beginning of this century.[20] At the end of the Cold War, Frank pleaded with the world to 'create a global system for the new millennium, one which preserves peace, fosters economic growth, and prevents the deterioration of the human physical and environmental condition'.[21] Almost thirty years later, peace, economic growth, and human, physical and environmental conditions remain riven with complications and limitations.

Despite this proliferation on the international stage, there is no generally accepted common definition of an international organisation.[22] Nevertheless three components are included in almost all definitions: firstly, that an international organisation is an association of states; secondly, that it was established under international law, that is, by an international agreement; and finally, that it has organs with capacity on the international stage to pursue common interests.[23] Well-known international organisations include the UN, the World Trade Organization and the International Monetary Fund. Theoretically, therefore, if the ICRC fulfils all three of these criteria it ought to be considered an international organisation.

This analysis takes each of the criteria outlined above to determine whether the ICRC ought to be considered an intergovernmental organization, akin to the UN. The UN is utilised throughout this analysis as it fulfils all three of the requirements for an entity to be defined as an 'international organisation', and whether the ICRC is, by its nature, an international organisation will therefore be determined largely by comparing it to the UN.

### (i) *Associated by States*

The first component of an international organisation is that it is associated by states. During the 1940s, against the backdrop of the Second World War, sovereign states began to join together at meetings and conferences to jointly engage in a fight against aggression. This is evidenced by the early outcomes of such gatherings, including the Dumbarton Oaks

[20] R McCorquodale, 'Beyond State Sovereignty: The International Legal System and Non-State Participants' (2006) *International Law: Revista colombiana de derecho internacional*, junio–noviembre, número 008, 103, 108.

[21] T Franck, 'United Nations Based Prospects for a New Global Order' (1990) 22 *New York University Journal of International Law and Politics* 601, 601–02.

[22] ND White, *The Law of International Organisations* (Manchester, Manchester University Press, 2005) 1; C Brölmann, *The Institutional Veil in Public International Law: International Organisations and the Law of Treaties* (Oxford, Hart Publishing, 2007) 13.

[23] M Virally, 'Classification of International Organizations: A Legal Approach' in G Abi-Saab, *The Concept of International Organizations* (UNESCO, Paris 1981) 51; P Gautier, 'The Reparation for Injuries Case Revisited: The Personality of the European Union' (2000) 4 *Max Planck Yearbook of United Nations Law* 331, 333; H Schermers and N Blokker, *International Institutional Law: Unity within Diversity*, 4th edn (Amsterdam, Martinus Nijhoff, 2003) 32-46; Brölmann (n 22) 17; J Klabbers, *An Introduction to International Institutional Law*, 2nd edn (Cambridge, Cambridge University Press, 2009) 6–12.

Conversations of 1944.[24] These Conversations led up to the UN Conference on International Organization, which was convened in San Francisco from 25 April to 26 June 1945, where fifty allied nations agreed to give certain powers to an international organisation, the UN.[25] The UN is a state-centric organisation, which continues to admit new Member States; the most recent state to be recognised by the General Assembly was South Sudan in 2011.[26]

The ICRC, as distinguished from the UN, is associated by Swiss nationals and is usually defined as a private organisation, as noted above. It does not have Member States and is therefore independent in its governance and operational decisions. The ICRC was 'born in private, among private people'.[27] Its instigator was Henry Dunant, whose experience of the aftermath of the Battle of Solferino in 1859 pushed him to consider how soldiers should fare following battles. Dunant imagined national societies of volunteers ready to help the wounded from all states whenever armed conflict broke out. He always intended therefore for the movement to be international. His reverie, backed in the initial months by General Dufour and Gustave Moynier, was of a cohort of volunteer nurses on battlefields, volunteers transporting the wounded, and soldiers being cared for in hospitals. In a speech to the Public Welfare Society on 9 February 1863 Dunant outlined his vision that such an international voluntary service needed a permanent committee with a covenant, supported by 'Europe's crowned heads', to 'adhere to some basic code of behaviour in wartime'.[28] The principle of voluntary service is now contained in the preamble to the Statutes of the IRCRCM.

On 17 February 1863 Dunant, Dufour, Moynier and two new supporters, Louis Appia and Theodore Maunoir, gathered and decided to become the International Committee for Relief to the Wounded, also known as the Committee of Five.[29] From February to October 1863 the Committee of Five worked to harness the support of ministers and royals in a number of

[24] H Kelsen, 'The Old and the New League: The Covenant and the Dumbarton Oaks Proposals' (1945) 39(1) *American Journal of International Law* 45; RC Hilderbrand, *Dumbarton Oaks: The Origins of the United Nations and the Search for Post War Security* (Durham, University of North Carolina Press, 1990).

[25] For a comprehensive account of the San Francisco conference, see S Schlesinger, *Act of Creation: The Founding of the United Nations: A Story of Superpowers, Secret Agents, Wartime Allies and Enemies, and their Quest for a Peaceful World* (New York, Basic Books, 2004); See also A Buzo, *Pacific Union: The Story of the San Francisco-Forty Fivers* (Monash University of Melbourne, Currency Press, 1995).

[26] UNGA, 'Admission of the Republic of South Sudan to Membership' (25 August 2011) Res A/RES/65/308.

[27] C Moorehead, *Dunant's Dream: War, Switzerland and the History of the Red Cross* (New York, Carol & Graf, 1999) 21.

[28] ibid, 14–15.

[29] ibid, 17.

European capitals for their international committee. On 26 October 1863 sixteen states and four philanthropic institutions sent representatives to a diplomatic conference, which adopted ten articles on the wounded and the neutrality of medical personnel.[30] They are contained in the 'Resolutions of the Geneva International Conference' and provide for each nation to establish a committee 'whose duty it shall be, in time of war and if the need arises, to assist the Army Medical Services by every means in its power'.[31] The resolutions also accepted the proposals made by Dunant and the Committee for the establishment of national committees.

The Committee of Five would have been a nonentity without state representatives and state support at the conference, including ratification of the articles agreed upon by states. Indeed, the following year, in 1864, the Swiss Federal Council, on the initiative of the Geneva Committee, invited the governments of Europe and several American states to a diplomatic conference.[32] The outcome of the conference was to be the 'Convention for the Amelioration of the Condition of the Wounded in Armies in the Field, Geneva, of 22 August 1864', which had sixteen state signatories. Pictet stated:

> It is difficult to imagine today the vast influence exercised by the first Geneva Convention on the evolution of the law of nations. For the first time in history, the States, in a formal and permanent document, accepted a limitation on their own power, for the sake of the individual and an altruistic ideal. For the first time, war had yielded to law.[33]

'The adoption of this text—the first modern international humanitarian law—by a dozen states enhanced the prestige of the ICRC and its founders, and gave it a moral and perhaps political force on the European scene'.[34] In 1875 the Committee of Five adopted the name the ICRC.[35]

Without the collaboration of states and state parties to a number of international conventions, the Committee of Five would never have become the ICRC. It would also not be the international presence that it is today. Although the Committee of Five were the original members of the ICRC, it was always Dunant's intention, and in fact need, for states to come together at the International Conference to support the initiatives as regards the wounded. The work of the International Conference was described in

[30] 'From the Battle of Solferino to the Eve of the First World War' (ICRC, 28 December 2004) www.icrc.org/eng/resources/documents/misc/57jnvp.htm.

[31] Resolutions of the Geneva International Conference (Geneva, 26–29 October 1863).

[32] D Schindler and J Toman, *The Laws of Armed Conflict: A Collection of Conventions, Resolutions, and Other Documents* (Leiden, Brill, 1998) 280–81.

[33] J Pictet, *Development and Principles of International Humanitarian Law* (Geneva, Henry Dunant Institute and Dordrecht, Martinus Nijhoff, 1985) 30, see also ch 2.

[34] Palmieri (n 13) 1276.

[35] See Introduction to the Resolutions of the Geneva International Conference (Geneva, 26–29 October 1863).

chapter 1, but, nevertheless, its significance should be emphasised. The International Conference cannot be matched, on the international stage, as a humanitarian forum. The presence of each component of the IRCRCM and the 194 state parties to the Geneva Conventions I, II, III and IV 1949 ensure that current issues in IHL and humanitarian needs are the focal point of each International Conference. To this end, although the ICRC cannot be defined as 'associated by states', it is, nevertheless, inextricably linked in its law and practice to states and the people living within them. The International Conference therefore supports the work of the ICRC and facilitates the drafting of conventions, to which states became signatories. The need for state consent for ICRC missions precludes a wholly autonomous ICRC, as is the case for the UN.

### *(ii) Established by International Agreement*

The second component of an international organisation is that it be established by international agreement between states. Under the Vienna Convention on the Law of Treaties 1969, as amended in 1986, an international agreement is concluded between states (or international organisations) in written form and governed by international law.[36] As regards an international organisation, such an agreement would be constitutional. As a caveat of such an organisation being established by an international agreement between states, those states must have freely consented to be bound by such an agreement. Schermers and Blokker stated that an organisation's functions and rights depend upon the constituting treaty provisions and the general limitations of international law.[37] An example of such a constitutional international agreement is the UN Charter, which describes the rights and obligations of Member States.[38]

The International Conferences, initially convened by the efforts of the Committee of Five, facilitated agreement upon the Geneva Conventions, under which the ICRC actions were mandated, including the protection of the wounded and sick in the field; wounded, sick and shipwrecked members of armed forces at sea; prisoners of war; and civilians who find themselves under the rule of a foreign power in the event of international conflict. Nowadays the ICRC receives instructions from the International Conferences—for example, to conclude a 'Study on Customary IHL', and

[36] Vienna Convention on the Law of Treaties (adopted 23 May 1969, entered into force 27 January 1980) 1155 UNTS 331.

[37] Schermers and Blokker (n 23) 992; See also A Cassese, *International Law in a Divided World* (Oxford, Clarendon Press, 1986) 86.

[38] United Nations, Charter of the United Nations, 24 October 1945, 1 UNTS XVI (UN Charter).

recently to study the provision of healthcare in armed conflict.[39] Directions to the ICRC to undertake such work are evidence of the freely expressed will of states to endow the ICRC with specific rights and duties.

### *(iii) Organs with Capacity on the International Stage*

The final element usually attributed to an international organisation is that it has organs with capacity on the international stage. The UN, for example, is not merely a forum for state interaction, as its organs act on the international stage, creating law, policy and practice in specific areas. The UN principal organs are the General Assembly, the Security Council, the Economic and Social Council (ECOSOC), the Secretariat, the International Court of Justice (ICJ) and the Trusteeship Council.[40] The UN also has specialised agencies for technical areas such as the International Labour Organization, the International Civil Aviation Organization (ICAO) and the Food and Agriculture Organization (FAO).[41] Finally, professionals, academics and staff can work in an individual capacity for a very specific mandate, in UN specialised agencies, such as the International Atomic Energy Agency (IAEA).[42] In the ICRC, the Presidency takes responsibility for its external relations.[43]

As we know from chapter 1, the ICRC is comprised of the Assembly, the Assembly Council and the Directorate (the executive body). Both the Assembly, with up to twenty-five co-opted members of Swiss nationality, and the Assembly Council are chaired by Peter Maurer, who has been President of the ICRC since 1 July 2012. He is assisted by a Vice-President, Christine Beerli. The Directorate, with five members, is chaired by the Director-General, Yves Daccord. These three organs

> have overall responsibility for ICRC policy, strategy and decisions related to the development of IHL. These bodies oversee all the activities of the organization, including field and headquarters operations and the approval of objectives

[39] In December 1995, the 26th International Conference of the Red Cross and Red Crescent officially mandated the ICRC to prepare a report on customary rules of international humanitarian law applicable in international and non-international armed conflicts. See 'Twenty-sixth International Conference of the Red Cross and Red Crescent, Geneva, 3–7 December 1995, Resolution 1: International Humanitarian Law: From Law to Action. Report on the Follow-up to the International Conference for the Protection of War Victims' (7 December 1995) www.icrc.org/eng/resources/documents/resolution/26-international-conference-resolution-1-1995.htm.

[40] For a general overview of the UN structure, see B Conforti and C Focarelli, *The Law and Practice of the United Nations*, 4th edn (The Hague, Martinus Nijhoff, 2010).

[41] KW Abbott and D Snidal, 'Why States Act through Formal International Organisations' (1998) 42(1) *Journal of Conflict Resolution* 3, 4.

[42] List of Specialised Agencies, www.un.org/en/sections/about-un/funds-programmes-specialized-agencies-and-others/index.html.

[43] ICRC Statutes, Art 11.

and budgets. They also monitor implementation by the Directorate of Assembly or Assembly Council decisions and are assisted in this task by a Control Commission and the internal and external auditors.[44]

## B. Private International Organisations

The second type of organisation to be examined are private international organisations. These are different from international organisations and NGOs. The ICRC's decision-making capabilities are in the hands of private individuals, rather than states. This indicates that the ICRC possesses some commonalities with private international organisations. In economic and market driven spheres, the globalisation of economic activity has meant the 'construction of private international regimes in many industry sectors as a form of self-regulation or rule setting in the absence of an overarching global political regime'.[45] The self-regulation and competence to establish rules that govern commerce shows that organisations do not always need Member States to control areas of international law and relations. Members of the private sector therefore often replace state-to-state negotiations or Member State-based international organisations.[46] Is it possible to draw parallels between private international organisations and the ICRC? This part of the chapter uses Intelsat Ltd, as an example of an existing private international organisation, to show how the ICRC might be consistent with the definition of such.

On 20 December 1961 UN General Assembly Resolution 1721 decided that global satellite communication should be made available on a non-discriminatory basis.[47] On 24 August 1964 the International Telecommunications Satellite Organisations (INTELSAT), a multilateral public intergovernmental treaty entity, was established by governments and operating entities signing an agreement.[48] On 30 November 1998 INTELSAT transferred working capital, five in-orbit satellites, one in-construction satellite and their associated orbital roles to a newly created company, New Skies NV. On 18 July 2001 INTELSAT became a private company called Intelsat Ltd. Intelsat provides satellite services worldwide that facilitate media and entertainment communications for media and network

[44] ICRC Decision Making Structures, https://www.icrc.org/en/document/icrc-decision-making-structures-0#.VOih50JZFNM.

[45] V Haufler, 'Private Sector International Regimes' in RA Higgot, GRD Underhill and A Bieler (eds), *Non-State Actors and Authority in the Global System* (London, Routledge, 2000) 122–23.

[46] ibid, 121.

[47] UNGA, 'International Co-operation in the Peaceful Uses of Outer Space' (20 December 1961) Res 1721 (XVI).

[48] Intelsat Ltd: About Us, www.intelsat.com/about-us/our-history/.

companies, multinational corporations, Internet service providers and government agencies.[49] Finally on 28 January 2005 it was sold to private investors.[50]

During the privatisation of INTELSAT a residual treaty organisation was instituted called the International Telecommunications Satellite Organization (ITSO).[51] It was charged with ensuring that the new owners of INTELSAT's satellite system preserve global connectivity and continue to serve those poor or under-served countries that lack the technological facilities to provide such a service. ITSO therefore relies on political and legal tools to accomplish its mandate.[52] Its Member States include most UN members.[53] The maintenance of an intergovernmental organisation within a private company was seen as necessary to protect the 'global connectivity and global coverage' of the system,[54] as it must safeguard 'non-discriminatory access to the [privatised] company's system' and ensure that privatised INTELSAT LLC 'serve[s] its lifeline connectivity customers'.[55] Is it possible to draw an analogy between Intelsat Ltd and the ICRC?

The ICRC possesses features akin to a private international organisation. Intelsat became a private company as necessitated by the demands of the market, whereas the ICRC was always a private enterprise but with state support. Nevertheless, in their functioning and infrastructure there are similarities; both need independent and non-political decision-making and, theoretically, both provide services worldwide without agenda. Indeed telecommunications, by the time of the privatisation, were considered a necessary part of all territories/states and the fear was that commercial enterprises could leave some developing states with no alternative service provider, 'cutting them off' from the rest of the world.[56] The role of the ICRC is likewise a necessary actor on the international stage. It has private Swiss citizens at the helm; its impartiality, neutrality and independence must be maintained. However, for INTELSAT/Intelsat Ltd, it was necessary to maintain government support. It is an intermingling of international organisation creation and private organisation functionality.

[49] ibid.

[50] ibid.

[51] K Katkin, 'Communication Breakdown? The Future of Global Connectivity after the Privatisation of INTELSAT' (2005) *International Journal of Communications Law and Policy* 1.

[52] ibid, 4–5.

[53] International Telecommunications Satellite Organization, www.itso.int.

[54] Katkin (n 51) 28.

[55] ITSO Agreement (17 November 2000) Arts III(b)(iii), IX(c)(ii) and (iii), www.itso.int/index.php?option=com_content&view=article&id=13&Itemid=208&lang=en.

[56] Intelsat Ltd (n 48).

## C. Non-Governmental Organisations

The final type of organisation to be considered is the NGO. Charnovitz and Amerasinghe define the ICRC as an NGO.[57] This section will clarify and argue against existing literature, which sees the ICRC as *just* an NGO. There is no generally accepted definition of the term NGO in international law.[58] If we take the list of elements of NGOs from just four academics it includes: independence; non-profit, non-use of or promotion of violence; formal existence and structure; public not private interests; transnational scope of activists; individuals join voluntarily; independent of states; self-appointed; exist outside of international law; consist of a small group of people; and represent the opinion of a relatively small number of people.[59] Indeed, confusingly, Kaczorowska states that the ICRC is an NGO, with personality similar to the UN.[60] This is significant and reinforces the analysis above that shows similarities between the UN and the ICRC in terms of its status as an organisation. The ICRC, critically, is more than just an NGO.

The term NGO is found in Article 71 of the UN Charter, which recognised the possibility of NGOs interacting with the UN.[61] It did not, however, provide any definition of such an organisation. In 1950 ECOSOC stated that: '[A]ny international organization which is not created by intergovernmental agreement shall be considered as an NGO.'[62] A simple argument would be that since the ICRC was not actually *created* by an intergovernmental agreement, it is therefore an NGO. We could add to this that the historical background of the ICRC shows that it emerged because of a profound normative change at a societal level, just like NGOs.[63]

[57] S Charnovitz, 'Nongovernmental Organizations and International Law' (2006) 100(2) *American Journal of International Law* 348, 348; CF Amerasinghe, *Principles of the Institutional Law of International Organizations*, 2nd edn (Cambridge, Cambridge University Press, 2005) 3, 6.

[58] A-K Lindblom, *Non-governmental Organizations in International Law* (Cambridge, Cambridge University Press, 2005) 36.

[59] S Hobe, 'Global Challenges to Statehood: The Increasingly Important Role of Nongovernmental Organizations' (1997–98) 5 *Global Legal Studies Journal* 191, 193–94; K Martens, 'Examining the (Non-) Status of NGOs in International Law' (2003) 1 *Indiana Global Law Studies Journal* 1, 1–2; Lindblom (n 58) 46–52; A-K Lindblom, 'NGOs and Non-State Actors in International Law' in B Reinalda (ed), *Ashgate Research Companion to Non-State Actors* (Surrey, Ashgate, 2011) 147–48.

[60] Kaczorowska (n 10) 181.

[61] S Charnovitz, 'Two Centuries of Participation: NGOs and International Governance' (1997) 18 *Michigan Journal of International Law* 183, 186. This article describes using UN criteria to define NGOs.

[62] ECOSOC, 'Review of Consultative Arrangements with NGOs' (27 February 1950) E/RES/ 288 (X) para 8; See also ECOSOC, 'Consultative Relationship between the UN and NGOs' (25 July 1996) E/RES/1996/31 para 12.

[63] K West, *Agents of Altruism: The Expansion of Humanitarian NGOs in Rwanda and Afghanistan* (Aldershot, Ashgate, 2001) 20.

Its creation was symptomatic of a feeling amongst people, in particular, the Committee of Five, not states, that some kind of external body was necessary during armed conflict. Furthermore, much like an NGO, the ICRC has a non-profit, independent identity. Finally, there are no Member States or state representatives in the ICRC, although it must be recalled that the ICRC is part of the International Conference, which adopts resolutions on the international stage.[64]

Recent international conferences, such as the World Humanitarian Summit, show that the role of NGOs on the international stage is developing.[65] In addition to international organisations, for example, NGOs too may participate at all stages of the negotiation processes at global conferences;[66] they seek to influence governmental representatives through informal lobbying, and advance international standards such as on human rights and the environment. The legal status of NGOs endows them with rights and obligations on the international stage, provides the possibility of acting before international courts and tribunals, allows them to enter formal relationships with international organisations and endows them with the ability to conclude agreements under international law.[67] The ICRC is privy to these rights too but, in addition, governments have accorded it rights that are typically only granted to intergovernmental organisations, including privileges and immunities on the international stage, and it has signed Headquarters Agreements with numerous states.[68] These rights are considered in depth in the ILP analysis in the next part of this chapter.

To conclude, the ICRC is not just an NGO. The ICRC mandate was created by states and is developed by the International Conference, and interpreted and applied by ICRC delegates on the ground. It provides the ICRC with authority on the international stage, as the guardian of IHL. The situations in which it works and the activities it undertakes develop over time. This is different to NGOs whose mandate is created by the people who found the organisation for the specific purposes of that body. For example, MSF, which is a private, international association, has the

[64] AS Muller, *International Organisations and their Host States: Aspects of their Legal Relationship* (The Hague, Kluwer Law International, 1995) 5.

[65] World Humanitarian Summit, Istanbul, May 2016, https://www.worldhumanitariansummit.org.

[66] A Gheciu, 'Divided Partners: The Challenges of NATO–NGO Cooperation in Peace building Operations' (2011) 17(1) *Global Governance* 95, 95–113; See also A Chadwick, 'The Emerging Roles of NGOs in the UN System: From Article 71 to a People's Millennium Assembly' (2002) 8(1) *Global Governance* 93.

[67] Lindblom (n 58) 149.

[68] 'Agreement between the International Committee of the Red Cross and the Swiss Federal Council to Determine the Legal Status of the Committee in Switzerland' (1993) 293 *IRRC* 152, Arts 1, 3, 4 and 5 (Headquarters Agreement 1993); See also MT Kamminga, 'The Evolving Status of NGOs under International Law: A Threat to the Inter-State System?' in P Alston (ed), *Non-State Actors and Human Rights* (Oxford, Oxford University Press, 2005) 93, 98–99.

mandate to 'bring[] humanitarian medical assistance to victims of conflict, natural disasters, epidemics or healthcare exclusion'.[69] Amnesty International has a mandate to 'to undertake research and action focused on preventing and ending grave abuses of these rights'.[70] Local NGOs aim to achieve specific purposes. For example, in the DRC, which forms the case study for this research, a local NGO Eben Ezer Ministries International (EMI) has been working with Children in Crisis, a London-based NGO, to support educational initiatives on the remote high plateau of South Kivu in eastern DRC.[71]

## D. The ICRC as a Sui Generis Entity

The ICRC is a private association with close ties to Switzerland, including its headquarters, the Swiss nationality of Committee members and senior staff, and frequent contacts with the Swiss Foreign Ministry.[72] These elements confer upon the ICRC a profile unique amongst NGOs and international organisations.[73] The subtleties and nuances of the establishment and functioning of the ICRC show that it cannot simply be defined as an international organisation, private international organisation or an NGO. From its inception the ICRC was not restricted to internal conflicts in Switzerland. Dunant's plan was for all wounded soldiers in all states to be afforded neutrality and medical care. The realisation of this vision came with the International Conference, an association of states, agreeing to the 1864 Convention and beginning a process of drafting and facilitating the adoption of international legal instruments from which the ICRC would derive rights and duties on the international stage. These aspects of its creation and its subsequent development set it apart from the UN, Intelsat Ltd and NGOs, such as Human Rights Watch and Amnesty International. It is concluded therefore that the ICRC can only be understood as a sui generis entity. The ICRC is an organisation that, through its principles of humanitarianism, neutrality and independence, is able to reach people on the ground.

[69] Medecins sans Frontières, www.msf.org/msf-activities.

[70] Statute of Amnesty International (as amended by the 31st International Council, meeting in Berlin, Germany, 18–22 August 2013, files.amnesty.org/AIStatute/AIStatuteAsAmendedAt2013ICM_EN.pdf.

[71] Democratic Republic of Congo, www.childrenincrisis.org/our-work/democratic-republic-congo; See also https://secure.thebiggive.org.uk/projects/view/12314/school-building--democratic-republic-of-congo.

[72] 'ICRC Directorate' (1 February 2014) www.icrc.org/eng/resources/documents/misc/icrc-directorate-010710.htm.

[73] See International Law Commission, 'First Report on the Responsibility of International Organisations' (26 March 2003) A/CN.4/532, para 21.

## III. INTERNATIONAL LEGAL PERSONALITY

This section focuses on the ILP of the ICRC, a status recognised by the Red Cross Conventions of 1949, the UN Security Council[74] and the International Criminal Tribunal for the former Yugoslavia (ICTY), the latter of which stated that it is generally acknowledged that the ICRC has ILP.[75] Partlett has argued that the ICRC 'has no historical or current connection to territory, nor any aspirations to Statehood. Rather it came to be recognised as having a measure of international personality in view of its special status under IHL.'[76] 'It is true that there are examples of domestic associations that came to be accepted as international persons. Thus the ICRC was formed as a private humanitarian initiative, sanctioned by a diplomatic conference in 1863. In 1915 it was formally established as a Swiss organization.'[77] Taking the analysis above as the foundation, it can be said that the ICRC has developed a dual character, as both a Swiss organisation and an organisation increasingly recognised as performing international functions. However, there is also scholarship that vehemently denies that the ICRC possesses ILP. The International Law Association Committee on Non-State Actors, for example, stated that: '[T]here are no absolutely compelling arguments for the ILP of the ICRC in the traditional sense of possessing international rights and duties and having the capacity to maintain its rights by bringing international claims.'[78] Moreover, it is recognised that 'individuals and corporate bodies also derive myriad

[74] 770 (13 August 1992) para 2; 771 (13 August 1992) paras 4, 5; 775 (28 August 1992); 776 (14 September 1992) para 2; 814 (26 March 1993) para 9; 1010 (10 August 1995) para 1; 1019 (9 November 1995) para 2; 1034 (21 December 1995) paras 4, 5; 1199 (23 September 1998) paras 4(c), 5(d), 5 (e); 1398 (15 March 2002) Preamble, para 4, 13; 1430 (14 August 2002) Preamble, para 6; 1434 (6 September 2002) Preamble, para 3; 1466 (14 March 2003) Preamble para 3.

[75] *Prosecutor v Simić et al* (Decision on the Prosecution Motion under Rule 73 for a Rule Concerning the Testimony of a Witness), ICTY Trial Chamber 27 July 1999, para 46; See also R Portmann, *Legal Personality in International Law* (Cambridge, Cambridge University Press, 2010) 110–14.

[76] K Partlett, *The Individual and the International Legal System: Continuity and Change in International Law* (Cambridge, Cambridge University Press, 2011) 34; See also C Dominicé, 'La Personalité Juridique International du CICR' in C Swinarski (ed), *Studies and Essays on International Humanitarian Law and Red Cross Principles in Honour of Jean Pictet* (The Hague, Martinus Nijhoff, 1984).

[77] D Bindschedler-Robert, 'Red Cross' (1983) 5 *EPIL* 250; Y Beigbeder, *The Role and Status of International Humanitarian Volunteers and Organisations* (Dordrecht, Martinus Nijhoff, 1991) 66; C Koenig, 'Observer Status for the International Committee of the Red Cross at the United Nations: A Legal Viewpoint' (1991) no 280 *IRRC*; A Schlögel, 'International Red Cross' in R Wolfrum (ed), *United Nations: Law Policies and Practice* (Dordrecht, Martinus Nijhoff, 1995) vol 2, 814–15; H-P Gasser, 'International Committee of the Red Cross (ICRC)' in R Wolfrum (ed), *The Max Planck Encyclopedia of Public International Law* (Oxford, Oxford University Press, 2009).

[78] T Gazzini (ILA Committee on Non-State Actors), 'A Unique Non-State Actor: The International Committee of the Red Cross' (Provisional Draft) (26–28 March 2009) 5.

rights from innumerable treaties and conventions are not classified as international persons by the same authors'.[79] Indeed treaties can be concluded by international organisations deprived of ILP, such as the Organization for Security and Co-operation in Europe (OSCE).[80] Finally, the IFRC derives similar or even more extraordinary rights from agreements with Switzerland and is still not classified as an international person.[81] Nevertheless, without personality, the entity itself, in this case the ICRC, does not have rights per se. This is critical to the investigation of the mandate of the ICRC as it is imperative to establish the extent to which the ICRC *itself* has powers beyond the states that sign up to the Geneva Conventions or attend the International Conference.

When an organisation is established it will be for a purpose, as a functioning entity with goals in mind, whether it is the Red Cross, the UN, or Oxfam. Personality is a legal concept enabling the community to distinguish between the entities that are capable of acting with legal effects in a given legal system. Organisations with ILP are not simply collections of states reliant on those states for any possible action, but rather they are actors in their own right; to this end, personality distinguishes organisations from other more traditional nineteenth-century notions of state cooperation, which were considered above.[82] When the founders, states or individuals, set it up they can intend for the organisation to function under its own personality, that is, they do not intend to rewrite the constituent document every time the organisation needs to undertake an activity not expressly provided for. The capacities and competences attributable to any given organisation vary according to the constituent document (ie express, and/ or implied powers) and can also be developed by the organisation, that is, a product of its separate will. For the ICRC to act independently and develop its own agenda on the international stage, therefore, it must be the case that it possesses ILP.

It is interesting to reflect on the fact that the Geneva Conventions were drafted around the same time as the UN Charter, with the same states and sometimes the same representatives involved in the negotiations. The ICJ *Reparations Case* found that the UN was intended to act autonomously, the question is whether such an intention is also the case for the ICRC? To be clear, if the question were posed today it would seem uncontroversial to suggest that the ICRC has a separate will, particularly given the autonomy

[79] N Leroux, 'Non-State Actors in French Legal Scholarship: International Legal Personality in Question' in J d'Aspremont (ed), *Participants in the International Legal System: Multiple Perspectives on Non-State Actors in International Law* (London, Routledge, 2011) 88.

[80] *Agreement on OSCE Kosovo Verification Mission*, Belgrade (16 October 1998) UN Doc S/1998/978.

[81] Leroux (n 79) 88–89.

[82] Sands and P Klein (n 3) 469.

of the headquarters in Geneva. This chapter considers the development of the practice of the ICRC and whether it is in line with the constituent document. Finally, it asks whether the ICRC can act ultra vires and what the consequences of such would be?

The most logical place to begin any analysis of ILP is the *Reparations Case* and the multitude of subsequent theories that seek to explain and rationalise the judgment. Four years after the creation of the UN, the ICJ was asked for an Advisory Opinion on whether the UN, as an international organisation, had the legal capacity to bring an international claim and whether it had specialist organs that exhibited a separate will to the will of its Member States.[83] The ICJ in the *Reparations Case* found that making treaties, claims, and the possession of privileges and immunities were essential to the functioning of the UN, so regardless of whether the UN Charter said it or not, those capacities were intended and essential to the UN. It therefore presumed that the UN had personality. The *Reparations Case* is the accepted 'test' for ILP but it is also widely accepted that the argument in the judgment is circular: the ICJ inferred from specific powers that the UN had ILP and then deduced from personality that it could bring an international claim. This has given rise to competing theories of ILP. The ICJ was careful to ground any 'progressive' change in international law upon the interests and needs of states to interact with such non-state entities.[84] As was stated in the introduction, the ICJ determined the ability of an organisation to have legal personality:

> In the opinion of the Court, the Organization was intended to exercise and enjoy, and is in fact exercising and enjoying functions and rights which can only be explained on the basis of the possession of a large measure of international personality and the capacity to operate upon an international plane.[85]

A state, for example, 'possesses the totality of international rights and duties recognized by international law, the rights and duties of an entity such as the Organization must depend upon its purposes and functions as specified or implied in its constituent documents and developed in practice'.[86] The *Reparations Case* failed, however, to determine whether a specific attribute of the UN was crucial to its finding of personality or whether it was a unique combination of factors.[87] Nevertheless, the ICJ continued to use this approach to ILP in a number of subsequent cases.[88]

[83] *Reparation for Injuries* (n 7) 178–79; Portmann (n 75) 105.

[84] GI Hernández, 'Non-state Actors from the Perspective of the International Court of Justice' in d'Aspremont (n 79) 142.

[85] *Reparations for Injuries* (n 7) 179.

[86] ibid.

[87] JE Alvarez, *International Organizations as Law-makers* (Oxford, Oxford University Press, 2005) 133.

[88] *Certain Expenses of the United Nations (Article 17 paragraph 2 of the Charter)*, (Advisory Opinion) [1962] ICJ Rep 151, 159; *Legal Consequences for States of the Continued Presence of South*

The court's overarching approach was to be one of pragmatic, progressive development.[89] The UN, and potentially other organisations, are to be considered, as 'communities' through which states participate in the international legal system and also as independent legal persons on an equal level to states.[90]

There are alternative understandings of ILP that have developed since the *Reparations Case*.[91] Sociological theory, for example, suggests that changing sociological circumstances on the international scene also impact upon ILP.[92] Indeed Portmann argues that the ICJ did not determine ILP directly from the UN Charter, rather it considered 'sociological observations', including 'factual changes on the international scene in order to open the possibility of including non-State entities into international law'.[93] The ICJ's *Reparation for Injuries* Advisory Opinion emphasised social developments as one of the main factors influencing its decision to find that the UN possessed ILP, in other words, its 'nature depends upon the needs of the community'.[94] The humanitarian principles of the ICRC make it an invaluable organisation for communities. Between 1863 and 1947 Moynier, Ador and Huber were key actors in the development and progression of the ICRC, and Sandoz remarks that, for these three men, 'the ICRC's role went without saying—it existed because it was needed, because it fulfilled a useful function in the international community'.[95] It is argued therefore that one cannot help but think the ICRC's international personality derives in equal part from the nature of the rights it enjoys under the Geneva Conventions I, II, III and IV 1949 and from the actual importance of the ICRC on the international stage.

Alternatively, personality may be established through intention, the constitution and the powers that implicitly follow. Traditionally,

*Africa in Namibia (South West Africa) notwithstanding Security Council Resolution 276 (1970)* (Advisory Opinion) [1971] ICJ Rep 16; *Interpretation of the Agreement of 25 March 1951 between the WHO and the Egypt* Case [1980] ICJ Rep 73, 89–90; *Legality of the Use by a State of Nuclear Weapons in Armed Conflict*, (Advisory Opinion) [1996] ICJ Rep 226; Vienna Convention on the Law of Treaties (with annex) concluded at Vienna on 23 May 1969, Art 31.

89 F Green, 'Fragmentation in Two Dimensions: The ICJ's Flawed Approach to Non-state Actors and International Legal Personality' (2008) 9(1) Melbourne Journal of International Law 47, 51.

90 R Collins, 'Non-State, Inter-state or Supra-State? The Peculiar Identity of the Intergovernmental Organization' in d'Aspremont (n 79) 315; DJ Bedermann, 'The Souls of International Organizations: Legal Personality and the Lighthouse at Cape Spartel' (1996) 36 *Virginia Journal of International Law* 371–74.

91 White (n 2) 114–15.

92 T Meron, 'Subjects of International Law: International Law in the Age of Human Rights' (2003) *Receuil des Cours de l'Academie de Droit International* 301, 371.

93 Portmann (n 75) 99–100, 104.

94 *Reparation for Injuries* (n 7) 178.

95 Y Sandoz, 'Max Huber and the Red Cross' (2007) 18(1) *Eur Journal of International Law* 171, 176.

in fact, the question of whether an organisation ought to be seen as an autonomous actor on the international stage came down to whether it had a separate will. The Advisory Opinion in the *Reparations Case* states that the rights of an organisation 'depend upon its purposes and functions as specific or implied in its constituent documents and developed in practice'.[96] For Kelsen, there is a simple 'formula' to look for to determine ILP: if its constituting treaty allows an organisation to enter into agreements, and establishes rights, duties and competences, then it has ILP.[97] For the ICJ, therefore, organisations are 'invested by the States which create them with powers, the limits of which are a function of the common interests whose promotion those States entrust to them'.[98] It is necessary for organisations to interpret their mandate so as to allow the achievement of their objects and purposes. To this end, the subsequent practice within organisations might not follow a strict interpretation of the constituent instrument.[99]

> The constituent instrument will usually provide that in the territory of each member State the organisation shall have the legal capacity it needs to carry out its functions, such as entering into contracts, buying and selling land and taking part in legal proceedings. The means, in effect, that each member must accord it the status of a corporation in its domestic law.[100]

This could be a simple method to find personality but it is unlikely that we would find such an explicit conferral of personality in a constituent treaty. Hartwig acknowledges the limits of such an approach, noting that it makes organisations dependent upon their members, despite an organisation's independence, rights and powers.[101] One has to question whether it would be possible for an organisation to function if it was wholly tied to the limited intentions of the founders. This seems unrealistic and self-defeating. Imagine if the Red Cross was restricted to the list of activities decided upon in the aftermath of the Second World War.

If we cannot subjectively know the intentions of the founders, perhaps we can determine whether personality exists objectively as a matter of law and can be based on an 'organisation-hood' that is parallel to 'statehood'.[102] By this theory, the objective fact of its existence means the

[96] *Reparation for Injuries* (n 7).

[97] H Kelsen, *General Theory of Law and State* (Cambridge, MA, Harvard University Press, 1945) 99 and 342.

[98] *Legality of the Use by a State of Nuclear Weapons in Armed Conflict* (Advisory Opinion) [1996] ICJ Rep 226 para 25.

[99] ibid; Vienna Convention on the Law of Treaties (adopted 23 May 1969, entered into force 27 January 1980) 1155 UNTS 331, Art 31(3)(b).

[100] A Aust, *Handbook of International Law*, 2nd edn (Cambridge, Cambridge University Press, 2010) 180–81.

[101] M Hartwig, *Die Haftung der Mitgliedstaaten* (Berlin, Springer, 1993) 37.

[102] F Seyersted, 'International Personality of International Organizations: Do their Capacities Really Depend upon their Constitutions?' (1964) 4 *Indian Journal of international Law* 1.

organisation has ILP. Seyersted identified the main criterion as the existence of a separate will of an organisation, but this does raise the problem of how to measure this separate will and the extent to which an organisation must have a will before it has personality.[103] Linked to such an idea is the proposal from Klabbers that we can *presume* that an organisation with certain elements possesses ILP.[104] This is seemingly the middle ground between the will theory and the objective theory. A number of academics support this perspective and, in terms of the ICRC, it is a sensible perspective to take in order to understand the ICRC and how it is possible for it to develop its practice legitimately and productively on the international stage. For example, White suggests that:

> [W]hile the existence of separate will is embodied in the concept of international legal personality, the extent of that will is to be found in the nature of those elements: for instance in the presence of majority voting in the organs; the width of purposes; the intrusiveness of powers; the nature of decision-making; and the depth of membership.[105]

In this regard, Klabbers and Wallendahl argue that will theory means that the organisation is 'born' with *potential* ILP but it is not until it acts or exercises powers that ILP is shown.[106] To put it another way, personality can be identified as soon as an organisation performs acts that can only be explained by the possession of personality.[107] This correlates with the *Reparations Case* where the ICJ stated that the UN was '*in fact enjoying …*'. Three elements of ILP were outlined in the *Reparation for Injuries* case: the capacity to make claims in respect of breaches of international law; the capacity to make treaties and agreements valid on the international plane; and the enjoyment of privileges and immunities from national jurisdictions.[108] Critically, however, these are just three examples of manifestations of personality and, as not all organisations have the same raison d'être, it is possible that an alternative set of actions could equally be deemed evidence of personality. Within each organization, therefore, we should look to its

[103] ibid.

[104] J Klabbers, 'Presumptive Personality: The European Union in International Law' in M Koskenniemi (ed), *International Legal Aspects of the European Union* (The Hague, Kluwer, 1998) 243–49.

[105] White (n 4) 30–31.

[106] J Klabbers and Å Wallendahl (eds), *Research Handbook on the Law of International Organisations* (Cheltenham, Edward Elgar, 2011) 36.

[107] J Klabbers, *An Introduction to International Institutional Law*, 2nd edn (Cambridge, Cambridge University Press, 2009) 49–51; J Klabbers, 'Presumptive Personality: The European Union in International Law', in M Koskenniemi (ed), *International Law Aspects Aspects of the European Union* (The Hague, Brill, 1998) 231.

[108] *Reparation for Injuries* (n 7) 179 and 188; I Brownlie, *Principles of Public International Law* (Oxford, Oxford University Press, 2003) 7; See also ILA, 'The Hague Conference 2010: Non-State Actors' (First Report of the Committee) (2010).

constitution *and practice* to find evidence of its international legal personality. Hence this section will examine the unique competences of the ICRC to determine whether it *is exercising* international legal personality.

Klabbers and Wallendahl argue that an organisation may be born with the potential for ILP but is not actually an international legal person until it performs acts that can only be explained by ILP. For the ICRC, therefore, we can look at what it was intended to do, its potential, and what is actually does. Consequently, the analysis of the ICRC demands answers to two questions: firstly, what was the intention at inception; and secondly, what does it do? The second question must be broken down into two parts. Firstly, does the ICRC possess the ability to make claims, negotiate international agreements, and possess privileges and immunities, like the UN? Secondly, does the ICRC possess functions and rights, unique to the ICRC, that can only be explained by personality, taking into account the Geneva Conventions and its practice. In order to answer these questions, this section consists of three substantive parts: intention, whether the ICRC was 'in fact' exercising functions and rights considered in the *Reparations Case*, and the intended and actual activities undertaken by the ICRC. The latter question is developed extensively throughout this book through legal and empirical analysis. The chapter will conclude by addressing the question of what may happen if the ICRC, as an ILP, usurps its mandate.

For some academics the diversity of functions performed by international organisations suggests that there is no set of capacities inherent within ILP,[109] whereas, for others, there is a presumption of certain inherent capacities so long as the international organisation is 'in a practical position to perform them'.[110] In other words, the corollary of ILP is the possession of rights and duties on the international stage, but these are not universal.[111]

Brownlie defines the three 'principal formal contexts' in locating ILP, which echo those in the *Reparation for Injuries* Advisory Opinion, including the capacity to make claims in respect of breaches of international law, the capacity to make treaties and agreements valid on the international plane, and the enjoyment of privileges and immunities from national jurisdictions.[112] These are functions and rights that can only be explained

[109] Sands and Klein (n 3) 473; I Rossi, *Legal Status of Non-Governmental Organizations in International Law* (Cambridge, Intersentia, 2010) 33.

[110] Amerasinghe (n 57) 101; F Seyersted, 'Objective International Personality of Intergovernmental Organizations: Do their capacities really depend upon the conventions establishing them?' (1964) 34 *Nordisk Tidsskrift International Ret* 3, 28, 55–56.

[111] Sands and Klein (n 3) 473–74; ILC, 'Documents of the Thirty-Seventh Session of the ILC, Yearbook of the ILC 1985, Volume II, Part One' (1985) A/CN.4/SER.A/1985/Add.1, Part 1, 112.

[112] *Reparation for Injuries* (n 7) 179 and 188; I Brownlie, *Principles of Public International Law* (Oxford, Oxford University Press, 2003) 7; See also ILA, 'The Hague Conference 2010: Non-State Actors' (First Report of the Committee) (2010).

on the basis of the possession of a large measure of ILP. Theoretically, therefore, if the ICRC exercises these functions and rights too, then it would be identifiable as having ILP. Within this, we can consider whether it was intended to exercise these functions and rights and whether they are, in fact, necessary to its functioning. Similarly, Leroux stated that: '[U]nder the so-called "restrictive" conception of international personality, international persons are those who can sign treaties, establish diplomatic relations with States and participate in the mechanism of international personality *de plano*.'[113]

## A. The ICRC was Intended to be an International Legal Person

> 'International organisations based on contractual foundations, where the member States remain to all intents and purposes the masters of the treaty, may have separate will, but the extent of it, and the possibility of its future development, are very limited. Other organisations based on constitutional foundations often possess, or have the potential to develop, significant separate wills. Constitutions have their foundation in an original contractual agreement between the partners, but thereafter the partners cease to be masters of the treaty but become subject to it. A constitution not only constitutes a political order and establishes political organs; it regulates that order in terms of the powers of different organs, in terms of the relations between institutions and the subjects of the order, and between the subjects themselves.[114]
>
> Once constitutions are established, they become living instruments, through a combination of practice, interpretation (by political and legal organs) and by amendment.[115]

The ICRC, as we know, was created by private individuals, who galvanised people, communities and states into agreeing to limit the methods and means of warfare and the provision of protection and assistance to those affected by armed conflict. The first Geneva Convention provided the ICRC with a twofold mandate: firstly, to oversee the conduct of armed conflict; and, secondly, to care for the casualties of war. The Convention endowed the ICRC with this role, a role that has been included in subsequent Geneva Conventions and Additional Protocols. We cannot conclude that states intended to keep control of the ICRC; this would be counterproductive, not least because the ICRC promises to act neutrally and independently in all armed conflicts. The original signatories and subsequent

[113] Leroux (n 79) 87.

[114] White (n 4) 70.

[115] ibid, 71; see also H Abromeit and T Hitzel-Cassagnes, 'Constitutional Changes and Contractual Revision: Principles and Procedures' (1999) 5 *European Law Journal* 23, 24–25, 28–32.

signatories were not just creating an organisation, like the UN Charter; they were agreeing to a whole host of limitations on sovereignty and actions outside of their own state. In addition, at the International Conference, states have agreed to IRCRCM Statutes, allowing the movement to act under its own will and endowing it with the ability to react to situations on the ground. To all intents and purposes therefore, one can argue that the ICRC is born of constitutive agreements, rather than simply contractual.

## B. The ICRC is in Fact an International Legal Person

### *(i) Claims*

The capacity of organisations to make claims in respect of breaches of international law is arguably the most reliable indicator of ILP.[116] Although the ICRC is somewhat unlikely to be called before international courts or make claims on the international stage, due to its principle of confidentiality, there are a limited number of examples that show that, if it wants to, the ICRC does have power to bring claims. For example, on 13 December 1961 an ICRC delegate, Georges Olivet, a Swiss national, and two volunteers, Mrs Vroonen and Mr Smeding, from the Katanga Red Cross, were killed in a Red Cross ambulance during a UN intervention in the Congo, now the DRC.[117] Olivet had reported that UN troops on guard at UN headquarters were stopping him getting by; he had wanted to negotiate a truce for the evacuation of civilians in the battle areas.[118] The UN and the ICRC established a commission charged with conducting an impartial and independent inquiry into the circumstances of the death of Olivet, Vroonen and Smeding.[119] The UN paid compensation to the ICRC, without admitting responsibility.

### *(ii) Treaties*

The ICJ took the power of the UN to conclude agreements with its members as a representation of the manifestation of distinct will.[120] This section

[116] T Gazzini, 'The Relationship between International Legal Personality and the Autonomy of International Organizations' in R Collins and ND White, *International Organisations and the Idea of Autonomy: Institutional Independence in the International Legal Order* (London, Routledge, 2011) 198.

[117] 'Following the Death of Georges Olivet: Delegate of the International Committee of the Red Cross' (1962) 2 *IRRC* 84, 84–88; See also 'In Memory of an ICRC Delegate' (1967) 7(74) *IRRC* 271; Beigbeder (n 77) 321.

[118] 'After the Death of Georges Olivet: Delegate of the International Committee of the Red Cross' (1962) 2 *IRRC* 21, 21–28.

[119] 'News Items' (June 1962) IRRC 295, 315.

[120] *Reparation for Injuries* (n 7) 178–79.

therefore concerns the treaties to which the ICRC is a party. The ICRC has concluded at least seventy-four Headquarters Agreements with host states and is currently working in over eighty countries that facilitate the independence of the ICRC and its delegates during missions. The ICRC argues these agreements are 'plainly treaties under international law'.[121] 'The very first Headquarter Agreement was signed between ICRC and the Government of the Cameroon in 1973 and laid the foundation for the agreements to come.'[122] The most recent Headquarters Agreement was signed on 24 November 2014 between the ICRC and Morocco.[123] Article 1 'Agreement between the International Committee of the Red Cross and the Swiss Federal Council to Determine the Legal Status of the Committee in Switzerland' of 19 March 1993, for example, recognised the 'international juridical personality and legal capacity' of the ICRC, which does not substantially differ in form or content from the host agreements concluded between the UN specialised agencies and Switzerland.[124]

The agreements create a legal framework for the provision of humanitarian assistance and protection by the ICRC in sovereign states. The ICRC has created a Standard Proposed ICRC Headquarter Agreement, which is used as a guideline for individual agreements.[125] Rona has argued that: '[B]y entering into agreements normally signed with IGOs, States chose to treat ICRC as an IGO and thereby allowing the organization to take part in international relations as a legal person.'[126] Not only have states signed up to the Geneva Conventions I, II, III and IV 1949 but they have also provided for specific roles within their territory within the Headquarters Agreements. Of course, this is still dependent on consent, but is a representation of the manifestation of distinct will.[127] However, although the ICRC has concluded international agreements, they are not subject to registration by the UN Secretary General in accordance with Article 102 of the UN Charter, as the UN states that, as the ICRC is not an international organisation, its agreements cannot be considered 'international agreements'

[121] ICRC Annual Report 2003, 21 in Partlett (n 76) 35 (the number of Headquarters Agreements has increased since this book was published); Letter from the ICRC Legal Division, 22 June 2001 (on file with A-K Lindblom) in A-K Lindblom, *Non-Governmental Organizations in International Law* (Cambridge, Cambridge University Press, 2005) 496.

[122] Beigbeder (n 77) 324.

[123] 'Morocco: ICRC Signs Headquarters Agreement with Government', https://www.icrc.org/en/document/morocco-icrc-signs-headquarters-agreement-government#.VOnRHkJZFNM.

[124] Headquarters Agreement 1993 (n 68).

[125] G Rona, 'The ICRC Privilege not to Testify: Confidentiality in Action' (*ICRC*, 28 February 2004) Annex 2.

[126] ibid.

[127] *Reparation for Injuries* (n 7) 178–79.

for the purposes of Article 102.[128] Despite the ability of the ICRC to conclude agreements with states, they will not be seen as such by the UN. Nevertheless, states that sign Headquarters Agreements consider them to be binding upon them.

### *(iii) Privileges and Immunities*

Finally, in the *Reparation for Injuries* Advisory Opinion, the ICJ considered the privileges and immunities of the UN, in the territory of each of its Member States, to be evidence of its ILP.[129] The Headquarters Agreements usually recognise the legal personality of the ICRC delegation or offices, the inviolability of its premises, the usual functional immunities and privileges related to the performance of official duties, tax exemption on ICRC salaries, exemption from custom duties, freedom of entry into the country, freedom of movement and communications, and freedom to transfer funds.[130] Finally ICRC delegates are authorised to display the emblem of the Red Cross and enjoy immunity from judicial process.[131] In a sense, therefore, the ICRC's legal status can be analogised to that of intergovernmental organisations and the legal status of ICRC delegates to those of intergovernmental civil servants.[132] The privileges and immunities of the ICRC are comparable to those of the UN, its agencies and other intergovernmental organisations.

The ICRC also enjoys immunity from legal process, which protects it from judicial and administrative proceedings.[133] This includes the right to confidentiality before international courts and tribunals, which was recognised in the *Simić Case* before the ICTY.[134] The court was asked whether a former ICRC interpreter who volunteered to give evidence before the ICTY could do so on behalf of the prosecutor's office. The ICTY answered the question of whether the ICRC possessed ILP and determined whether an employee could be called as a witness or whether the ICRC had a right under international law to confidentiality. The ICTY stated that 'it is widely acknowledged that the ICRC, an independent humanitarian organisation

[128] 'Article 102, Repertory, Supplement 5, Volume V (1970–1978): ANNEX Registration and Publication of Treaties and International Agreements: Regulations to give Effect to Article 102 of the Charter of the United Nations', para 6.

[129] *Reparation for Injuries* (n 7) 178–79.

[130] ICRC Headquarters Agreement 1993, Arts 1, 3–5; See also ICRC, *Discover the ICRC* (booklet) (Geneva, September 2005).

[131] G Rona, 'The ICRC's Status: In a Class of its Own' (*ICRC*, 17 February 2004) www.icrc.org/eng/resources/documents/misc/5w9fjy.htm; Beigbeder (n 77) 325.

[132] See Headquarters Agreement between the Federal Military Government of the Federal Republic of Nigeria and the ICRC, 5 July 1988 (Art XIII).

[133] S Jeannet, 'Non-disclosure of Evidence before International Criminal Tribunals: Recent Developments Regarding the ICRC' (2001) 50 *ICLQ* 649.

[134] Simić ICTY (n 75) para 49.

enjoys a special status in international law, based on the mandate conferred upon it by the international community', to this end it is 'generally acknowledged that the ICRC, although a private organization under Swiss law, has ILP'.[135]

The ICTY found that the ICRC has a position not only under the Geneva Conventions but also under customary international law.[136] Moreover, according to the Rules of Procedure for the International Criminal Court (ICC), information provided by the ICRC is privileged, and consequently not subject to disclosure, unless the ICRC waives this privilege or the information is contained in public statements and documents of the ICRC.[137]

The International Criminal Tribunal for Rwanda confirmed in *Prosecutor v Tharcisse Muvunyi* that international law has granted the ICRC 'the exceptional privilege of non-disclosure of information' relating to the ICRC's activities.[138] In addition, 'such privilege is not granted to national Red Cross societies', which further evidences the unique position of the ICRC's right to confidentiality.[139] Moreover, Amnesty International or Save the Children, for example, would not be able to claim similar rights.[140] The right to confidentiality supports the ICRC's ability to maintain its neutrality and independence. It assures states, when entering into Headquarters Agreements, that the ICRC keeps information between itself and the state confidential. Finally, in addition to the ICTY recognition of ICRC personality, under Rule 73 of the ICC Rules of Procedure, the ILP of the ICRC is recognised.[141]

## C. The Functions and Rights of the ICRC

If we turn, therefore, to its 'powers', what capacities and competences does the ICRC have? At the beginning of this chapter, it was noted that powers can be express, implied and developed by the organisation itself, that is, as a product of its separate will. It is this third component which is particularly significant throughout this book: what does the ICRC do, as

[135] ibid, para 46; G Rona, 'The ICRC Privilege not to Testify: Confidentiality in Action' (*ICRC*, 28 February 2004) https://www.icrc.org/eng/resources/documents/article/other/5wsd9q.htm.

[136] Simić ICTY (n 75) paras 73–74; 'Trial Chamber III Rules that ICRC Need Not Testify before the Tribunal' (Press Release, The Hague, 8 October 1999) JL/P.I.S./439-E.

[137] ICC, 'Rules of Procedure and Evidence', adopted by the Assembly of State Parties (3–10 September 2002) ICC-ASP/1/3, Rule 73(4).

[138] *Prosecutor v Tharcisse Muvunyi* (Judgment and Sentence), ICTR-2000-55A-T (12 September 2006).

[139] ibid.

[140] ibid, s 16.

[141] Rule 73 Rules of Procedure and Evidence of the ICC, ICC-ASP/1/3.

a product of its separate will? Remembering, of course, that separate will, 'must be exercised within the legal framework of the constituent document, but those documents are notoriously open textured, allowing for organic growth by the organisation itself, disembodied from the will of each member State'.[142]

The Geneva Conventions I, II, III and IV 1949, Additional Protocols and IRCRCM Statutes, consented to by states, provide the international mandate for the ICRC and are often explicit in terms of outlining specific roles that the ICRC may undertake. The provisions of the Geneva Conventions I, II, III and IV 1949 enable it to bring humanitarian aid to victims of war, exchange messages between prisoners of war and their families, trace the fate of disappeared people, and care for the wounded and sick.[143]

These functions allow the ICRC to protect and assist victims of armed conflict. However, if we look at the ICRC Strategy 2015–2018 it is evident that the ICRC's work on the ground is developing beyond these specific provisions.[144] The current objectives include:

1. Strengthen the ICRC's capacity to protect through law, operations and policy;
2. Enhance the ICRC's distinctive response to growing needs;
3. Secure the widest possible support for ICRC action;
4. Contribute to a more significant response by the movement to large-scale emergencies; and
5. Adapt and strengthen organisational capacities to sustain growth and the continued relevance of ICRC action.

Humanitarian assistance can describe methods 'to alleviate human suffering during war time'.[145] The 'aim of the ICRC's assistance programmes is to preserve life and restore the dignity of individuals and communities affected by armed conflict or other situations of violence', as the humanitarian mission is at the heart of the ICRC's activities on the international stage.[146] Indeed, the first of the seven fundamental principles of the IRCRCM is humanity.

The activities that can be undertaken by the ICRC stem from Common Article 3 and Article 9 of Geneva Conventions I, II and III 1949 and Article 10

[142] White (n 4) 32.

[143] See D Fleck, *The Handbook of International Humanitarian Law*, 2nd edn (Oxford, Oxford University Press, 2008) paras 117, 503, 513, 516, 524–25, 542, 562, 564, 576, 584, 591, 706, 710, 734, 816 and 1422.

[144] 'ICRC Strategy 2015–2018: Adopted by the ICRC Assembly 24 June 2014', https://www.icrc.org/eng/assets/files/publications/icrc-002-4203.pdf.

[145] West (n 63) 13.

[146] ICRC, 'Assistance for People Affected by Armed Conflict and other Situations of Violence' (ICRC Geneva, February 2011) 2, 13.

of Geneva Convention IV 1949. Under Common Article 3(2) of Geneva Conventions I, II, III and IV 1949 'an impartial humanitarian body, such as the International Committee of the Red Cross, may *offer its services* to the Parties to the conflict'.[147] This provision is somewhat open ended; it therefore affords the ICRC wide discretion to act in NIAC. Article 18(2) Additional Protocol II provides that:

> If the civilian population is suffering undue hardship owing to a lack of the supplies essential for its survival, such as foodstuffs and medical supplies, relief actions for the civilian population which are of an exclusively humanitarian and impartial nature and which are conducted without any adverse distinction shall be undertaken subject to the consent of the High Contracting Party concerned.

In terms of international armed conflicts, Geneva Conventions I, II, III and IV 1949 each state that:

> The provisions of the present Convention constitute no obstacle to the humanitarian activities which the International Committee of the Red Cross or any other impartial humanitarian organisation may, subject to the consent of the Parties to the conflict concerned, undertake for the protection of wounded and sick, medical personnel and chaplains, and for their relief.

The commentary to Article 9 Geneva Convention I states that:

> All humanitarian activities are covered in theory, and not only those for which express provision is made. They are, however, covered subject to certain conditions with regard to the character of the organization undertaking them, their own nature and object and, lastly, the will of the Parties to the conflict.[148]

In addition, as regards the activities of the ICRC, Article 81(1) Additional Protocol I 1977 states that:

> The Parties to the conflict shall grant to the International Committee of the Red Cross all facilities within their power so as to enable it to carry out the humanitarian functions assigned to it by the Conventions and this Protocol in order to ensure protection and assistance to the victims of conflicts; the International Committee of the Red Cross may also carry out *any other humanitarian activities* in favour of these victims, subject to the consent of the Parties to the conflict concerned.[149]

Article 23 of Geneva Convention IV 1949 provides that parties to an international armed conflict and other transit states are required to 'allow free passage' to medical supplies, items for religious worship and religious

[147] Emphasis added.

[148] 'Article 9 Commentary: Convention (I) for the Amelioration of the Condition of the Wounded and Sick in Armed Forces in the Field' (Geneva, 12 August 1949) www.icrc.org/ihl/1a13044f3bbb5b8ec12563fb0066f226/bcb0d20422c82f18c12563cd00420459?OpenDocument.

[149] Emphasis added.

goods intended for civilians of other parties to the conflict, even if from the enemy side.[150] They must also allow 'consignments of essential foodstuffs, clothing and tonics intended for children under fifteen, expectant mothers and maternity cases'. This is subject to the condition that the party is satisfied that the consignments are unlikely to be diverted, particularly for military purposes. Moreover, the consignments must be forwarded as quickly as possible, subject to 'technical arrangements' under the control of the power permitting free passage.[151] Finally, under Article 30 of Geneva Convention IV 1949, 'humanitarian organisations must be granted all facilities possible' such that they can carry out their humanitarian functions.[152]

In addition to the provisions on humanitarian assistance contained in the Geneva Conventions I, II, III and IV 1949, the Seville Agreement introduced the idea of 'Lead Agency' into the IRCRCM. It means that the ICRC has specific areas in which it will take the lead in relief operations.[153] Under Article 5(1) of the Seville Agreement 1997 the term 'direct results of a conflict' is said to include the time 'beyond the cessation of hostilities and extends to situations where victims of a conflict remain in need of relief until a general restoration of peace has been achieved'. This detailed explanation of 'direct results of a conflict' is key to any understanding, analysis or critique of the roles of the ICRC beyond those described in the Geneva Conventions I, II, III and IV 1949.

The Geneva Conventions I, II, III and IV 1949 'not only place primary legal obligations on warring parties, but legitimise the role of "impartial" humanitarian organisations, such as the ICRC, in promoting the protection of and providing relief assistance to, non-combatants'.[154] Under the Geneva Conventions I, II, III and IV 1949 and Additional Protocol I the ICRC also has the mandate to perform functions traditionally performed

[150] See H-P Gasser, 'Protection of the Civilian Population' in D Fleck (ed), *The Handbook of International Humanitarian Law*, 2nd edn (Oxford, Oxford University Press, 2008) paras 503, 513.

[151] Under Geneva Convention IV, Art 61, relief consignments must be 'exempt in occupied territory from all charges, taxes or customs duties unless these are necessary in the interests of the economy of the territory'. In addition, the occupying power must facilitate their free passage and rapid distribution.

[152] Gasser (n 150) para 516, see also paras 524–25 on humanitarian assistance.

[153] Council of Delegates (ICRC), 'Agreement on the Organization of the International Activities of the Components of the International Red Cross and Red Crescent Movement—The Seville Agreement' (Council of Delegates, ICRC, 25–27 November 1997) www.icrc.org/eng/resources/documents/misc/57jp4y.htm, preamble (Seville Agreement) Arts 4.3, 4.4, 5.3.1, 5.4 and 6.1.2.

[154] N de Torrente, 'Humanitarian Action under Attack: Reflections on the Iraq War' (2004) 17(1) *Harvard Human Rights Journal* 2 in KF Abiew, 'Humanitarian Action under Fire: Reflections on the Role of NGOs in Conflict and Post-Conflict Situations' (2012) 19(2) *International Peacekeeping* 203, 205.

by protecting powers, as a neutral humanitarian organisation.[155] A protecting power is intended to secure the supervision and implementation of the Geneva Conventions I, II, III and IV 1949 and Additional Protocols. Traditionally a protecting power was appointed by a state, which was party to the conflict, to safeguard the respective interests during the conflict. The ICRC can replace a contracting power and perform its functions or it can enjoy protecting power status; in both situations it is afforded automatic powers to carry out its activities, thus putting the ICRC on same footing as a state. The difference is that the ICRC is neutral and must work in the interests of all sides to a conflict. Indeed, under Article 6 of the ICRC Statutes 'the ICRC shall maintain relations with government authorities and any national or international institution whose assistance it considers useful'.

There are other conditions placed on the right to provide humanitarian assistance. Organisations undertaking humanitarian action 'must be concerned with the condition of man, considered solely as a human being without regard to the value which he represents as a military, political, professional or other unit. And the organization must be impartial.'[156] Its activities must be purely humanitarian in character; they must be concerned with human beings as such, and must not be affected by any political or military consideration.[157] These stipulations firstly give humanitarian organisations criteria for authorising their involvement in conflict, and secondly, they provide apparatus for organisations to secure humanitarian access. That is to say, the ICRC uses its reputation for neutrality and independence to gain access to those in need. It also encourages states to cooperate in the provision of humanitarian aid.

In addition to the right to provide humanitarian assistance, the ICRC has the right to take humanitarian *initiatives*. This is a much broader right than that contained in the legal provisions discussed above. Under paragraph 4(2) of the ICRC Statutes, 'the ICRC may take *any humanitarian initiative* which comes within its role as a specifically neutral and independent institution and intermediary, and may consider any question requiring examination by such an institution'.[158] This broad power of initiative is

[155] Geneva Convention I, Art 10; Geneva Convention II, Art 10; Geneva Convention III, Art 10; Geneva Convention IV, Art 11; Additional Protocol I, Art 5(3)–(4).

[156] 'Art 9 Commentary' (n 148); see Right to Humane Treatment, Art 27 Geneva Convention IV; Geneva Convention IV, Arts 55 and 56 provide that the occupying power has the duty to ensure food, medical supplies, medical and hospital establishments and services, and public health and hygiene to populations in the occupied territory. Under Additional Protocol I, Art 69, this duty was extended to include the duty to ensure bedding, means of shelter and other supplies essential to the survival of the civilian population; see Gasser (n 150) para 562, 564, 576.

[157] 'Art 9 Commentary' (n 148).

[158] Emphasis added.

also found in the Statutes of the IRCRCM, which again state that the ICRC 'may take any humanitarian initiative which comes within its role as a specifically neutral and independent institution and intermediary' and it must 'endeavour at all times—as a neutral institution whose humanitarian work is carried out particularly in time of international and other armed conflicts or internal strife—to ensure the protection of and assistance to military and civilian victims of such events and of their direct results'.[159]

This right to humanitarian initiative is flexible and therefore practical as 'no one can foretell what a future war will consist of, under what conditions it will be waged and to what needs it will give rise'.[160] It is therefore right that 'a door should be left open to any initiative or action, however unforeseeable today, which may help effectively in protecting, caring for and aiding the wounded and sick'.[161] According to Ratner: '[T]his significant grant of authority, while not legally binding on States—which must consent to the ICRC's involvement—has permitted the ICRC to visit detainees in countries not experiencing war and work in States and on issues where human rights law, not IHL, is the governing legal framework.'[162] This latter statement, concerning the development of the role of the ICRC into situations where IHRL is the governing legal framework, is considered in chapter 3.[163]

## D. Conclusions on Personality

The development of the ICRC as an international legal person is evidenced by a number of factors. These include the conclusion of several international treaties between the ICRC and states or international organisations, including Headquarter Agreements; recognition by its host country of Switzerland, as well as many other states, in Headquarter Agreements; enjoyment by the ICRC of immunities from the jurisdiction of several states; the maintenance of diplomatic relations between the ICRC, states and other organisations; and finally, the recognition by the ICTY in the *Simić* case of the international legal status of the ICRC. The ICRC has also brought claims against subjects of international law, such as the UN.

ILP is a necessary part of any international organisation that needs to act autonomously. That is, once created by individuals, as with the Committee

159 IRCRCM Statutes, Art 5(2)(d) and 5(3); ICRC Statutes, Art 4(2).

160 'Art 9 Commentary' (n 148).

161 ibid; see B Jakovlijević, 'The Right to Humanitarian Assistance—Legal Aspects' (1987) 27 *IRRC* 469, 471; 'Guiding Principles on the Right to Humanitarian Assistance' (1993) 33 *IRRC* 519.

162 SR Ratner, 'Law Promotion Beyond Law Talk: The Red Cross, Persuasion, and the Laws of War' (2011) 22(2) *European Journal of International Law* 459, 464.

163 See chapter 3.III.

of Five or states, as with the UN, an organisation is intended to act to pursue the objectives set out for it at its inception. It is through its actions thereafter that outsiders can see that it has ILP. For the ICJ, in the *Reparations* case, it saw the UN making treaties and so on as evidence of it exercising its ILP. To a lesser extent, we can see the ICRC undertaking similar practice. In addition, the ICRC has the power to undertake other humanitarian protection and assistance activities. An organisation with ILP may also develop its competences through practice. It can therefore interpret and act upon its own mandate. The rest of this book focuses on whether and the extent to which the ICRC is developing its practice beyond the activities specified in the Geneva Conventions.

The process of interpreting the mandate goes from the field, to Geneva and back. The team on the ground has to plan ahead each year and identify the projects it wishes to undertake, the objectives of such, the impact they will have and how that impact will be measured.[164] These reports are area specific and will then be compiled with reports from other parts of the region. They are then presented to the Director of Operations in Geneva who will consider the reports. In practice, therefore, there is a working relationship between the ICRC delegates on the ground and the Geneva offices. To this end, exploratory or innovative proposals must be justified; in other words, delegates on the ground must justify every project and initiative to Geneva. The only decisions that are predominantly taken on the ground are security related; such decisions are taken close to the people on the ground, rather than at the Geneva headquarters.

The ICRC derives its mandate from the Geneva Conventions and the Statutes of the movement. The Assembly of the ICRC, composed of Members of the ICRC, decides on the content of the Statutes.[165] Regarding the interpretation of the articles pertaining to the roles, relations with the movement or outside of the movement, the Assembly also makes such interpretation, but the interpretation cannot go against what was established in the Statutes of the movement. In addition, other individuals will use the Statutes without necessarily interpreting them. By example, legal advisers and Heads of Delegations can use the Statutes to negotiate access or an agreement with the authorities, such as during the negotiation of a new Headquarters Agreement.The Statutes are rarely the subject of any interpretation per se. What is subject to interpretation may be whether a country is or is not in a situation of armed conflict and what, if any,

[164] 'ICRC Overview of Operations 2015' (Geneva, ICRC, 2014) https://www.icrc.org/en/document/icrc-presents-record-budget-2015-meet-vastly-expanding-needs#.VOn1i0JZFNM.

[165] ICRC Statutes, Art 17.

rights of initiative the ICRC may have in such a context.[166] Closely related to such interpretation is a recent issue facing the ICRC, namely its interpretation of its role in what it terms 'other situations of violence', that is, situations under the threshold of applicability of IHL in which the ICRC may have a statutory right of initiative.[167] In practice, this means that the ICRC will can refer to its mandate as coming from the Statutes of the ICRC rather than Common Article 3.

Another potential point of contention is the signature of Headquarters Agreements recognising the privileges and immunities accorded to ICRC staff, as some states may not recognise the ICRC's ILP and would, as a consequence, fail to agree that ICRC staff should benefit from any privileges and immunities. Ultimately, the ICRC has to persuade its hosts of the added value of its presence and of the importance of allowing it to act according to its principles. No law or statute alone can overcome a state's decision not to allow the ICRC to operate within its borders.

For the ICRC, therefore, interpretation of the mandate comes from within when thinking about its international mandate. The specific mandate between the ICRC and a given host state will be unique to that state. It is, therefore, for the ICRC itself and its delegates and host states to decide upon the humanitarian protection and assistance to be provided. The ICRC can review its own roles and responsibilities as they are found in its Statutes, while keeping in mind that it cannot 'take [a] decision contrary to the [Statutes of the Movement] or to the resolutions of the [Conference]'.[168] There is no doubt that the Conference can review the Statutes of the movement under Article 10(3), but it is not clear whether it could review the mandate of the ICRC by changing the relevant articles of the Statutes of the movement. This is unclear because the roles and responsibilities of the ICRC found in the IRCRCM Statutes are a copy–paste of the ICRC Statutes and such modification procedure is not specifically allowed, nor prohibited, in the Statutes. Amending the relevant articles of the IRCRCM Statutes could be perceived as modifying the corresponding articles in the ICRC Statutes and Article 11(6) prohibits such modification, as it states that: '[T]he International Conference shall not modify either the Statutes of the International Committee or the Constitution of the Federation nor take decisions contrary to such statutes.'

[166] S Vité, 'Typology of Armed Conflicts in International Humanitarian Law: Legal Concepts and Actual Situations' (2009) 91 *IRRC* 69.

[167] 'Interview with Kathleen Law and of the ICRC: Internal Conflicts or other Situations of Violence—What Is the Difference for Victims?' (10 December 2012) https://www.icrc.org/eng/resources/documents/interview/2012/12-10-niac-non-international-armed-conflict.htm; ICRC, 'Enhancing Protection: For Civilians in Armed Conflict and Other Situations of Violence' (Geneva, ICRC, 2012).

[168] IRCRCM Statutes, Art 11(6).

### *(i) Responsibility of the ICRC for Breach of Mandate?*

One consequence of the judgment that the UN has ILP was that the International Law Commission questioned whether international organisations should be held responsible for their actions. Early discussions merely led to the determination that retaining the distinction between states and other actors in the area of responsibility was necessary.[169] It was not until 2002, after the adoption of the ILC Articles on State Responsibility, that the ILC began work on the responsibility of international organisations.[170] The articles were adopted on 5 August 2011 and referred to the General Assembly, which welcomed the work and annexed the articles to a resolution.[171]

The question here is whether the ICRC would fall under the Draft Articles on the Responsibility of International Organisations.[172] If states were to accuse the ICRC of not abiding by its mandate, are there any consequences? Hypothetically, if there was a problem between a state and the ICRC regarding its mandate, it could be related to the fact that the state is displeased with the ways in which the ICRC operates in said state. This situation could be interpreted as if the ICRC is not abiding by its mandate or more specifically, not according to what was agreed with the authorities. For the ICRC, this could have an impact on obtaining access to the victims it seeks to help. At the moment the most serious consequence for the ICRC is that the state could withdraw its consent. In 1986, for example, the ICRC delegation was asked to leave South Africa following a decision by the 25th International Conference of the Red Cross and Red Crescent to suspend the participation of the South African authorities at the conference.[173] On 1 February 2014, 'the Sudanese authorities suspended the ICRC's activities in Sudan …, citing technical issues, and asked the organization to review the country agreement that sets out its legal and diplomatic

[169] First Report by Mr A El-Erian, Special Rapporteur, 'Relations Between States and Inter-Governmental Organizations', Document A/CN.4/161 and Add.1, in *ILC Yearbook* (1963) vol II, A/CN.4/SER.A/1963/ADD.1, 159, 184; Report by Mr R Ago Chairman of the Sub-Committee on State Responsibility, 16 January 1963, *ILC Yearbook* (1963) vol II, A/CN.4/SER.A/1963/ADD.1, Annex I, Document A/CN.4/152, 234.

[170] International Law Commission, 'Report on the Work of its Fifty-Second Session' (2000) A/55/10, Ch.IX.A.1, para 729; United Nations General Assembly Resolution 56/82 (12 December 2001) para 8.

[171] Draft Articles on the Responsibility of International Organizations, with Commentaries 2011, *ILC Yearbook* (2011) vol II, part two; United Nations General Assembly Resolution 66/100 (9 December 2011).

[172] Adopted by the International Law Commission at its sixty-third session, in 2011, and submitted to the General Assembly as a part of the Commission's report covering the work of that session (A/66/10).

[173] 'South Africa: ICRC Honoured for Work during Apartheid Era' (13 November 2003) https://www.icrc.org/eng/resources/documents/misc/5t9klb.htm.

status in the country'.[174] The ICRC negotiated a new agreement that has been in force since August 2014.[175]

## IV. CONCLUSION

This chapter has shown that it is difficult to define the legal nature of the ICRC, but it can be said to be a sui generis entity. The definition of the ICRC as an international organisation could have helped justify, or perhaps explain, the autonomous expansion of ICRC functions into long-term projects. The ICRC shares aspects of international organisations, private international organisations and NGOs and it has a relationship with sovereign states. This includes the role of states in the movement and the International Conferences. It is also a private association made up of Swiss individuals. In fact, it has close ties to Switzerland, including its location, the nationality of Committee members and senior staff, and frequent contacts with the Swiss Foreign Ministry. It is this unique status that sets it apart from other organisations. This is compounded by its reputation as an impartial, neutral and independent organisation. The ICRC markets itself as an organisation to be trusted by all parties—by states because of its confidentiality and by the people on the ground because of its neutrality and independence.

As a humanitarian organisation, the ICRC is focused on the protection and assistance of those in need. This chapter has explored its organisational structure and its relationship with the IRCRCM. Ultimately the ICRC has evolved from an NGO, which it essentially was when it was established by five Swiss nationals, to a Swiss organisation, recognised as such under the Swiss Civil Code (in 1993 Switzerland signed an agreement with the ICRC which conferred privileges and immunities upon the organization). These agreements give the ICRC a status somewhat akin to an international organisation. To this end, the ICRC cannot be characterised into a specific definition, which other organisations fit neatly into. It has evolved over time and developed relationships with states to facilitate and fulfil its humanitarian mandate. To support the claim that the ICRC is not easily definable, we can look to Article 5 of the IRCRCM Statutes, which states that the ICRC is 'an independent humanitarian organization having a *status of its own* [emphasis added]'. Academic commentary

[174] 'Sudan: ICRC Signs Country Agreement with Government' (28 August 2014) https://www.icrc.org/en/document/sudan-icrc-signs-country-agreement-government#.VOn9EUJZFNM.

[175] ibid.

supports this finding that the ICRC is both an NGO and an international organisation,[176] or suggests that it is sui generis.[177]

In the wider context of this book, although the ICRC does, in fact, have a unique organisational structure and legal nature, the pertinent question is whether it possesses ILP. This aids the critical analysis of whether the ICRC has legitimately, or otherwise, extended its protection and assistance mandates beyond activities outlined in the Geneva Conventions I, II, III and IV 1949 and the ICRC Statutes, the latter of which can be amended by the International Conference. The Geneva Conventions I, II, III and IV 1949, Additional Protocols and the ICRC Statutes confer rights and duties on the ICRC. The ICRC is able to make claims on the international stage and enter into international agreements with states, and it also enjoys certain privileges and immunities, all of which were considered to be evidence of the UN possessing ILP in the *Reparation for Injuries* Advisory Opinion.

Will theory tells us that traditionally the possession of ILP correlates to the 'powers' of an organisation, express or implied, as necessary to fulfil the obligations of the organisation on the international stage. However, it is arguable that if the ICJ were to consider the 'powers' of the UN today, it would not concentrate so much on the UN Charter but on the practice of the UN. Just as the UN has continued to develop its functions on the international stage, the ICRC has also been forced to adapt its humanitarian role to respond to international and NIAC armed conflicts. It is this development of competencies to which this book turns to in the following chapters.

The intention of the founders and the state parties to the Geneva Conventions has been for the ICRC to participate in the international community, not least as a creator of international humanitarian law, to which states consent to be bound. The ICRC acts as an independent person, through its delegates and the Assembly, Presidency and Directorate situated in Geneva. The Headquarters Agreements concluded between the ICRC and host states support the argument that the ICRC has ILP. If we were to reflect on the *Reparation for Injuries* Advisory Opinion, it seems to be beyond doubt that the ICRC 'is intended to exercise and enjoy, and is to this day exercising and enjoying functions and rights that can only be explained on the basis of the possession of international legal personality'.[178]

In order to take this book forward, into an analysis of the developing roles of the ICRC, it must be emphasised that there is a distinction to be

[176] C Koenig, 'Observer Status for the ICRC at the United Nations: A Legal Viewpoint' (1991) 280 *IRRC* 47.

[177] J-P Lavoyer and L Maresca, 'The Role of the ICRC in the Development of International Humanitarian Law' (1999) 4 *International Negotiation* 501, 508.

[178] *Reparation for Injuries* (n 7) 179.

drawn between the mandate the ICRC gets from the Geneva Conventions and Additional Protocol I and II, its international mandate, and that that comes from its status as a Swiss Association, consisting of Swiss nationals, who are able to make autonomous decisions. In addition, a distinction must be drawn between the mandate the ICRC gets from the Geneva Conventions and the one it gets from its Statutes: the latter being agreed at the International Conferences and more likely to adapt to changes on the international stage. Finally, it is the Headquarters Agreements that allow the ICRC to work in a state, but they are secret and difficult to access, much like Status of Forces Agreements between the UN and host states.[179] The exact content of each individual Headquarters Agreement cannot be known.

In terms of its work, therefore, Member States have some say in the presence of the ICRC on their territories, but not concerning its overarching projects, such as Health Care in Danger, as agreed to at International Conferences. The ICRC is still grappling with establishing its right of initiative in such internal troubles, as it gets this from the IRCRCM Statutes, not the Geneva Conventions I, II, III and IV 1949 or Additional Protocols I and II 1977.

Overall, ILP is an essential component of the ICRC's ability and willingness to forge its own path in the interests of humanitarian assistance and protection. If the ICRC needed the consent of all state parties at International Conferences, or a new set of Geneva Conventions or IRCRCM/ICRC Statutes were necessary for it to undertake new roles in states affected by conflict, this would render the ICRC useless. The utility of the ICRC as a humanitarian actor comes in part from the international law component of its mandate, that is, a mandate to which states have consented to by signing up to the Geneva Conventions. It also comes from state consent at the International Conferences and the conclusion of Headquarters Agreements. The mandate, which is essential to its functionality, comes from decisions made on the ground by delegates coming face to face with humanitarian disasters and partly from the ICRC Assembly, Directorate and Presidency in Geneva.

[179] Report of the Secretary-General, 'Model Status-of-Forces Agreement for Peace-Keeping Agreements' (9 October 1990) A/45/594.

# 3

# *The ICRC and International Law in Armed Conflict and other Situations of Violence*

## I. INTRODUCTION

THE BATTLEFIELD EXPERIENCE of Henry Dunant, which inspired the creation of the ICRC, is a far cry from the armed conflict situations seen across the world today. Nevertheless, the ICRC continues to strive to provide protection and assistance to victims of armed conflict. In a 2016 report, the ICRC looked at its operational experiences and considered the theory and practice of the its approach to humanitarian assistance in protracted conflict.[1] This chapter begins with an analysis of the normative and legal development of the laws of war. After the Second World War, the ICRC and the UN institutionalised the traditional binary distinction between the laws of war and peace. As a consequence, in the post-war years, the development of *jus in bello, jus ad bellum* and IHRL was undertaken by two distinct organisations. That situation prevailed until 1968, when the International Conference on Human Rights took place in Tehran.[2] This pre-empted a number of UN General Assembly resolutions and Secretary-General Reports on the respect for human rights in armed conflicts. In other words, the international community recognised that IHL does not cover all circumstances during armed conflict and that it is also necessary to draw on IHRL for the protection of populations. The synergy between these two legal frameworks is therefore a consequence of both the changing nature of conflict and the humanitarian core of both IHL and IHRL. To this end, this chapter examines whether the provisions in the Geneva Conventions I, II, III and IV 1949 and the ICRC Statutes provide enough scope for the ICRC to respond meaningfully to the

[1] ICRC, 'Protracted Conflict and Humanitarian Action: Some Recent ICRC Experiences (Geneva, ICRC, 2016).

[2] Proclamation of Tehran, 'Final Act of the International Conference on Human Rights, Teheran' (22 April–13 May 1968) UN Doc A/CONF. 32/41.

needs of people during and after armed conflicts and other situations of violence.[3] It also considers the ICRC within the wider international community and posits that it is inevitable, perhaps necessary, for other legal frameworks to apply during the same situations in which the ICRC is working. It finds that the ICRC will be pragmatic in its dialogue and use the legal framework best suited to communicating humanitarian values to try and ensure that all actors in international and NIAC respect 'humanity'. This principle and its implications for the work of the ICRC are also considered in chapters 4 and 5.

## II. THE NORMATIVE AND LEGAL DEVELOPMENT OF THE LAWS OF WAR

The *jus ad bellum* and *jus in bello* both regulate the use of force, firstly by circumscribing its legality and, secondly, by limiting the means and methods used in warfare, aiming at preventing total war and preventing unnecessary suffering.[4] The spirit of both normative frameworks is to minimise human suffering through the regulation of the use of force.[5] The principle of humanity theoretically fosters a reciprocal relationship between parties at war, as fighting ought to be based on notions of chivalry and civilised behaviour.[6] In fact, during the Thirty Years War, which began in 1618 and which Kunz referred to as the first 'total war', there were basic rules of humanity such as the distinction between civilians and combatants.[7] However the *jus ad bellum* affords the aggressor and the victims of the use of force unequal status before the law, whereas all people are afforded the protections of the *jus in bello*.[8]

The *jus in bello* is purely humanitarian, it comprises a set of treaty-based and customary rules that govern belligerents' rights and duties in the conduct of hostilities, including on the legality of methods and means of warfare and the safeguarding of protecting persons, notably those *hors de*

[3] Geneva Convention I, Art 9; Geneva Convention II, Art 9; Geneva Convention III, Art 9; Geneva Convention IV, Art 10; Additional Protocol I, Art 81; Additional Protocol II, Art 18; ICRC Statutes, para 4(2); IRCRCM Statutes, Art 5(2)(d).

[4] A Eide, 'International Law, Dominance, and the Use of Force' (1974) 11(1) *Journal of Peace Research* 1, 4.

[5] See generally G Best, *Humanity in Warfare: The Modern History of the International Law of Armed Conflicts* (London, Weidenfeld & Nicolson, 1980).

[6] C Droege, 'The Interplay between International Humanitarian Law and International Human Rights Law in Situations of Armed Conflict' (2007) 40 *Israel Law Review* 310, 313; See also Instructions for the Government of Armies of the United States in the Field (Lieber Code) 24 April 1863.

[7] JL Kunz, 'The Laws of War' (1956) 50(2) *American Journal of International Law* 313, 313.

[8] ibid 318.

*combat*, prisoners of war and civilians not taking part in hostilities. These rules are based on basic axioms of IHL, including military necessity, the principle of distinction and proportionality.[9]

The Battle of Solferino 1859 stimulated international focus on the laws of war and led to the creation of the first internationally agreed upon legal framework for the conduct of hostilities. The Convention for the Amelioration of the Condition of the Wounded in Armies in the Field was adopted in Geneva on 22 August 1864.[10] Pictet stated that this treaty, and subsequent Geneva Conventions, 'are all founded on respect for the individual and for his dignity: they embody the principle of selfless relief, without discrimination, to all human beings in distress whether they be wounded, prisoners of war or shipwrecked, and thus defenceless and no longer to be regarded as enemies'.[11] Whilst in Europe the Battle of Solferino led to the adoption of new laws of war, across the Atlantic US President Lincoln was signing the Lieber Code. The Lieber Code was adopted in 1863 and concerned how the Union forces should conduct themselves during armed conflict.[12] Shortly after the adoption of the Lieber Code, the 1868 St Petersburg Declaration was adopted, which prohibits the use of certain types of weapons in war.[13] Progress in the codification of the laws of war was later made at the Brussels Conference in 1874 and stimulated the adoption of the Hague Convention on land warfare of 1907.[14] These laws aim to protect human beings, either from each other or from certain weapons. In terms of this book, it is important to note that these laws considered physical injury only to soldiers, rather than the impact of war on civilians. It was the world wars of the twentieth century that drew international interest and attracted the attention of the ICRC to the inadequacies of the existing legal frameworks for the protection of victims of armed conflicts.

The ICRC offered assistance in the Third Carlist War in Spain (1872–76), the insurrection in Herzegovina (1875), and during periods of violence

[9] C Greenwood, 'Historical Development and Legal Basis' and S Oeter, 'Methods and Means of Combat' in D Fleck, *The Handbook of International Humanitarian Law*, 3rd edn (Oxford, Oxford University Press, 2013) 35ff, 126–36.

[10] For a good outline of the laws of war prior to 1864, see D Schindler, 'The International Committee of the Red Cross and Human Rights' (1979) 208 *IRRC* 3, 3–5; See also P Bossier, *History of the International Committee of the Red Cross: From Solferino to Tsushima* (Geneva, Henri Dunant Institute, 1985).

[11] JS Pictet, 'The New Geneva Conventions for the Protection of War Victims' (1951) 45(3) *American Journal of International Law* 462, 462.

[12] Lieber Code (n 6) Art 152.

[13] Declaration Renouncing the Use, in Time of War, of Explosive Projectiles under 400 Grammes Weight (St Petersburg, 29 November/11 December 1868).

[14] 1907 Hague Convention IV Respecting the Laws and Customs on War on Land (adopted 18 October 1907, entered into force 26 January 1910).

in Argentina (1890), Brazil (1894), Venezuela (1894–95) and Macedonia (1903).[15] During the 10th International Conference in Geneva, the adoption of the resolution XIV recognised that the ICRC might intervene in social disturbances and revolutions.[16] This was never adopted into a legal instrument. Nevertheless, Schindler stated that the ICRC

> [i]ndependently of the development of international humanitarian law [and the emergence of the international law of human rights] … has acted also in various other ways to protect the victims of armed conflicts and, as a consequence, to work for the defence of human rights… [and] has also carried out a wide range of relief operations to bring aid to persons affected by international or non-international conflicts and to the victims of internal strife and tension.[17]

The assassination of Franz Ferdinand and Germany's declaration of war against Russia in the summer of 1914 began four years of conflict during which all states flouted the laws of war, until war officially ceased with the Treaty of Versailles on 28 June 1918. Critically, 'before 1914 the ICRC only reflected on war; after that date it also became one of the actors in war'.[18] Unfortunately, although the First World War showed the insufficiency of the laws of war, the ideology of extreme pacifists afterwards caused it to be fashionable to ignore the problem. Indeed, Kunz argued that 'it was part and parcel of an officially created illusion of wishful thinking fostered by States and utopian writers'.[19]

It took a few years for war to be back on the international agenda. The Pact of Paris, also referred to as the Kellogg–Briand Pact 1928, reflected a 'feeling' in the international community. It did not 'outlaw' or 'abolish' war, even for its signatories, rather it contained a 'renunciation of war as an instrument of national policy'.[20] Mr Kellogg's circular letter stated that 'every state retains the inherent right to self-defense, and is itself the only judge to decide whether there is a given case of self-defense'. War remained lawful therefore as a means of a legally permissible self-defence, a measure of collective action, as between signatories of the Pact and

[15] G Torreblanca, 'The International Committee of the Red Cross and Human Rights Law' in R Kolb and G Gaggioli (eds), *Research Handbook on Human Rights and Humanitarian Law* (Cheltenham, Edward Elgar, 2013) 549; See also S Sivakumaran, 'International Humanitarian Law' in D Moeckli, S Shah and S Sivakumaran (eds), *International Human Rights Law* (Oxford, Oxford University Press, 2010) 30–39.

[16] R Perruchoud, *Les Résolutions des Conférences Internationales de la Croix-Rouge* (Geneva, Henry Dunant Institute, 1979) in Torreblanca (n 15) 549.

[17] D Schindler, 'The International Committee of the Red Cross and Human Rights' (1979) 208 *IRRC* 5.

[18] D Palmieri, 'An Institution Standing the Test of Time? A Review of 150 Years of the History of the International Committee of the Red Cross' (2012) 94 *IRRC* 1273, 1278.

[19] JL Kunz, 'The Chaotic Status of the Laws of War and the Urgent Necessity for their Revision' (1951) 45(1) *American Journal of International Law* 37, 38.

[20] ibid 46.

non-signatories and as against a signatory who has broken the Pact by resorting to war in violation of its provisions.[21]

Article 7 of the International Law Association's Articles of Interpretation of the 1928 Pact of Paris provided that: '[T]he pact does not affect such humanitarian obligations as are contained in general treaties, such as the Hague Conventions 1899 and 1907, the Geneva Conventions of 1864 and 1906, and the International Convention relating to the Treatment of Prisoners of War 1929.'[22] The hope for the Pact, therefore, 'was that in the long run this change in international law would induce governments and people to view war in a new way and that this moral, social and psychological change would profoundly affect the occurrence of hostilities'.[23] For the ICRC, its raison d'être in 1859 was to assist the victims of armed conflicts. By 1928 there was a focus on the abolition of war, but whilst the Pact recognised that peace was the ideal, it acknowledged certain circumstances may arise whereby a state may lawfully use force.

Unfortunately, on 1 September 1939, just over a decade after the adoption of the Pact, Germany invaded Poland, thus beginning the Second World War and from 1939 to 1945 the laws of war 'were regularly and on a mass scale violated by all the belligerents'.[24] So shocking were the violations that Veale postulated that the conduct of the Second World War threatened a new 'advance to barbarism'.[25] Kunz echoed such a fear in 1956, when he stated that: '[W]e have arrived where we started, in the sixteenth century, at the threat of total, lawless war, but this time with weapons which may ruin all human civilization, and even threaten the survival of mankind on this planet.'[26]

For the ICRC, its work during the Second World War focused on activities to protect and assist prisoners of war. The Geneva Convention 1929 included rules governing the treatment of prisoners of war, but civilians, including those held in concentration camps, were not protected under IHL.[27] During the Second World War the ICRC sent delegates to France, Germany, Poland and the United Kingdom; their principal role was to visit prisoners of war, although access was routinely denied by Germany.[28]

[21] H Lauterpacht (ed), *International Law: A Treatise by L Oppenheim*, vol II, 6th edn (London, Longmans, Green and Co, 1947) 149–50.

[22] ILA, *Briand–Kellogg Pact of Paris (August 27, 1928): Articles of Interpretation as adopted by the Budapest Conference, 1934, together with the report of the relevant proceedings* (London, Sweet & Maxwell, 1934) Art 7.

[23] Q Wright, 'The Outlawry of War and the Law of War' (1953) 47(3) *American Journal of International Law* 365, 369.

[24] HJ Morgenthau, *Politics Among Nations* (New York, Knopf, 1948) 218.

[25] FJP Veale, *Advance to Barbarism: The Development of Total Warfare from Sarajevo to Hiroshima* (Original Publication, 1953) www.vho.org/aaargh/fran/livres10/VEALAdvance.pdf.

[26] Kunz (n 7) 313.

[27] Geneva Convention 1929 Relative to the Treatment of Prisoners of War.

[28] '1939–1945: Descent into Hell' (11 May 2010) https://www.icrc.org/eng/who-we-are/history/second-world-war/overview-2-world-war.htm.

The ICRC also struggled to carry out its visits to prisoners of war in the Philippines, the Dutch East Indies and Borneo, Singapore and Thailand as the Japanese authorities refused accreditation to delegates.[29] This prevented ICRC delegates from working in an 'official' capacity. Sadly, these circumstances led to accusations of spying against ICRC delegates trying to bring relief to prisoners of war in Borneo; Dr Matthaeus Visher and his wife, after a mockery of a trial, were sentenced to death by a Japanese naval court, and beheaded.[30]

The international community sought a solution to the violations of *jus in bello* and *jus ad bellum*, and on 14 August 1941 the Atlantic Charter was completed. It spoke of a 'wider and permanent system of general security', which would 'afford to all nations the means of dwelling in safety within their own boundaries' at the war's end.[31] This idea pre-dated the UN but arguably pre-empted the collective security provisions of the UN Charter.

The ICRC was, and still is, *the* humanitarian organisation. Before the League of Nations or the UN, states had seen fit to sign up to The Hague and Geneva Conventions. The UN was created out of the ashes of the Second World War and, on the one hand, was a protector of state sovereignty and territorial integrity, whilst, buried in Article 55 of the UN Charter, it had the ability to develop human rights law. In 1943 Corbett published an article in the *American Journal of International Law*, which stated that: '[M]ost plans of post-war settlement advocate curtailment of national sovereignty and propose extensive and vigorous supranational organization'—the world legal order needed a community of states or individual human beings, or in the alternative, an amalgamation of both.[32] For many, the UN is the epitome of such a supranational organisation. Ultimately, however, such an ideal was to be realised through the ICRC, not the UN. The ICRC's amalgamation of state participation, in the International Conferences, and the neutrality and independence afforded by the ICRC members being Swiss nationals, not Member States, makes it best placed to take into account state and human interests. Of course, much existing academic analysis suggests that the UN was intended to fulfil Corbett's proposal for a 'supranational organisation', one that would continue to prevent and

[29] J Crossland, *Britain and the International Committee of the Red Cross 1939–1945* (London, Palgrave Macmillan, 2014).

[30] 'The ICRC in WW II: Overview of Activities' (ICRC, 2 February 2005) www.icrc.org/eng/resources/documents/misc/history-world-war-2-overview-020205.htm; see also 'ICRC in WW II: Delegations throughout the World' (ICRC, 4 February 2005) www.icrc.org/eng/resources/documents/misc/57jnwt.htm.

[31] E Luard, *A History of the United Nations*, vol 1: *The Years of Western Domination, 1945–1955* (Hong Kong, Macmillan, 1982) 17.

[32] PE Corbett, 'World Order: An Agenda for Lawyers' (1943) 37(2) *American Journal of International Law* 207, 210.

address insecurity and violations of international law. This book aims to change such presuppositions and posit the potential of the ICRC to build security in the face and aftermath of armed conflict.

This chapter now turns to the institutionalisation of the binary distinction between the laws of war and the law of peace. Following the atrocities of the Second World War there were two distinct beliefs as regards the laws of war: (i) war should be outlawed; or (ii) the laws of war should be significantly developed. The proponents of the first belief questioned the necessity of the laws of war, if war was to be outlawed.[33] The question therefore was whether there was a need for such laborious preparation of new conventions to be implemented during hostilities when every endeavour was being made to abolish war?[34] The vigorous and perhaps dominant scholarly opinion in the period following the Second World War was that it was undesirable to deal with the actual conduct of war, as it would weaken the central drive to eliminate war entirely.[35] Arguably this opinion was institutionalised with the adoption of the UN Charter and the establishment of a new international organisation.

Pictet argued that the debates as to whether to develop the laws of war or not echoed those following the First World War and the conclusion at that time was that 'so long as States maintain powerful armies, they obviously do not rule out the possibility of war breaking out once more'.[36] In fact, at the same time, quite separate from the debates surrounding the development of two distinct legal frameworks, it was suggested that there is in fact an inherent relationship between the *jus ad bellum* and the *jus in bello*. The requirement, for example, for military necessity appears in both.[37] This relationship is explored later in this chapter.

The UN's resolve not to undermine its determination to prevent war, or rather not to work on laws of war, was embedded in the UN law developed by the International Law Commission (ILC) in 1948. In fact, a survey of international law by Professor Lauterpacht, which covered the 'whole field of international law' in accordance with Article 18 of the Statute of the ILC, did not mention the laws of war.[38] During the First Session of the ILC 1949

> it was considered that if the Commission, at the very beginning of its work, were to undertake this study [on the laws of war], public opinion might interpret this

[33] Wright (n 23) 365.

[34] Pictet (n 11) 463.

[35] Schindler (n 10) 7; see also R Kolb, 'The Relationship between International Humanitarian Law and Human Rights Law: A Brief History of the 1948 Universal Declaration of Human Rights and the 1949 Geneva Conventions' (1998) 324 *IRRC* 409.

[36] Pictet (n 11) 463.

[37] Kunz (n 7) 316.

[38] H Lauterpacht, *International Law: Being the Collected Papers of Hersch Lauterpacht*, vol 1: *The General Works*, ed E Lauterpacht (Cambridge, Cambridge University Press, 2009) 445.

> action as showing a lack of confidence in the efficiency of the means at the disposal of the United Nations for maintaining peace.[39]

It was left, therefore, to the ICRC to continue its work on the development of the laws of war; this led to the adoption of the Geneva Conventions I, II, III and IV 1949.

In 1956 Kunz suggested that, although there had been a new positive law created in the Geneva Conventions 1949, there were 'doubts whether the laws of war dealing with the actual conduct of war, including methods and weapons, [had] any value at this juncture of history and whether there [was] any chance for their revision'.[40] Despite this negative perspective, Kunz went on to state that:

> Rules for the actual conduct of war are absolutely necessary, even in time of peace, because they correspond not only to humanitarian sentiments, but to military necessity; they are a requisite pre-condition for the punishment of war crimes: and are needed today to guarantee the survival of civilization and even, perhaps, the physical survival of humanity.[41]

The times before the First World War, the interwar years and after the Second World War all had their own trials and tribulations and the situation on the ground stimulated legal developments. It has been shown that following the Second World War the ICRC was the actor willing to take responsibility for the development of a legal framework to regulate the conduct of hostilities. The ICRC is continually developing the laws of war. Following the end of the Second World War it helped develop the Geneva Conventions, in the 1970s it produced the Additional Protocols and most recently it has published a study on customary IHL.[42] The developments of these new laws reflect not only the changing nature of conflict, as described in the Introduction, but also the changing needs of people on the ground during conflict.

## III. INTERNATIONAL HUMAN RIGHTS LAW IN ARMED CONFLICT

One of the most relevant matters under discussion in this chapter is that despite distinct beginnings, it now is widely accepted that human

[39] '(1949) ILC Yearbook 281 paragraph 18' in F Kalshoven, 'Reaffirmation and Development of International Humanitarian Law Applicable in Armed Conflicts: The Conference of Government Experts, 24 May–12 June 1971' (1971) 2 *Netherlands Yearbook of International Law* 68, 68; See also H Lauterpacht, 'The Revision of the Laws of War' (1952) 29 *British Yearbook of International Law* 360.

[40] Kunz (n 7) 321.

[41] ibid, 322.

[42] J-M Henckaerts and L Doswald-Beck, *Customary International Humanitarian Law*, vol 1: *Rules* (Cambridge, Cambridge University Press, 2005).

rights and IHL frameworks overlap during armed conflict.[43] This chapter questions whether, as the guardian of IHL, the ICRC has been impacted by this shift or whether it was, in fact, a driver of change. We can look to ICJ jurisprudence, Geneva Convention commentaries and academic debate to unpick the question of the relationship between the ICRC and human rights. As a succinct overview of the matters at hand, in 2004, whilst determining the legal consequences arising from the construction of the wall being built by Israel, the ICJ confirmed the applicability of IHRL to situations of military occupation.[44] It stated, by thirteen votes to two, that 'some rights may be exclusively matters of IHL; others may be exclusively matters of IHRL; yet others may be matters of both these branches of international law'.[45] Furthermore the commentaries to the Geneva Conventions identify when the Geneva Conventions reflect specific human rights guarantees. They include, for example, the inalienability of rights;[46] treatment of protected persons;[47] prohibition of torture and corporal punishment;[48] penal procedure;[49] civil capacity;[50] and complaints and petitions from internees.[51] The question is how these legal developments impact on the work of the ICRC in terms of its mandate and on the ground. Beyond the generalised idea in the international community that there are inherent overlaps between IHL and human rights law, Milanovic argued that the current debate has progressed and no longer focuses on the relationship between the two legal regimes, as such, but on 'the relationship of the particular norms belonging to the two regimes that are

[43] 'Final Act of the International Conference on Human Rights, Teheran' (n 2); UNGA, 'Respect for Human Rights in Armed Conflict' (19 December 1968) Res 2444 (XXIII); UNGA, 'Respect for Human Rights in Armed Conflict' (9 December 1970) Res 2674 (XXV); *Legality of the Use by a State of Nuclear Weapons in Armed Conflict* (Advisory Opinion) [1996] ICJ Rep 226, para 25; *Legal Consequences of the Construction of a Wall in the Occupied Palestinian Territory* (Advisory Opinion) [2004] ICJ Rep 136, para 137; *In the Case Concerning Armed Activities on the Territory of the Congo (DRC v Uganda)*, Judgment, ICJ Reports 2005, para 207. This judgment was reinforced in *Application of the International Convention on the Elimination of all Forms of Racial Discrimination (Georgia v Russian Federation)*, Provisional Measures Order, ICJ Rep 2008, paras 111–12; See also C Droege, 'Elective Affinities? Human Rights and Humanitarian Law' (2008) 90 *IRRC* 501, 503ff; W Schabas, '*Lex Specialis*? Belts and Suspenders? The Parallel Operation of Human Rights Law and the Law of Armed Conflict, and the Conundrum of Jus ad Bellum' (2007) 40 *Israel Law Review* 592.

[44] *Legal Consequences of the Construction of a Wall in the Occupied Palestinian Territory* (n 43) paras 106–13.

[45] ibid, para 106.

[46] Geneva Convention I, Art 7; Commentary on Geneva Convention I, 82; Geneva Convention III, Art 3; Commentary on Geneva Convention III, 91; Geneva Convention IV, Art 8; Commentary on Geneva Convention IV, 78.

[47] Geneva Convention IV, Art 27; Commentary on Geneva Convention IV, 200.

[48] Geneva Convention IV, Art 32; Commentary on Geneva Convention IV, 223.

[49] Geneva Convention III, Art 99; Commentary on Geneva Convention III, 470; Geneva Convention IV, Art 71; Commentary on Geneva Convention IV, 353.

[50] Geneva Convention IV, Art 80; Commentary to Geneva Convention IV, 374.

[51] Geneva Convention IV, aRt 101; Commentary to Geneva Convention IV, 436.

controlling specific factual situations'.[52] Milanovic identifies specific situations in which IHL and IHRL both apply during armed conflict, including lawfulness of preventive detention, and necessity in targeting and transformative occupation.[53] Taken in this light, IHL is not simply a *lex specialis* of human rights law.[54]

The ICRC was founded upon the principle of humanity and mandated as the guardian of IHL. This chapter approaches the conundrum of the impact and relevance of these normative shifts to the ICRC from a theoretical and legal standpoint, to provide critical insight into the current legal framework that underpins the work of such a valuable humanitarian organisation.

Teitel's famous book, *Humanity's Law*, posits that 'humanitarian legalist discourse offers an alternative set of principles and values for global governance'.[55] The international legal order is a myriad of actors including states, intergovernmental organisations, regional human rights bodies, NGOs, civil society and individuals—the list is potentially endless—but the common entity in each is human beings. Global governance, therefore, can logically benefit from a humanitarian focus as the principle of humanity alone is insufficient as a tool for protection and assistance from states or other self-interested actors. The ICRC provides a pathway for individuals and communities suffering through or recovering from conflict to have 'humanity' as the focus of protection and assistance decision-making, which can translate into concrete actions on the ground. In order to remain useful for people on the ground, therefore, Torreblanca posits that:

> [T]he ICRC's own mandate—and the provisions' wording that enshrined it—seem to acknowledge the need for great flexibility in contexts where the dynamics of the conflicts and situations of internal violence may require from the ICRC fast changes and adaptation in order to fulfil its pivotal aim, that is, the protection of persons affected by these events.[56]

That is, the ICRC needs to draw on more than IHL on the ground.

Although much of the interview data informs later analysis in the book, it is pertinent, perhaps revelatory, to state that the ICRC delegates

[52] M Milanovic, 'A Norm Conflict Perspective on the Relationship between International Humanitarian Law and Human Rights Law' (2010) 14 *Journal of Conflict and Security Law* 459, 462.

[53] ibid.

[54] R Jennings and A Watts (eds), *Oppenheim's International Law*, 9th edn (London, Longman, 1992) para 636; S Sivakumaran, 'International Humanitarian Law' in D Moeckli, S Shah and S Sivakumaran (eds), *International Human Rights Law* (Oxford, Oxford University Press, 2010) 532–35.

[55] RG Teitel, *Humanity's Law* (Oxford, Oxford University Press, 2011) 35.

[56] Torreblanca (n 15) 546–47.

on the ground do, in fact, utilise IHRL in their dialogue with community stakeholders and non-state armed groups.[57] If IHL and the rules applicable to the situation are not convincing the actors of their responsibilities to others, in particular civilians, the ICRC may draw on other 'humanitarian' legal frameworks including IHRL. Given that the ICRC mandate is to protect and assist, broadly speaking, it seems logical that it would draw on a myriad of legal sources to convince those on the ground to respect civilians. To this end, the practice of the ICRC supports Teitel's conjecture that there is a 'humanity's law' that underpins the exigencies of IHL, IHRL and international criminal justice.

This chapter will now turn to consider the development of IHRL and its relationship with the laws of armed conflict. The purpose of this section is to show that the international community recognised that despite protestations following the end of the Second World War of 'never again', wars were continuing to occur. Unfortunately, neither the ICRC nor the UN were prepared for the myriad of conflicts occurring *within* states. The UN pursued the human rights in armed conflict agenda. The UN human rights in armed conflict agenda of 1968 and the following decade, building up to the adoption of Additional Protocol I and II 1977, are analysed in terms of ICRC involvement in the development of each organisation's legal framework.[58] These significant legal developments show the beginnings of an inherent and necessary overlap between IHL and IHRL and ultimately the development of the role of the ICRC.

The first two chapters of this book showed that the ICRC's mandate has developed to include 'other situations of violence'. In such situations IHRL would apply, not IHL. Before this chapter can analyse the impact of IHRL on the mandate of the ICRC, it is important to introduce the normative and legal content of IHRL and its relationship with armed conflict. The common understanding is that modern human rights can be traced back to the visionaries of the Enlightenment who sought a more just relationship between the state and its citizens.[59] Human rights remained a subject of national law until after the Second World War and the adoption of the Universal Declaration of Human Rights (UDHR) in 1948.[60] Just one year

[57] Interview 003.

[58] See XVIth International Red Cross Conference, London, 1938, 'Resolution XIV: Role and Activity of the Red Cross in Time of Civil War' in S Sivakumaran, *The Law of Non-International Armed Conflict* (Oxford, Oxford University Press, 2012) 36.

[59] L Doswald-Beck and S Vité, 'International Humanitarian Law and Human Rights Law' (1993) 293 *IRRC* 94, 94–119.

[60] Universal Declaration on Human Rights (adopted 10 December 1948 UNGA Res 217 A(III)) (UDHR); Droege (n 6) 313; for an overview of the development of the UN human rights legal framework, see R Provost, *International Human Rights and Humanitarian Law* (Cambridge, Cambridge University Press, 2002); for a simple and brief overview of human rights in war, see R Baxter, 'Human Rights in War' (1977) 31(2) *Bulletin of the American Academy of Arts and Sciences* 4.

later, the four Geneva Conventions were adopted. At the time, although 'general political statements referred to the common ideal of both bodies of law, there was no understanding that they would have overlapping areas of application'.[61] Indeed historically IHL and IHRL were two distinct legal frameworks and there was little interaction between them.[62] IHRL concerns the inherent rights of the person to be protected at all times against abusive power, whereas IHL regulates the conduct of parties to an armed conflict.[63] Another basic distinction to note is that human rights apply between a state and its own nationals, whereas the Geneva Conventions I, II, III and IV 1949 do not generally apply to the relations of a state with its own nationals. Rather their objectives are to govern relations between a belligerent and enemy civilians who, as a result of the occupation of the territory of the state of which they are nationals, are under the control of the adverse power.[64] Of course, there is an exception in Common Article 3. It must also be made clear that the UDHR 1948 presupposed application in times of peace, as this was what the UN sought to achieve.[65] The UDHR 1948 therefore completely bypasses the question of respect for human rights in armed conflicts, and at the same time human rights were scarcely mentioned during the drafting of the Geneva Conventions I, II, III and IV 1949.[66]

It was suggested earlier in the chapter that IHL and IHRL share common ground in their 'humanitarian core', or as Teitel would call it, 'humanity's

[61] Droege (n 6) 314.

[62] See S Sivakumaran, 'Re-envisioning the International Law of Armed Conflict' (2011) 22(1) *European Journal of International Law* 219, 234; see also AH Robertson, 'Humanitarian Law and Human Rights' in C Swinarski (ed), *Studies and Essays on International Humanitarian Law and Red Cross Principles in Honour of Jean Pictet* (The Hague, Martinus Nijhoff, 1984).

[63] For 'doctrinal' discussions on the relationship between IHL and IHRL, see Schindler (n 10); Robertson (n 62) 793; H-P Gasser, 'International Humanitarian Law' in H Haug, *Humanity for All, the International Red Cross and Red Crescent Movement* (Geneva, Henry Dunant Institute, 1993) 507–08; Doswald-Beck and Vité (n 59); H Krieger, 'A Conflict of Norms: The Relationship between Humanitarian Law and Human Rights Law in the ICRC Customary Law Study' (2006) 11(2) *Journal of Conflict and Security Law* 265; S Sayapin, 'The International Committee of the Red Cross and International Human Rights Law' (2009) 9(1) *Human Rights Law Review* 95; M Milanovic, 'A Norm Conflict Perspective on the Relationship between International Humanitarian Law and Human Rights Law' (2010) 14(3) *Journal of Conflict and Security Law* 459; I Scobbie, 'Principle or Pragmatics? The Relationship between Human Rights Law and the Law of Armed Conflict' (2010) 14(3) *Journal of Conflict and Security Law* 449.

[64] Kolb (n 35).

[65] ECOSOC, 'Report of the Drafting Committee to the Commission on Human Rights, suggestions submitted by the representative of France (R Cassin)' (1 July 1947) UN Doc E.CN.4/21, 48 and 68; 'Draft International Declaration of Human Rights (E/8OO)' (29 October 1948) UN Doc A/C.3/SR.116, 268; 'Draft Article 26 Economic and Social Council, Third Year, Seventh Session, Supplement No 2, page 11' and 'Doc A/C.3/SR.152 page 639' in Kolb (n 35); Droege (n 6) 314.

[66] Schindler (n 10); see also LG Lossier, 'The Red Cross and the International (sic) Declaration of Human Rights' (1949) *5 IRRC* 184.

law'.[67] Pictet characterised humanitarian law as 'that considerable portion of international law which is inspired by a feeling for humanity and is centred on the protection of the individual in time of war'.[68] Droege stated that: '[H]uman rights and humanitarian law share a common ideal, protection of the dignity and integrity of the person, and many of their guarantees are identical, such as the protection of the right to life, freedom from torture and ill-treatment, the protection of family rights, economic and/or social rights.'[69] Furthermore, Kellenberger, former President of the ICRC, has stated that: '[T]he common underlying purpose of international humanitarian and IHRL is the protection of the life, health and dignity of human rights.'[70]

Okimoto argued that although the UN Charter does not specifically mention the laws of war, Articles 1(3) and 55 allow the Security Council to take decisions that would ensure respect for the Geneva Conventions I, II, III and IV 1949 if a state party is not complying with them.[71] Ignatieff argued that there are also synergies between the UDHR 1948 and the Geneva Conventions 1949, as the UDHR 1948 was 'part of a wider reordering of the normative order of post war international relations, designed to create firewalls against barbarism'.[72] The 1949 Geneva Conventions were to prove, along with the UDHR 1948, 'one of the two main moral pillars for international relations after 1945'.[73] Morsink argues that: '[T]here is a clear reminiscence of war in the debates on the Universal Declaration. It is probably fair to say that for each of the rights, [the delegates] went back to the experience of the war as the epistemic foundation of the particular right in question.'[74] Moreover, the application of the Geneva Conventions I, II, III and IV 1949 should not deprive people of their human rights.

[67] Teitel (n 55).

[68] J Pictet, *Development and Principles of International Humanitarian Law* (Geneva, Henry Dunant Institute and Dordrecht, Martinus Nijhoff, 1985) 1.

[69] Droege (n 6) 312.

[70] Address by Jakob Kellenberger, President of the ICRC, 'International Humanitarian Law and Other Legal Regimes: Interplay in Situations of Violence' (2003) 85 *IRRC* 645, 646.

[71] K Okimoto, *The Distinction and Relationship between* Jus ad Bellum *and* Jus in Bello (Oregon, Hart Publishing, 2011) 119.

[72] M Ignatieff, *Human Rights as Politics and Idolatry* (Princeton, Princeton University Press, 2001) 5.

[73] Diplomatic Conference for the Establishment of International Conventions for the Protection of War Victims, 'Final Record of the Diplomatic Conference of Geneva of 1949' (Geneva, 21 April–12 August 1949) vol II, section A, 165–66, 323, 619ff, 692–95 (delegates' notes) and 813; Kunz (n 7) 322; DP Forsythe, *The Humanitarians: The International Committee of the Red Cross* (Cambridge, Cambridge University Press, 2005) 55.

[74] J Morsink, 'World War Two and the Universal Declaration' (1993) 15 *Human Rights Quarterly* 357, 358.

The President of the Geneva Conventions conference, Max Petitpierre, also spoke of the parallelism between the common ideal of the Geneva Conventions and the UDHR 1948. He stated that:

> Our texts are based on certain of the fundamental rights proclaimed in it- respect for the human person, protection against torture and against cruel, inhuman or degrading punishments or treatment. Those rights find their legal expression in the contractual engagements that your Governments have today agreed to undertake. The UDHR and the Geneva Conventions are both derived from one and the same ideal.[75]

In 1968 the 'Final Act of the International Conference on Human Rights' stated that: '[P]eace is the underlying condition for the full observance of human rights and war is their negation.'[76] The subsequent General Assembly Resolution 2444 (XXIII) of 1968 urged the Secretary-General to study measures for a better application of existing law and described the need for new instruments to better protect civilians, prisoners and combatants in all armed conflicts.[77] Interestingly, despite the title of the resolution being 'Respect for Human Rights in Armed Conflicts', it only mentions IHL, except for a statement in the preamble that war amounts to a negation of human rights.[78] It is curious, therefore, how the General Assembly hoped to better apply IHRL to situations of armed conflict.

The UN's interest in increasing the legal framework applicable during NIACs was ignited during the Korean conflict and the invasion of Hungary by Soviet troops.[79] The preamble to Geneva Convention I states

[75] Final Record of the Diplomatic Conference of Geneva of 1949 (n 73) 536; See also JAC Gutteridge, 'The Geneva Conventions of 1949' (1949) 26 *British Yearbook of International Law* 300, 325; GIAD Draper, 'The Relationship Between the Human Rights Regime and the Law of Armed Conflict' (1971) 1 *Israel Yearbook on Human Rights* 205.

[76] 'Final Act of the International Conference on Human Rights' (n 2) para 10, states that: '[M]assive denials of human rights, arising out of aggression or any armed conflict with their tragic consequences, and resulting in untold human misery, engender reactions which could engulf the world in ever growing hostilities. It is the obligation of the international community to co-operate in eradicating such scourges'; Proclamation of Tehran, 'Final Act of the International Conference on Human Rights, Teheran' (22 April–13 May 1968) UN Doc A/CONF. 32/41, 3; for a general overview of this period, see K Suter, *An International Law of Guerrilla Warfare: The Global Politics of Law-Making* (Basingstoke, Palgrave Macmillan, 1984); Sivakumaran (n 58) ch 2.

[77] 'Final Act of the International Conference on Human Rights, Tehran' (n 2) paras 2-3; Kalshoven (n 39) 70; see discussion in Schindler (n 10) 3; see also S Miyazaki, 'The Application of the New Humanitarian Law' (1980) 20 *IRRC* 184, which focuses on IHL and human rights in NIAC; AS Calogeropoulos-Stratis, 'The Humanitarian Dimension of War: Protection of the Individual, whether Military or Civilian' (1992) 32 *IRRC* 183.

[78] UNGA, 'Respect for Human Rights in Armed Conflict' (19 December 1968) Res 2444 (XXIII).

[79] UNGA, 'Question of Atrocities Committed by the North Korean and Chinese Communist Forces Against United Nations Prisoners of War in Korea' (3 December 1953) Res 804 (VIII); UNGA, 'Invasion of Hungary by Soviet Troops' (12 December 1958) Res 1312 (XIII) UN Doc A38/49.

that in all armed conflicts the inhabitants and belligerents are protected in accordance with 'the principles of the law of nations derived from the usages established among civilized peoples, from the laws of humanity and from the dictates of the public conscience'. It was recognised by the Conference of Government Experts that convened in 1971 to consider the 'Reaffirmation and Development of International Humanitarian Law Applicable in Armed Conflicts' that the Geneva Conventions were 'not sufficiently broad in scope to cover all armed conflicts'. Furthermore the conference stated that: 'States parties to the Geneva Conventions sometimes fail to appreciate their responsibility to take steps to ensure the respect of these humanitarian rules in all circumstances by other States, even if they are not themselves directly involved in an armed conflict.'[80] This Resolution 2444 and General Assembly Resolution 2675 (XXV) (1970) 'with their various protections for the civilian population were considered to reflect the state of customary international law applicable to all armed conflicts'.[81] Indeed Kellenberger stated that: '[I]n political terms, the 1968 resolution signalled the international community's recognition that armed conflicts "continued to plague humanity" despite the UN Charter's prohibition on threats or use of force in international relations.'[82]

The Secretary-General wrote two reports on the 'Respect for Human Rights in Armed Conflicts' in 1969 and 1970, at the request of the General Assembly. These reports postulated that human rights instruments, in particular the International Covenant on Civil and Political Rights 1966 (ICCPR),[83] afforded more comprehensive protection to persons in times of armed conflict than the Geneva Conventions alone.[84] In fact, a couple of months after the second report, the UN General Assembly confirmed that human rights continue to apply in situations of armed conflict.[85] Subsequently, the General Assembly directed the Human Rights Commission to consider the Secretary-General's report on 'Respect of Human Rights in Armed Conflicts'.[86] The UN Secretariat worked in close

[80] ICRC, 'Reaffirmation and Development of International Humanitarian Law Applicable in Armed Conflicts: The Conference of Government Experts, 24 May–12 June 1971' 37 www.loc.gov/rr/frd/Military_Law/pdf/RC-conference_Vol-8.pdf.

[81] Sivakumaran (n 62) 223–24.

[82] Address by Jakob Kellenberger, President of the ICRC, 'Protection Through Complementarity of the Law' (27th Annual Round Table on Current Problems of International Humanitarian Law, San Remo, Italy, 4–6 September 2003) www.icrc.org/eng/resources/documents/statement/5rfgaz.htm.

[83] International Covenant on Civil and Political Rights (adopted 16 December 1966, entered into force 23 March 1976) 999 UNTS 171 (ICCPR).

[84] Report of the Secretary General, 'Report on the Respect for Human Rights in Armed Conflict' (20 November 1969) UN Doc A/7729, ch 3; Report of the Secretary General, 'Respect of Human Rights in Time of Armed Conflicts' (18 September 1970) UN Doc A/8052, annex 1.

[85] UNGA, 'Principles for the Protection of Civilian Populations in Armed Conflict' (9 December 1970) UN Doc A/8028 Basic; GA Res 2675.

[86] UN Doc A/8052 (n 84).

cooperation with the ICRC during the process.[87] The two reports influenced the preparation of new draft treaties by the ICRC, which became Additional Protocols I and II. Meanwhile the UN continued its human rights in armed conflict agenda.[88]

In terms of Additional Protocols I and II, from 1974 to 1977 the Diplomatic Conference on the Reaffirmation and Development of International Humanitarian Law took place in Geneva.[89] The world in which the Additional Protocols were launched was very different from the one in existence following the end of the Second World War and the adoption of the Geneva Conventions I, II, III and IV 1949. In particular, the Third World had risen up against colonialists; the 'capitalist' and 'socialist' blocs were engaged in a battle of wills, later to be named the 'Cold War'; and the Vietnam conflict was still fresh in the minds of the international community.[90]

Prior to the Diplomatic Conference the ICRC advocated a parallel approach to the rules governing international armed conflict and NIAC, but with the focus of the world on the armed national liberation movements it was impossible to achieve consent for such a proposition.[91] There were therefore two protocols, one on international armed conflict and one on NIAC.[92] The protocols updated the rules on the conduct of hostilities,

[87] See Miscellaneous, 'Human Rights in Armed Conflicts' (1970) 10 *IRRC* 220.

[88] Res 2444 (XXIII) (n 78); UNGA, 'Respect for Human Rights in Armed Conflict' 16 December 1969) Res 2597 (XXVI); (9 December 1970) Res 2677 (xxv); (9 December 1970) Res 2676 (xxv); (9 December 1970) Res 2674 (XXV); (20 December 1971) Res 2852 (XXVI); (20 December 1971) Res 2853 (XXVI); (20 December 1972) Res 3032 (XXVII); (12 December 1973) Res 3102 (XXVIII); (14 December 1974) Res 3319 (XXIX); (15 December 1975) Res 3500 (XXX); UNGA, 'Basic Principles for the Protection of Civilian Populations in Armed Conflicts' (9 December 1970) Res 2675 (XXV); UNGA, 'Basic Principles of the Legal Status of the Combatants Struggling against Colonial and Alien Domination and Racist Regimes' (12 December 1973) Res 3103 (XXVIII); Report of the Secretary General, 'Respect for Human Rights in Armed Conflicts' (20 November 1969) UN Doc A/7720; UN Doc A/8052 (n 84); (1971) UN Doc A/8370; (20 September 1972) A/8781; (1973) A/9123; (1974) A/9669; (11 November 1975) A/10195/Add.1.

[89] For details of the preparatory work on the Additional Protocols, see M Bothe, KJ Patsch and WA Solf, with M Eaton, *New Rules for Victims of Armed Conflicts: A Commentary on the Two 1977 Protocols Additional to the Geneva Conventions of 1949* (The Hague, Martinus Nijhoff, 1982); C Pilloud, Y Sandoz, C Swinarski and B Zimmerman, *Commentary on the Additional Protocols of 8 June 1977 to the Geneva Conventions of 12 August 1949* (The Hague, Martinus Nijhoff, 1987).

[90] R Kosirnik, 'The 1977 Protocols: A Landmark in the Development of International Humanitarian Law' (1997) 320 *IRRC* 483, 483.

[91] 'Report submitted to the 21st International Conference of the Red Cross (Istanbul, 6–13 December 1969)' (1969) 51 *IRRC* 33, 33–35.

[92] For an overview of the significant developments in the law contained in Additional Protocol I, see GH Aldrich, 'New Life for the Laws of War' (1981) 75(4) *American Journal of International Law* 764; AP Heike Spieker, 'Twenty-five Years after the Adoption of Additional Protocol II: Breakthrough or Failure of Humanitarian Legal Protection?' (2001) 4 *Yearbook of International Humanitarian Law* 129.

which afforded non-combatants and civilians enhanced protection.[93] Moreover the UN General Assembly called on states to become parties to the 1977 Additional Protocols.[94] UN bodies were also called upon to work for a strengthening of IHL: reaffirmation and progressive codification of IHL (standard setting), ensuring prosecution and punishment of persons who have committed serious violations of that law, and increasing respect on the part of parties to specific conflicts for their obligations under IHL, that is, humanitarian diplomacy.[95]

## IV. CONCLUSION

Since the creation of the ICRC the landscape of war has changed. Traditionally IHL was the law in force during armed conflict and when there was no war the landscape was peaceful and IHL did not apply. The nature of NIAC and protracted armed conflict has changed this. Nowadays conflict ebbs and flows; within a sovereign state some areas can be considered 'at war' whilst others are 'at peace'. Not only can these labels change from place to place but one area can sometimes be engaged in armed conflict, then not, then perhaps engaged in armed violence not amounting to a conflict, and so on. The application of laws to each situation has therefore become increasingly complex.

This chapter has shown that human rights law, including the soft law created by the General Assembly resolutions on human rights in armed conflicts, has developed and is now applicable at all times. Indeed, a 'human-being-oriented approach' to international law, as identified in the *Tadić* Appeals Chamber decision, now prevails.[96] The inherent overlaps between human rights and IHL therefore lead to the convergence of legal frameworks. The differing normative basis of the UN and ICRC explored earlier in the chapter appears therefore to have been subsumed by the necessary development of the laws and rules applicable during international armed conflict and NIAC. This analysis will feed into the next chapter of the book, which considers human security. The development of human rights since the end of the Second World War is part of a wider human-centric progression within the international community. Human

[93] Additional Protocol I, Arts 35–67; Additional Protocol II, Arts 13–17.

[94] UNGA, 'Status of the Protocols Additional to the Geneva Conventions of 1949 and Relating to the Protection of Victims of Armed Conflicts' (9 December 1994) Res 49/48; UNGA, 'Resolution of the United Nations General Assembly on the 1977 Additional Protocols' (12 December 2000) A/RES/55/148.

[95] UNGA, 'United Nations Resolution on the Development of International Humanitarian Law: Respect for Human Rights in Armed Conflicts' (1977) Res A/C.6/32/L.6.

[96] *Prosecutor v Tadić* (Appeals Chamber Decision on Defence Motion for Interlocutory Appeal on Jurisdiction) ICTY-1995-IT-49-I-AR72 (2 October 1995) para 97.

rights fit into a jigsaw, so to speak, of human-centric norms. The ICRC is an important organisation within this human-centric paradigm, as the Geneva Conventions I, II, III and IV 1949 and the ICRC Statutes underpin the ICRC as an international actor, legal person and 'guardian' of IHL. Legally the ICRC is still unique, as was shown in chapters 1 and 2, but the humanitarian norms that filter through international law, per se, are relevant to the ICRC.

It appears that the ICRC applies IHRL when necessary to promote its humanitarian agenda, despite there being no reference to IHRL in its mandate, a theory that will explored further in the empirical analysis later in the book. The ICRC is increasingly working in situations not amounting to armed conflicts, and interviewees disclosed that, where there is a need to impart the message of humanity, they will refer to IHRL in order to convince non-state armed groups of the importance of humanity in armed violence. This book is conscious of the fact that the ICRC is a humanitarian actor, tasked with the provision of humanitarian assistance and protection during international armed conflict and NIAC. It also shows, however, that such a limited idea of what the ICRC is and does fails to reflect the full corpus of situations in which the organisation acts and the activities that it undertakes. Analysis of the ICRC must, therefore, draw on the existing knowledge we have of the ICRC, its mandate and principles, and reflect on broader 'humanitarian' notions to see whether they impact on the organisation. Moving into the next chapter, therefore, these considerations must be kept in mind, as the argument moves from the ICRC mandate in terms of treaty and statute law to how it is being interpreted and implemented on the ground today. What broader ideas and activities is the ICRC seemingly drawing on in its work? Is it interpreting its mandate more broadly than in the past?

# 4

# *Humanity as a Core Principle of the Red Cross and Red Crescent Movement*[1]

## I. INTRODUCTION

THE FUNDAMENTAL PRINCIPLES of the IRCRCM are included in the preamble to the Statutes of the IRCRCM. They include, as stated earlier, humanity, impartiality, neutrality, independence, voluntary service, unity and universality.[2] One aim of the principles is to ensure that all national societies are a 'solid and well-built edifice'.[3] The ICRC has a responsibility to act in all situations of armed conflict and violence and in order to do so it needs to be accepted by all actors.[4] It is well known that the ICRC acts within politically and legally sensitive areas; it is able to do so because of its reputation for humanity and impartiality in the eyes of parties to conflicts and other actors. As regards the latter, in theory, therefore, the ICRC does not engage in political debates, or activities that could undermine its credibility, unity and strength. It also does not make its assistance conditional upon the legitimacy of the recourse to arms, as its aim is to assist rather than denounce.[5] Furthermore the ICRC does not allow 'its activities to be coordinated by the UN or anyone else, claiming its

1 I would like to thank Emma Fowler (University of Lincoln) for her research assistance in summer 2016.

2 ICRC, *The Fundamental Principles of the Red Cross and Red Crescent* (Geneva, ICRC, 1996).

3 See J Pictet, 'The Fundamental Principles of the Red Cross: Commentary' (Geneva, International Federation of Red Cross and Red Crescent Societies, 1979) 6.

4 For further discussion on the neutrality and independence of the ICRC, see K Anderson, 'Humanitarian Inviolability in Crisis: The Meaning of Impartiality and Neutrality for UN and NGO Agencies Following the 2003–2004 Afghanistan and Iraq Conflicts' (2004) 17 *Harvard Human Rights Journal* 41; P Krahenbuhl, 'The ICRC's Approach to Contemporary Security Challenges: A Future for Independent and Neutral Humanitarian Action' (2004) 86 *IRRC* 505; D Thurer, 'Dunant's Pyramid: Thoughts on the "Humanitarian Space"' (2007) 89 *IRRC* 47; E Wortel, 'Humanitarians and their Moral Stance in War: The Underlying Values' (2009) 91 *IRRC* 779.

5 Y Sandoz, 'The Red Cross and Peace: Realities and Limits' (1987) 24(3) *Journal of Peace Research: Special Issue on Humanitarian Law of Armed Conflict* 287, 288.

historically unique position as the custodian of the Geneva Conventions I, II, III and IV 1949 and Additional Protocols'.[6] In addition to remaining impartial, it is important that the ICRC acts as a neutral and independent actor, outside the political sphere, which allows it to intervene in humanitarian situations, even between a government and its people. The ICRC is clear that neutrality is not indifference; rather the ICRC 'believes that it must steer clear of political controversies and keep its action distinct from the political or military agendas of any one actor'.[7] The ICRC insists on 'dialogue with all parties to armed conflict in order to reach and improve the lives of those most in need'.[8] The provision of humanitarian assistance must always be neutral, that is, for all sides of the conflict. States are under an obligation to allow free passage through their territories of goods intended for the civilians of another party to the conflict.[9]

This chapter engages critically with the fundamental principle of humanity and describes its application by the ICRC in contemporary settings. It examines legal and theoretical conceptualisations of humanity within and beyond the ICRC. It finds that humanity is an ethical and legal principle that underpins humanitarian protection and assistance, whilst being reinforced and supported by the other principles, particularly neutrality and independence.

## II. HUMANITY

Humanity is, at its very core, a call for human beings to be put first by states, perhaps also by each other. Traditionally the notion of humanity manifested itself in the laws of war through notions of chivalry, distinction, necessity and proportionality.[10] Ultimately, it is this author's belief

[6] TG Weiss, 'Humanitarian Action in War Zones' in J Nederveen Pieterse, *World Orders in the Making* (Basingstoke, Macmillan, Institute of Social Studies, 1998) 43.

[7] P Krähenbühl (ICRC Director of Operations), 'Challenges for Humanitarian Action in Situations of Armed Conflict and Internal Violence' (IRCRCM (Council of Delegates), Seoul, Republic of Korea, 16–18 November 2005).

[8] ICRC, 'Strengthening Legal Protection for Victims of Armed Conflict: Draft Resolution and Report' (31st International Conference of the Red Cross and Red Crescent, Geneva, October 2011) 31IC/11/5.1.1, 28–29 www.icrc.org/eng/assets/files/red-cross-crescent-movement/31st-international-conference/31-int-conference-strengthening-legal-protection-11-5-1-1-en.pdf.

[9] Geneva Convention IV, Art 23; Additional Protocol I, Art 70(2); J-M Henckaerts and L Doswald-Beck, *Customary International Humanitarian Law*, vol 1: *Rules* (Cambridge, Cambridge University Press, 2005) Rule 55; See also Hague Convention V, Art 14 which states that humanitarian assistance for the sick or wounded is not considered to be a violation of neutrality even if it benefits only the sick and wounded from one party to the conflict.

[10] T Gill, 'Chivalry?: A Principle of the Law of Armed Conflict' in M Matthee, B Toebes and M Brus (eds), *Armed Conflict and International Law: In Search of the Human Face* (The Hague, TMC Asser Press, 2013) ch 2.

that as human beings we have an inherent understanding of humanity. Even if our humanity is put into question, the very fact that we recognise 'inhumanity' is evidence of our empathy towards one another. In this regard, an absence of humanity is perhaps easier to identify than the positive existence of such. Inhumanity is more than 'bad behaviour' towards another and, to this end, 'crimes against humanity' provide a sensible reference point for understanding inhumane treatment.[11] It is the 'positive' idea of humanity that needs more thought. The ICRC definition of humanity states that 'its purpose is to protect life and health and to ensure respect for the human being'.[12] If we take the mandate of the ICRC, for example, then its rights to visit prisoners of war or provide healthcare to wounded soldiers are clearly linked to this part of the principle of humanity. This book addresses, in part, whether 'protection' and 'assistance' have had to adapt to new types of conflict and broader humanitarian concerns, in order to uphold the principle of humanity.

It is almost impossible to provide a concise and agreeable definition of humanity. Perhaps it refers to human beings collectively, the state of being human or the quality of being humane.[13] In which case, acts of 'inhumanity' could be identified as 'massacres, persecution, forced displacement, arrests, attacks on civilians, and excessive use of force by police and denial of freedom or of self-determination'.[14] Perhaps the most pragmatic way to think about humanity, and for that matter, inhumanity, is 'you know it when you see it', but in terms of legal analysis this is not particularly helpful. If you ask someone to define 'humanity' one would imagine the response might take some time to articulate. Ask an international lawyer, particularly one with a background in IHL, and perhaps they would cite the Martens clause or crimes against humanity, as defined in the Rome Statute.[15] Or perhaps they might remind you that the principle of humanity is a cornerstone of the IRCRC and that it theoretically fosters a reciprocal relationship between parties at war, as fighting ought to be

[11] There are exciting and interesting developments in literature on this matter. See M Bergsmo and S Tianying (eds), *On the Proposed Crimes Against Humanity Convention* (Brussels, Torkel Opsahl Academic E-Publisher, 2014); T Rodenhäuser, 'Beyond State Crimes: Non-State Entities and Crimes Against Humanity' (2014) 27(4) *Leiden Journal of International Law* 913; A Chehtman, 'Contemporary Approaches to the Philosophy of Crimes Against Humanity' (2014) 14(4–5) *International Criminal Law Review* 813; J-A Wemmers, *Reparation for Victims of Crimes Against Humanity: The Healing Role of Reparation* (London, Routledge, 2014).

[12] IRCRCM Statutes.

[13] Oxford Dictionary, www.oxforddictionaries.com/definition/english/humanity.

[14] R Coupland, 'Humanity: What Is it and How Does it Influence in International Law' (2001) 83 *IRRC* 969, 971.

[15] Hague Convention Concerning the Laws and Customs of War on Land, 18 October 1907, 36 Stat 2227 (Martens clause); Rome Statute of the International Criminal Court (adopted 17 July 1998, entered into force 1 July 2002) 2187 UNTS 3 (Rome Statute) Art 7.

based on notions of chivalry and civilised behaviour.[16] As was stated in chapter 3, the *jus in bello* is purely humanitarian, based on the basic axioms of IHL, including military necessity, the principle of distinction and proportionality.[17] Turns argues that:

> [T]he principle of humanity is, so to speak, the other side of the coin: it counterbalances military necessity by decreeing that the horrors of war must, to the extent possible, and without unduly hindering the attainment of lawful military objectives, be alleviated by considerations of humanitarianism, such as the protection of enemy soldiers who have surrendered. The balance between military necessity and humanity is not always easy to strike.[18]

## III. HISTORY OF THE PRINCIPLE OF HUMANITY

It is fair to say that the meaning of 'humanity' remains ambiguous, despite the 'laws of humanity' being evoked as early as 1868 in the St Petersburg Declaration, which 'prohibited the use of bullets that would explode on impact with a soldier's body', as the useless aggravation of suffering was seen as contrary to 'humanity' and the 'progress of civilization'.[19]

Three decades later, at the 1899 Hague Peace Conference a Russian diplomat, Fryodor Fyodorovich Martens, successfully introduced a clause into the preamble of The Hague Convention (II) with Respect to the Laws and Customs of War on Land. It was also included in The Hague Convention (IV), developed at the Peace Conference of 1907. The clause states that:

> The inhabitants and the belligerents must remain under the protection and the rule of the basic principles of the law of nations, as they result from the usages established among civilised peoples, from the laws of humanity and the dictates of public conscience.[20]

[16] The Statutes of the International Red Cross and Red Crescent Movement were adopted by consensus at the Twenty-Fifth International Conference of the Red Cross, meeting in Geneva in October 1986 (IRCRCM Statutes); C Droege, 'The Interplay between International Humanitarian Law and International Human Rights Law in Situations of Armed Conflict' (2007) 40 *Israel Law Review* 310, 313; see also Instructions for the Government of Armies of the United States in the Field (Lieber Code) 24 April 1863.

[17] C Greenwood, 'Historical Development and Legal Basis' and S Oeter, 'Methods and Means of Combat' in D Fleck, *The Handbook of International Humanitarian Law*, 3rd edn (Oxford, Oxford University Press, 2013) 35ff, 126–36.

[18] D Turns, 'Targets' in ND White and C Henderson (eds), *Research Handbook on International Conflict and Security Law: Jus ad Bellum, Jus in Bello and Jus Post Bellum* (Cheltenham, Edward Elgar, 2013) 344.

[19] Declaration Renouncing the Use, in Time of War, of Explosive Projectiles under 400 Grammes Weight, St Petersburg, 29 November–11 December 1868.

[20] Restated in Geneva Convention I, Art 63; Geneva Convention II, Art 62; Geneva Convention III, Art 142 and Geneva Convention IV, Art 158; Also present in Additional Protocol I,

Eight years after the adoption of The Hague Convention (IV) there was a mass killing of Armenians in the Ottoman Empire. The terminology used to describe this event was that they were crimes against humanity and civilisation.[21] Such terminology continues to permeate international criminal law today. (Although, technically, 'the use of this specific term at Nuremberg was suggested by a leading scholar, Hersch Lauterpacht, to Robert Jackson, the US delegate to the London Conference, who was subsequently appointed chief US prosecutor at Nuremberg'.)[22] These crimes were thus defined as:

> Murder, extermination, enslavement, deportation, and other inhumane acts committed against any civilian population, before or during the war, or persecutions on political, racial, or religious grounds in execution of or connexion with any crimes within the jurisdiction of the Tribunal [ie either 'crimes against peace' or 'war crimes'], whether or not in violation of the domestic law of the country where perpetrated.

Nowadays, in fact, the nexus between crimes against humanity and armed conflict is no longer required, as crimes against humanity can be committed outside of armed conflict. Indeed, 'customary international law bans crimes against humanity whether they are committed in time of war or peace'.[23] The application of the principle of humanity in the legal sphere has therefore developed over time. This chapter examines whether such developments have impacted on the ICRC.

In chapter 3, the relationship between the laws of war and peace, and the ICRC, was explored, ultimately showing that there is significant convergence in law and practice between the two. To this end, humanity, too, is a concept that permeates both war and peace; in the same way that the ICRC may refer to IHRL, the principle of humanity may, perhaps, overarch all functions of the ICRC.

Art 1(2) but 'laws' was replaced by 'principles' and Additional Protocol II preamble, para 4; Convention on Prohibitions or Restrictions on the Use of Certain Conventional Weapons Which May Be Deemed to Be Excessively Injurious or to Have Indiscriminate Effects (10 October 1980) 1342 UNTS 137 Preamble, para 5.

[21] For the full text of the note, see the 'Dispatch of the US Ambassador in France, Sharp, to the US Secretary of State, Bryan, of 28 May 1915' in *Papers Relating to the Foreign Relations of the United States, 1915, Supp* (Washington, US Government Printing Office, 1928) 981.

[22] See on this point M Koskenniemi, 'Hersch Lauterpacht and the Development of International Criminal Law' (2004) 2 *Journal of International Criminal Justice* 811.

[23] See on this point the dictum of the ICTY, *Prosecutor v Tadić* (Appeals Chamber Decision on Defence Motion for Interlocutory Appeal on Jurisdiction) ICTY-1995-IT-49-I-AR72 (2 October 1995) 141.

## IV. THE IRCRCM DEFINITION OF HUMANITY

Under the Statutes of the movement the ICRC's concept of humanity is defined as follows:

> The International Red Cross and Red Crescent Movement, born of a desire to bring assistance without discrimination to the wounded on the battlefield, endeavours, in its international and national capacity, to prevent and alleviate human suffering wherever it may be found. Its purpose is to protect life and health and to ensure respect for the human being. It promotes mutual understanding, friendship, cooperation and lasting peace amongst all peoples.[24]

Chapters 1 and 2 explored the legal status and foundations of the IRCRCM Statutes and the mandate of the ICRC. What is the significance of the Fundamental Principles to the ICRC and the state parties to the Geneva Conventions I, II, III and IV 1949? Bugnion states that:

> Just like the Statutes, the Fundamental Principles form part of the constitutive rules of the Red Cross. At the regulatory level, they perform the same function as the Statutes do at the institutional level: they provide the cement without which the edifice of the Movement would fall apart. Even more than the statutory rules, the principles stand for belief in certain basic ideals which transcend not only national borders but also political, economic, religious, ideological and racial differences; they preserve the bond of solidarity without which the Movement would lose its meaning.[25]

Bugnion also argues that 'while the States themselves are not bound to adhere to the Fundamental Principles, they are obliged to allow Red Cross and Red Crescent organizations to do so'.[26] This conclusion is supported by Article 2(4) of the IRCRCM Statutes, which states that: '[T]he States shall at all times respect the adherence by all the components of the Movement to the Fundamental Principles.'

In 1956 Pictet stated that 'humanity' is a 'further example of the poverty of language'.[27] To this end, humanitarianism is 'simply this attitude of humanity laid down as a social doctrine and extended to mankind as a whole'.[28] Humanitarianism 'combines the elements of secular humanism and religious traditions, … promotes an approach which places individual human beings at the forefront while at the same time putting emphasis

24 IRCRCM Statutes.
25 F Bugnion, 'Red Cross Law' (1995) 308 *IRRC* 491, 507.
26 ibid.
27 J Pictet, *Red Cross Principles* (Geneva, ICRC, 1956) 14–31.
28 ibid.

on mercy, charity and compassion'.[29] For this author, the ICRC principle of humanity, if followed to the letter of the Statutes of the movement, fails to reflect the reality of inhumanity seen around the world today. If humanitarian action were restricted to the battlefield, to take one example, then the utility of humanitarianism would be ineffective for civilians affected by armed conflict and other situations of violence the world over. Fortunately, in the IRCRCM Statutes humanity also includes the 'prevention and alleviation of suffering wherever it may be found', which adds credence to the view that 'humanity' is to be determined in light of the situation on the ground.

## V. JUDICIAL INTERPRETATIONS OF HUMANITY

There are key references to principles or laws of humanity in preambles to various conventions[30] and General Assembly resolutions.[31] An oft-cited judicial reference to humanity is found in the *Corfu Channel* case, in which the ICJ relied on certain 'general and well-recognized principles', including 'elementary considerations of humanity, even more exacting in peace than in war'.[32] Earlier, in the *Naulilaa* case, the arbitral tribunal 'applied principles of humanity to limit the scope of permissible reprisals'.[33] The ICJ has also referred to provisions of the UN Charter concerning the protection of human rights and fundamental freedoms, as a basis for the

[29] V Bilkovà, 'Ensuring Human Security in Armed Conflicts: The Role of Non-State Actors and its Reflection in Current International Humanitarian Law' in C Ryngaert and M Noortman, *Human Security and International Law: The Challenge of Non-State Actors* (Cambridge, Intersentia, 2014) 36.

[30] See especially preamble to the Hague Convention Concerning the Laws and Customs of War on Land, 18 October 1907, 36 Stat 2227: 'Until a more complete code of the laws of war has been issued, the High Contracting Parties deem it expedient to declare that, in cases not included in the Regulations adopted by them, the inhabitants and the belligerents remain under the protection and the rule of the principles of the law of nations, as they result from the usages established among civilized peoples, from the laws of humanity, and the dictates of the public conscience.' This is known as the Martens clause.

[31] 'Declaration on the Prohibition of the Use of Nuclear and Thermo-Nuclear Weapons', UNGA Res 1653(XVI) (24 November 1961).

[32] *Corfu Channel Case* (*UK v Albania*) (Merits) [1949] ICJ Rep 4, 22. The statement referred to Albania's duty to warn of the presence of mines in its waters. See also *Case Concerning Military and Paramilitary Activities in and against Nicaragua* (Merits) [1986] ICJ Rep 14, 112–14.

[33] 'Responsibilité de l'Allemagne à Raisons des Dommages Causés dans les Colonies Portuguaises du sud de Afrique, 2 RIAA 1013, 1026 (1928)' in T Meron, 'The Martens Clause, Principles of Humanity, and Dictates of Public Conscience' (2000) 94(1) *Americal Journal of International Law* 78, 82.

legal status of considerations of humanity.[34] Interestingly, however, Judge Tanaka, in his dissenting opinion, stated that:

> As outstanding examples of the recognition of the legal interests of States in general humanitarian causes, the international efforts to suppress the slave trade, the minorities' treaties, the Genocide Convention and the Constitution of the International Labour Organisation are cited.

We consider that in these treaties and organisations common and humanitarian interests are incorporated. By being given organisational form, these interests take the nature of 'legal interest' and require to be protected by specific procedural means.[35]

One of the key cases that is often cited in reference to 'humanity' is the *Case Concerning Military and Paramilitary Activities in and against Nicaragua*.[36] What was seen as an assault on the internal affairs of Nicaragua was defended, by the United States, as provision of humanitarian assistance. However, the ICJ held that: '[T]he aim of its assistance was not to prevent and alleviate human suffering. Moreover, it was provided in a discriminatory fashion, only to the Contras and their dependents. As such, it did not satisfy the criteria required to qualify as humanitarian assistance.'[37] What is important to this book is that the court explicitly recognised that the provision of strictly humanitarian assistance to persons or forces in another country could in no way be considered illicit, provided that such assistance conformed to the Fundamental Principles of the Red Cross, in particular those of humanity and impartiality:

> An essential feature of truly humanitarian aid is that it is given without discrimination of any kind. In the view of the Court, if the provision of humanitarian assistance is to escape condemnation as an intervention in the internal affairs of Nicarauga, not only must it be limited to the purposes hallowed in the practice of the Red Cross, namely to prevent and alleviate human suffering, and to protect life and health and to ensure respect for the human being; it must also, and above all, be given without discrimination to all in need.[38]

The most recent articulation of crimes against humanity can be found in Article 7 of the Rome Statute on Crimes against Humanity. Article 7(1) states that:

> '[C]rime against humanity' means any of the following acts when committed as part of a widespread or systematic attack directed against any civilian population, with knowledge of the attack:

[34] In *South West Africa* (Second Phase) ICJ Rep 1966, 6, 34, the Court held that humanitarian considerations were not decisive.

[35] ibid 252–3, 270, 294–9.

[36] *Case Concerning Military and Paramilitary Activities in and against Nicaragua* (Merits) [1986] ICJ Rep 14.

[37] ibid.

[38] ibid, 115.

> (a) Murder; (b) Extermination; (c) Enslavement; (d) Deportation or forcible transfer of population; (e) Imprisonment or other severe deprivation of physical liberty in violation of fundamental rules of international law; (f) Torture; (g) Rape, sexual slavery, enforced prostitution, forced pregnancy, enforced sterilization, or any other form of sexual violence of comparable gravity; (h) Persecution against any identifiable group or collectivity on political, racial, national, ethnic, cultural, religious, gender as defined in paragraph 3, or other grounds that are universally recognized as impermissible under international law, in connection with any act referred to in this paragraph or any crime within the jurisdiction of the Court; (i) Enforced disappearance of persons; (j) The crime of apartheid; (k) Other inhumane acts of a similar character intentionally causing great suffering, or serious injury to body or to mental or physical health.

The specifics of such actions are given further elaboration under Article 7(2) of the Rome Statute. The Rome Statute goes some way to framing the concept of humanity, as it identifies what humanity is not. It specifies which acts are 'against' humanity. For Teitel, there are a myriad of cases that consider the definition and application of crimes against humanity, from the ICJ,[39] the ICTY,[40] European Court of Human Rights,[41] the Inter-American Court of Human Rights[42] and domestic courts.[43] It is beyond the purpose of this book to consider the jurisprudence in depth, but what it shows is that the concept of humanity applies globally and is seemingly timeless; it is, in the words of Teitel, 'humanity's law'.[44] This book will, however, delve into the concept of humanity and its relationship with ICRC humanitarian assistance and protection.

The question remains, however: what does humanity look like? And as a 'humanitarian' actor, what is the ICRC truly striving to achieve? It must be something beyond absence of the crimes described in the Rome Statute.

[39] *Legality of the Threat or Use of Nuclear Weapons* (Advisory Opinion) [1996] ICJ Rep 679, para 24; *Legal Consequences of the Construction of a Wall in the Occupied Palestinian Territory* (Advisory Opinion) [2004] ICJ Rep 136 para 86, 106; *Case Concerning Armed Activities on the Territory of the Congo (DRC v Uganda)*, Judgment, ICJ Reports 2005, 116; *Case Concerning the Application of the Convention on the Prevention and Punishment of the Crime of Genocide (Bosnia and Herzegovina v Serbia and Montenegro)* (Judgment) [2007] ICJ Rep 43.

[40] *Prosecutor v Kordić and Cerkez* (Judgment/Trial Chamber) ICTY IT-95-14/2 (26 February 2001) para 23; *Prosecutor v Tadić* (Appeals Chamber Decision on Defence Motion for Interlocutory Appeal on Jurisdiction) ICTY-1995-IT-49-I-AR72 (2 October 1995); See also *Prosecutor v Martić* (Review of the Indictment Pursuant to Rule 61) ICTY No IT-95-11-R61 (13 March 1996) para 13; See also the *Prosecutor v Furundžija* (Judgment) ICTY IT-95-17/1-T (10 December 1998) para 137.

[41] *Isayeva v Russia*, App No 57950/00 (Judgment) (ECtHR 24 February 2005).

[42] *Abella v Argentina*, Case 11.137, Rep No 5/97, IAmCtHR OEA/Ser L/V/II.95 Doc 7 Rev (13 April 1998).

[43] *Al-Skeini v Secretary of State for Defence* [2007] UKHL 26.

[44] See in particular RG Teitel, *Humanity's Law* (Oxford, Oxford University Press, 2011) 40–72.

For this author the answer lies in a gradual 'creep' of human-centric concepts and ideas that have gradually permeated international law and the international community over the past twenty-five years. Sovereignty as responsibility, human security and RtoP, taken together, provide key evidence that there is an increasing awareness and willingness to take the plight of civilians seriously and as central issues in decisions about intervention, protection and assistance. Of course, for the ICRC 'intervention' in any militaristic sense is not an option, but in terms of establishing its presence, through the consent of the government and a Headquarters Agreement, intervention is crucial to its utility as a humanitarian actor. The extent to which the ICRC has developed into roles akin to human security is considered in chapter 5.

## VI. NEUTRALITY AND INDEPENDENCE

In addition to the principle of humanity, neutrality is included in the Statutes of the IRCRCM. This section will consider how neutrality informs and guides the protection and assistance offered by the ICRC. Cassese has argued that:

> [T]he attitude of neutrality adopted in 1804–15 by the USA towards the countries engaged in the Napoleonic wars and, subsequently, the stand of Britain and other European countries in relation to the American Civil War (1861–5) greatly contributed to the development of a set of rules striking a fairly felicitous compromise between conflicting interests.[45]

'Neutrality is defined in international law as the status of a State which is not participating in an armed conflict between other States.'[46] According to Neff:

> [A]longside the law of war—and in some ways in close partnership to it—was the full flowering of the law of neutrality, which, for the first time, emerged in the full light of juridical respectability as a sort of counterpart to the unrestricted right of States to resort to war on purely political grounds.[47]

The ICRC is given the status of a neutral state and, as such, is governed by the elements of neutrality outlined below.[48] In the Geneva Convention

[45] A Cassese, *International Law*, 2nd edn (Oxford, Oxford University Press, 2004) 401–02.

[46] Fleck (n 17) para 1101–55; See also H Haug, *Humanity for All: The International Red Cross and Red Crescent Movement* (Vienna, Henry Dunant Institute/Paul Haupt Publishers, 1993) 461–64.

[47] S Neff, 'A Short History of International Law' in M Evans, *International Law*, 4th edn (Oxford, Oxford University Press, 2014) 18.

[48] See also BA Rieffer-Flanagan, 'Is Neutral Humanitarianism Dead? Red Cross Neutrality: Walking the Tightrope of Neutral Humanitarianism' (2009) 31 *Human Rights Quarterly* 888; D Plattner, 'ICRC Neutrality and Neutrality in Humanitarian Assistance' (1996) 26(311) *IRRC* 161.

1864, neutrality is contained in a number of provisions. Under Article 1 'ambulances and military hospitals shall be recognized as neutral'; Article 2 states that: '[H]ospital and ambulance personnel, including the quartermaster's staff, the medical, administrative and transport services, and the chaplains, shall have the benefit of the same neutrality when on duty, and while there remain any wounded to be brought in or assisted'; and Article 5 states that: '[I]nhabitants of the country who bring help to the wounded shall be respected and shall remain free. Generals of the belligerent Powers shall make it their duty to notify the inhabitants of the appeal made to their humanity, and of the neutrality which humane conduct will confer.' Under Article 14 of The Hague Convention V, humanitarian assistance for the sick or wounded is not considered as being a violation of neutrality even if it benefits only the sick and wounded from one party to the conflict.[49] Cassese further argued that the 'institution of neutrality gradually fell into decline' following the Second World War.[50] Nevertheless, the Geneva Conventions of 1949 and Additional Protocol I of 1977 describe the ICRC as an impartial humanitarian body or organisation, specifically; they state that 'an impartial humanitarian body, such as the International Committee of the Red Cross' may carry out humanitarian activities.[51] The IRCRCM Statutes state that the ICRC is a 'neutral institution' and a 'specifically neutral and independent' institution and intermediary.[52]

The ICRC must not, therefore, participate in hostilities. This includes helping or hindering either party. It must also 'keep out of political, racial, religious or ideological controversy in all circumstances'.[53] 'In other words, neutrality means standing apart from contending parties or ideologies, so that everyone will trust you. It is a means to an end, not an end in itself.'[54] The concept of neutrality is therefore of paramount importance to any developments of the ICRC mandate. Chapters 1 and 2 above showed that the ICRC takes its mandate from Conventions, IRCRCM Statutes and its right to 'humanitarian initiative', which enable it to act in a number of situations and contexts. Chapter 3 showed that the ICRC is no longer restricted to working in contexts where IHL applies, as there is a growing overlap between IHL and IHRL. This humanisation of international law has impacted the international community through the inception and development of human-centric norms including human security and

[49] Hague Convention V.

[50] Cassese (n 45) 403.

[51] See Geneva Conventions I, II, III and IV 1949, Common Art 3; Geneva Convention I, II, III and IV 1949, Arts 9/9/9/10 and Additional Protocol I, Art 5(3).

[52] See IRCRCM Statutes, Art 5 (2)(d) and (3).

[53] M Harroff-Tavel, 'Neutrality and Impartiality—The Importance of these Principles for the International Red Cross and Red Crescent Movement and the Difficulties Involved in Applying Them' (1989) 29(273) *IRRC* 536, 537.

[54] ibid.

RtoP. The key aspect of such developments for the ICRC is that it is inherently limited by the principle of neutrality. Whilst humanity, as a principle, can be developed, stretched and interpreted broadly, as will be argued in chapter 5, the extent to which the ICRC can engage in such developments, and thus apply new concepts of humanity to its mandate, will always be restricted by its principle of neutrality.

Thus the initial concern was whether fighting parties would attack medical personnel helping wounded soldiers. Fundamentally, medical personnel should not be viewed as combatants. Hence the ICRC tried to convince belligerents that humanitarian assistance to injured soldiers in its various forms is not to be thought of as interference or a violation of neutrality.[55] Akin to the principle of neutrality is that of non-discrimination, adverse distinction based on race, nationality, religious belief or political opinion is prohibited in the treatment of prisoners of war,[56] civilians[57] and persons hors de combat.[58] Parties to the conflict shall treat all protected persons with the same consideration, without distinction based on race, religion, sex or political opinion.[59] The key to its functioning is that the ICRC be seen as neutral, to enable it to reach those who need its protection and assistance. Its neutrality also allows it to 'negotiate rights for prisoners and captors alike, creating a human rights culture and ensuring compliance with fundamental rights and freedoms'.[60] In addition, when the ICRC believes that there has been a breach of IHL, it will make representations to the requisite authority in confidence.[61] The ICRC must maintain neutrality to carry out its humanitarian work effectively. 'Only where there is general confidence, confidence of the authorities and the population, can the institutions of the Movement have unimpeded access to conflict and disaster victims and obtain the necessary support for their protection and assistance activities.'[62]

According to Rhona Smith: '[T]he Geneva Conventions are at the forefront of the work of the Red Cross in conflict situations but other rights

[55] J Pictet, *Development and Principles of International Humanitarian Law* (The Hague, Martinus Nijhoff, 1985).

[56] Geneva Convention III, Art 16.

[57] Geneva Convention IV, Art 13; Geneva Conventions I, II, III and IV 1949, Common Art 3.

[58] Geneva Conventions I, II, III and IV 1949, Common Art 3.

[59] Geneva Conventions I, II, III and IV 1949, Common Art 3; Geneva Convention IV, Art 27; Additional Protocol I, Art 75.

[60] R Smith, *Textbook on International Human Rights Law*, 6th edn (Oxford, Oxford University Press, 2013) 160.

[61] D Weissbrodt, 'Humanitarian Law in Armed Conflict: The Role of International Nongovernmental Organizations' (1987) 24(3) *Journal of Peace Research* 297, 300.

[62] H Haug, 'Neutrality as a Fundamental Principle of the Red Cross' (1996) 36(315) *IRRC* 627, 628.

such as food, shelter, and water also characterize their operations.'[63] This proposition that ICRC work is expanding beyond the strict delineation of roles prescribed in the Geneva Conventions I, II, III and IV 1949 forms much of the argument in this book. This concept of neutrality fed into the guiding principles of the movement and, ultimately, the IRCRCM Statutes. Jean Pictet, who stated that the ICRC should 'never take sides in hostilities or engage at any time in controversies of a political, racial, religious or doctrinal nature', has offered the most concise conception of ICRC neutrality.[64] David Forsythe explained that: '[T]he ICRC tries to avoid, or minimize, or balance if possible whatever impact its humanitarian protection may have on the power and status of states and the various factions engaged in power struggles.'[65] How, then, does the ICRC maintain its neutrality?

> The challenge for an organisation such as the ICRC is to carve out a neutral space where it can carry out its activities while limiting its impact as much as possible. Given the global environment, including the War on Terrorism, the ICRC must carefully calculate how its actions will impact others in the international community while maintaining its neutral image.[66]

The extent to which this is possible will be considered alongside analysis of the ICRC's expanding humanitarian protection and assistance mandate.

The increasing complexity of modern armed conflict and armed violence require the ICRC to gain and maintain the trust not only of states but also NSAs. The ICRC therefore relies on its reputation for neutrality and independence to facilitate dialogue and a relationship between all parties. Indeed 'principled humanitarian action is the foundation of the ICRCs success in reaching people and gaining acceptance by State and non-State parties to conflict'. It is this acceptance that gives the ICRC access and the ability to help.[67] In addition to the fulfilment of the fundamental principles, consent is also essential to the protection and assistance work of the ICRC. In 2012 Henckaerts reported that: '[T]oday there is much discussion about the requirement to obtain consent from the parties to the conflict in order to access conflict zones and, in particular, about the prohibition on withholding such consent on arbitrary grounds.'[68] 'If the survival of the

[63] Smith (n 60) 160.

[64] C Moorehead, *Dunant's Dream: War, Switzerland and the History of the Red Cross* (New York, Carol & Graf, 1999) 561.

[65] See DP Forsythe, *The Humanitarians: The International Committee of the Red Cross* (Cambridge, Cambridge University Press, 2005) 173–74.

[66] Rieffer-Flanagan (n 48) 890.

[67] Ban Ki-Moon, 'The ICRC and the Changing Humanitarian Landscape' (2012) 94 *IRRC* 1251, 1252.

[68] J-M Henckaerts, 'Reports and Documents-Bringing the Commentaries on the Geneva Conventions and their Additional Protocols into the Twenty-first Century' (Winter 2012) 94 *IRRC* 1551, 1553.

population is threatened and a humanitarian organisation fulfilling the required conditions of impartiality and non-discrimination is able to remedy this situation, relief actions must take place.'[69] State practice and the 'ICRC Study on Customary IHL' show that if action can be shown to be humanitarian and impartial, then governments cannot arbitrarily refuse assistance.[70] This is particularly the case in extreme situations, where a lack of supplies would result in starvation.[71] Article 18 AP II refers to the consent of the High Contracting Party for the delivery of supplies.

The fundamental principles of the IRCRCM should ensure the acceptance by states of the ICRC providing humanitarian assistance and, in doing so, the safe working environment of ICRC delegates. However, it is important to note that, on the ground, the activities of the ICRC are continually disturbed, hindered and halted by targeted attacks against humanitarian personnel, by complicated and lengthy visa regimes, and by humanitarian workers needing permits for travel to certain areas.[72] If neutrality cannot be upheld, then the 'warring parties—local warlords, bandits and thieves, religious fanatics, thugs and terrorists—are willing to kidnap, bomb and kill humanitarian aid workers, thereby escalating the dangers of relief work in the field'.[73] These incidents are evidence of the need for the ICRC to maintain its reputation for neutrality and impartiality, and to ensure that states consent to its presence.

## VII. CONCLUSION

One purpose of the ICRC is to uphold humanity, but what does this mean? Is it that the ICRC must react to inhumanity, prevent inhumanity or create the circumstances for a positive realisation of humanity? If it is the latter, then what does humanity look like? According to Drucilla Cornell: '[H]umanity must always retain its ideality; it can never be figured once

[69] C Pilloud, Y Sandoz, C Swinarski and B Zimmerman, *Commentary on the Additional Protocols of 8 June 1977 to the Geneva Conventions of 12 August 1949* (The Hague, Martinus Nijhoff, 1987) 1479.

[70] ICRC, 'Rule 55: Access to Humanitarian Relief for Civilians in Need', https://www.icrc.org/customary-ihl/eng/docs/v1_rul_rule55.

[71] Additional Protocol I, Art 54; see also Bond J, 'International Conflict and Article 3 of the Geneva Conventions' (1971) 48 *Denver Law Journal* 266; HP Gasser, 'International Non-International Armed Conflict: Case Studies of Afghanistan, Kampuchea, and Lebanon' (1982) 31 *American University Law Review* 911; R Barber, 'Facilitating Humanitarian Assistance in International Humanitarian and Human Rights Law' (2009) 91 *IRRC* 371, 372.

[72] Humanitarian Practice Network, 'Operational Security Management in Violent Environments' (London, Overseas Development Institute, 2010) 39–40.

[73] See K Anderson, 'Humanitarian Inviolability in Crisis: The Meaning of Impartiality and Neutrality for UN and NGO Agencies Following the 2003–2004 Afghanistan and Iraq Conflicts' (2004) 17 *Harvard Human Rights Journal* 41, 42.

and for all. We are responsible for an ideal that can never be realized and yet is always being configured and contested.'[74] For this author, humanity is about something beyond IHL or human rights law. The humanity and inhumanity of humans extends beyond the direct recipients of aid or the victims of inhumanity and, as such, responses to inhumanity must go beyond the judicial. Theoretical and legal concepts of humanity are of little practical use in protecting and assisting those on the ground. To this end, the ICRC is the 'champion' of humanity, making real life changes on the ground to protect or bring humanity to those suffering the effects of armed conflict and other situations of violence.

Today, it is insufficient to consider humanity simply as an IHL term, as a reference point for the banning of certain weapons or the maintenance of neutrality. Humanity must be understood in a more purposive sense and, to this end, the extent to which the principle of humanity feeds into broader humanity, or human-centric, ideas is considered in chapter 5. For this author, and others, humanity is the common denominator of IHL and IHRL.[75] The extent to which it permeates emerging concepts on the international stage, including sovereignty as responsibility, human security and RtoP, is considered below.

Through its dissemination of IHL, the ICRC ensures that states and NSAs think about the interests of individual human beings. The provisions of the Geneva Conventions I, II, III and IV 1949 enable The ICRC to bring humanitarian aid to victims of war, exchange messages between prisoners of war and their families, trace the fate of disappeared people, and care for the wounded and sick. The ICRC has developed its activities from its traditional focus on the mere survival of victims of war, to a more comprehensive assistance and protection role, which not only seeks to protect victims of armed conflict, but also to provide for their basic needs. The application of humanity and neutrality to the ICRC is considered throughout the next two chapters which investigate whether the ICRC is able to work outside or beyond of its mandate. As stated at the beginning of this chapter, this chapter is a preface to an analysis that draws on broader notions of humanity and the actual practice of the ICRC, the latter being defended through the use of qualitative interviews with ICRC delegates.

[74] D Cornell, 'Facing Our Humanity' (2003) 18(1) *Hypatia* 170, 172.
[75] Teitel (n 44).

# 5

# *New Humanitarian Horizons for the ICRC*

## I. INTRODUCTION

AT THE BEGINNING of this book it was theorised that humanitarian protection and assistance are currently inextricably linked with the concept of human security. For this author there is a noticeable shift in the international legal order, a 'humanisation' of existing public international law. This shift places human beings as the beneficiaries of law. For Peters, this makes 'humanity' a '*Grundnorm*' of an otherwise still state-based system.[1] Oberleitner makes a connection between the concept of humanity and human security, which is a key component of this book.[2] Oberleitner's text is not focused specifically on the ICRC but his conjecture that humanity and human security are inextricably linked, as they each focus on making human beings the reference point for decisions, is echoed throughout this book.[3] This chapter builds on the analysis provided in chapter 3, which presented the humanisation of international law.

The book shows that 'humanity' features in a number of concepts that emerged in the latter part of the twentieth century and considers whether the ICRC is guided by such developments, that is, whether its interpretation of its mandate appears to reflect a broader concept of humanity, namely outside of armed conflicts. Or perhaps, but this may be stretching the investigation too far, whether the ICRC has actually driven 'humanisation' developments on the international stage. The definition of humanity in the IRCRCM Statutes is no longer reflective of the full corpus of human needs on the ground given the type of conflicts we see today and, as such, it provides a reference point to explore whether ICRC work is reflective of a wider concept of humanity.

Teitel has stated that: '[H]umanity law redefined security in a manner that transcends the traditional distinction between war and peace,

[1] A Peters, 'Humanity as the Alpha and Omega of Sovereignty' (2009) 20(3) *European Journal of International Law* 513.
[2] G Oberleitner, *Human Rights in Armed Conflict: Law, Practice, Policy* (Cambridge, Cambridge University Press, 2015) ch 16.
[3] ibid, 235.

conceptualizing conflict along a continuum of situations that require ongoing protection of those who are affected or threatened.'[4] The existence of 'inhumanity' is an issue for individual people, for example prisoners of war deprived of food or civilians trapped in a city without access to healthcare. Inhumanity could also refer to a lack of safe drinking water, caused by natural disaster or armed conflict, which the government refuses to remedy, for whatever reason. It could refer to sexual violence as a weapon of war, which is a recognised crime against humanity.[5] Whatever inhumanity might be, the methods and means to establish 'humanity' are not cut-and-dry. This chapter examines the extent to which the humanisation of international law and new concepts of humanity inform, guide or are inspired by the work of the ICRC.

Since the end of the Cold War, new concepts have emerged on the international stage, which, at their heart, recognise and seek to remedy 'inhumanity' in its various guises. This chapter takes sovereignty as responsibility and human security as key concepts that encompass the idea that humans ought to be front-and-centre when considering the behaviour of states, security and appropriate responses to armed conflict. The foundations of these concepts are reflective of humanitarian fears that permeate national, organisational and individual consciences, particularly armed conflicts that facilitate violations of the four core crimes—war crimes, crimes against humanity, genocide and ethnic cleansing.

This chapter introduces the sovereignty as responsibility concept and describes how it links to the overall concept of human security. This includes outlining the expansion of 'threats' to security, from the traditional idea that the use of force against a sovereign states was the highest threat to security, to a concept of threats that includes threats to the day-to-day lives of individuals and communities. The Human Development Report (HDR) 1994 definition of human security has continued to be discussed at international forums and a 'Common Understanding' of human security was agreed upon in the General Assembly in 2012.[6]

As armed conflict has changed, so too has the practice of the ICRC. The international community has also redirected its concerns to look closely at what is happening within the sovereign borders of states, especially in places often only open to citizens and the Red Cross, the latter by virtue of its reputation as an organisation that will keep quiet about what it sees. As the ICRC develops the roles it undertakes, and responds to increasingly complex and protracted situations, is it threatening to void the relationship

[4] RG Teitel, *Humanity's Law* (Oxford, Oxford University Press, 2011) 109.

[5] Rome Statute, Art 7(g).

[6] Report of the Secretary General, 'Follow-up to General Assembly Resolution 66/290 on Human Security' (23 December 2012) UN Doc A/68/685 para 4 (Common Understanding).

with states that both parties rely on? Is human security, although an important and worthy cause, a step too far for the agenda of the ICRC?

## II. SOVEREIGNTY AS RESPONSIBILITY

A consequence of the traditional state-centric paradigm of international law was that discourse on security focused on military defence of state sovereignty and territorial integrity. Despite the establishment of a number of intergovernmental organisations after the Second World War, international law remained a 'system of legal norms, procedures and institutions of the States, for the States and by the States'.[7] Indeed state sovereignty is the principle that defines the modern state system.[8] There are a myriad of concepts of state sovereignty, but it is the European model, described in the Treaty of Westphalia 1648, which remains the dominant concept today.[9] Indeed, the Westphalian idea of sovereignty has rarely been challenged in principle.[10] In fact, since 1648 the international stage has been a place for sovereign states to come together as persons or subjects of international law.[11] However, there have been developments in what it means to be a sovereign state since 1648. While Westphalian sovereignty was traditionally dynastic, nowadays, popular rule is important in

[7] M Noortman, 'Human Securities, International Laws and Non-State Actors: Bringing Complexity Back In' in C Ryngaert and M Noortman, *Human Security and International Law: The Challenge of Non-State Actors* (Cambridge, Intersentia, 2014) 16.

[8] C Weber, *Simulating Sovereignty: Intervention, the State and Symbolic Exchange* (Cambridge, Cambridge University Press, 1995) 4, 9; R Thakur, *The United Nations, Peace and Security: From Collective Security to the Responsibility to Protect* (Cambridge, Cambridge University Press, 2006) 276; See J-M Coicaud, 'Deconstructing International Legitimacy' in H Charlesworth and J-M Coicaud (eds), *Fault Lines of International Legitimacy* (Cambridge, Cambridge University Press, 2010) 38; H Melber, 'In the Footsteps of Hammerskjöld: The United Nations and Interventions for Security and Development' (2012) repository.up.ac.za/bitstream/handle/2263/20767/Melber_Footsteps(2012).pdf?sequence=1.

[9] See Montevideo Convention on the Rights and Duties of States, 26 December 1933 (1934) 165 LNTS 19; See also TJ Biersteker and C Weber, *Sovereignty as a Social Construct* (Cambridge, Cambridge University Press, 1996).

[10] SD Krasner, 'Sharing Sovereignty: New Institutions for Collapsed and Failing States' (2004) 29(2) *International Security* 85, 85.

[11] A Nussbaum, *A Concise History of the Law of Nations* (rev edn, New York, MacMillan, 1954) 115; P Reuter, *International Institutions* (London, George Allen and Unwin, 1958) 42–43 (trans JM Chapman from the French *Institutions Internationales* (Paris, Presses Universitaires de France, 1955); C de Visscher, *Theory and Reality in Public International Law* (Princeton, Princeton University Press, 1968) 3–18; P Taylor, *International Cooperation Today: The European and Universal Pattern* (London, Elek, 1971) 28; D Kennedy, 'International Law and the Nineteenth Century: History of an Illusion', (1996) 65 *Nordic Journal of International Law* 385, 406–08; C Brölmann, *The Institutional Veil in Public International Law: International Organisations and the Law of Treaties* (Oxford, Hart Publishing, 2007) 37–38; R Collins, 'Modern-Positivism and the Problem of Institutional Autonomy in International Law' in R Collins and ND White, *International Organisations and the Idea of Autonomy: Institutional Independence in the International Legal Order* (London, Routledge, 2011) 22.

the recognition of a collective entity as a legitimate member of the international community.[12] In fact, the requirements to be a 'legitimate' member of international society have continued to change over time. Years ago, for example, Christianity was required to be seen as a legitimate state. Nowadays it is democracy, liberal economic structures and capitalism.[13] Slaughter argues that: '[M]embership of the UN is no longer validation of sovereign status and a shield against unwanted meddling in the internal affairs of the State. … Membership recognises States as international actors that must work in concert and take action against threats to human security.'[14] During the twentieth-century totalitarian states committed themselves to secular ideology or religious radicalism, whilst liberal states saw sovereign power limited by social contracts and constitutions, and finally the spread of democracy meant that more states became increasingly accountable to their citizens.[15]

In the Westphalian sovereignty paradigm, states have an external and internal identity.[16] External sovereignty concerns the relationship between states, as legal persons, whereas internal sovereignty concerns the state and its relationship with NSAs within its territory.[17] Non-intervention in the domestic affairs of other states is a structural and substantive component of external sovereignty.[18] The principle of non-intervention was codified and enshrined in Article 2(7) of the UN Charter. This article, and Article 2(4), which prohibits the use of force, reflect concerns within the international community following the Second World War that the aims of military intervention by states could include overthrowing governments, changing borders or disrupting the economic, political and social infrastructure of a state.[19] Internal sovereignty concerns the 'dignity, justice,

[12] See P Allott, *Eunomia: New Order for a New World* (Oxford, Oxford University Press, 1990) 306–09 which offers, according to Charlesworth and Coicaud (n 8), a critical interpretation of the phenomenon of popular rule.

[13] Charlesworth and Coicaud (n 8) 40.

[14] A-M Slaughter, 'Security, Solidarity, and Sovereignty: The Grand Themes of UN Reform' (2005) 99(3) *American Journal of International Law* 619, 620.

[15] T Jacobsen, C Sampford and R Thakur (eds), *Re-envisioning Sovereignty: The End of Westphalia?* (Aldershot, Ashgate, 2008) 2.

[16] CB Badescu, *Humanitarian Intervention and the Responsibility to Protect: Security and Human Rights* (New York, Routledge, 2011) 38–39.

[17] A Peters, 'Humanity as the A and Ω of Sovereignty' (2009) 20(3) *European Journal of International Law* 513, 514, 515–16.

[18] DP Fidler, 'Revolt Against or from Within the West? TWAIL, the Developing World, and the Future Direction of International Law' (2003) 2 *Chinese Journal of International Law* 29, 34–36; See also C Harding and CL Lim, *Renegotiating Westphalia: Essays and Commentary on the European and Conceptual Foundations of Modern International Law* (The Hague, Martinus Nijhoff, 1999) 5–6; DP Fidler, 'The Return of the Standard of Civilisation' (2001) 2 *Chicago Journal of International Law* 140.

[19] UNGA, 'Declaration on the Inadmissibility of Intervention and Interference in the Internal Affairs of States' (9 December 1981) A/RES/36/103, 79.

worth and safety' of citizens.[20] The UN Secretary-General argued that these values should be at the heart of any collective security system for the twenty-first century, but too often states have failed to respect and promote them.[21] Moreover the sovereign state must work with international organisations, NGOs and non-military government agencies towards development.[22] This chapter considers to what extent the traditional Westphalian/external concept of sovereignty has been usurped by ideas of responsibility for the people within states, that is, human-centric security.

During the twentieth century sovereignty came to symbolise and encompass not merely a state-centric international legal order: the focus was increasingly on happenings inside the borders of other states. In 1996, Deng argued that: '[E]ffective sovereignty implies a system of law and order that is responsive to the needs of the national population for justice and general welfare.'[23] A decade later, Chimni stated that, although the 'State is the principal subject of international law, the relationship between State and international law continually evolves, as each era sees the material and ideological reconstitution of the relationship between State sovereignty and international law'.[24] Falk argued that states must protect the welfare of their own people and fulfil their obligations to the wider international community.[25]

It was Kofi Annan, as UN Secretary-General, who arguably had the biggest impact on the sovereignty as responsibility paradigm. In 1999, Kofi Annan published a 'landmark' article entitled 'Two Concepts of Sovereignty' in *The Economist*, where he articulated that state sovereignty was being 'redefined', as 'States are now widely understood to be instruments at the service of their people's, and not vice versa'.[26] Annan argued that we should recognise that the aim of the UN Charter is to 'protect individual human beings, not to protect those who abuse them'.[27] This is a position repeated by Annan in subsequent UN reports, including 'We the Peoples: The Role of the United Nations in the Twenty-first Century' in 2000

[20] Report of the Secretary General's High-Level Panel on Threats, Challenges and Change, 'A More Secure World: Our Shared Responsibility' (2 December 2004) UN Doc A/59/565, 22 (High-level Panel).

[21] ibid, para 30.

[22] M De Larrinaga and MC Doucet, 'Sovereign Power and the Bio Politics of Human Security' (2008) 39(5) *Security Dialogue* 517, 525.

[23] FM Deng, S Kimaro, T Lyons, D Rothchild and W Zartman (eds), *Sovereignty as Responsibility: Conflict Management in Africa* (Washington DC, Brookings Institution, 1996) 18.

[24] BS Chimni, 'Third World Approaches to International Law: A Manifesto' (2006) 8 *International Community Law Review* 3, 7.

[25] R Falk, 'Revisiting Westphalia, Discovering Post-Westphalia' (2002) 6(4) *Journal of Ethics* 311, 327.

[26] K Annan, 'Two Concepts of Sovereignty', *The Economist*, 18 September 1999, www.economist.com/node/324795; see also Bellamy AJ, *Global Politics and the Responsibility to Protect: From Words to Deeds* (London, Routledge, 2011) 10.

[27] Annan (n 26).

and the Report of the Secretary-General's High-Level Panel on Threats, Challenges and Change, 'A More Secure World: Our Shared Responsibility 2004'.[28] Annan reminded the international community that being a sovereign state is as much about responsibilities to the population within the territorial borders as it is about inter-state relations. When states sign the UN Charter, they 'not only benefit from the privileges of sovereignty but also accept its responsibilities'.[29] The High-level Panel Report 2004 was written by a panel of experts who had examined the major threats and challenges the world was facing in the broad field of peace and security. The threats identified included economic and social issues insofar as they relate to peace and security. The panel made recommendations for the elements of a collective response. The report appealed for a 'new security consensus' and concluded that threats to security 'go far beyond States waging aggressive war', as threats are to people and not just states, including 'conflict between and within States'.[30] According to Slaughter, the panel considered the 'reconception of security, solidarity and even sovereignty'.[31]

The 4th Vienna Workshop on International Constitutional Law in 2008 stated that 'sovereignty, or security, or for that matter, a state's existence, can only be a means to an end—the end being the protection of the people, but never an end in and of itself'.[32] This juxtaposition on the international stage between the traditional Westphalian sovereignty paradigm and the sovereignty as responsibility concept raises an important issue: if individuals are to be the referent object or normative unit of security, where is human security situated within the traditional state-centric security paradigm?[33]

In terms of the ICRC, sovereignty as responsibility reiterates a principle that has guided its actions on the ground since its inception in 1864,

[28] Report of the Secretary General, 'We the Peoples: The Role of the United Nations in the Twenty-first Century' (New York, UN, 2000) (We the Peoples) 68; High-level Panel (n 20) para 201.

[29] High-level Panel (n 20), para 21.

[30] ibid, part 1.

[31] Slaughter (n 14) 619.

[32] 4th Vienna Workshop 2008. The Workshop title was 'Constitutional Limits to Security' and was the 4th Workshop on International Constitutional Law, 16–17 May 2008, Vienna University, Faculty of Law; the workshop objective was to 'develop criteria how to limit and/or balance security within the constitutional design' and was open to students, lawyers and practitioners. See 'ICL Workshop' (16–17 May 2008) www.internationalconstitutionallaw.net/fourth_workshop; H Eberhard, K Lachmayer, G Ribarov and G Thallinger (eds), *Constitutional Limits to Security: Proceedings of the 4th Vienna Workshop on International Constitutional Law* (Bergasse, Facultas Verlags, 2009) 132, 140.

[33] We the Peoples (n 28) 7, in which human security is identified as 'complimentary' to state security; R Banakar (ed), *Rights in Context: Law and Justice in Late Modern Society* (Farnham, Ashgate, 2010) 260.

that is, humanity. For the ICRC, the state has always had responsibilities to civilians. Perhaps sovereignty as responsibility is a reconceptualisation of the Westphalian paradigm, but ultimately the international legal order will remain state-centric. Nevertheless, it is evidence of progress in understanding the detrimental impact that a 'closed' sovereign state can have for the people living within it.

The fact that responsibility for the lives of 'civilians' and the local population lies with the state during peace and times of armed conflict shows the importance of 'humanity' to the international legal order and international law more broadly. The recognition of the responsibilities of the state to its citizens suggests that the ICRC approach, its principles of neutrality, impartiality and humanity, in particular, are inherent to the wider international legal order.

## III. HUMAN SECURITY

The theory of human security broadly understood encompasses the protection of the individual from threats that may be external or internal, emanating from the state or its absence (ie a so-called failed state), man-made or caused by nature. The spirit of human security is a normative plea for people, rather than states, to be placed at the centre of decisions on security. The European definition of security, based on the Westphalian model, focused exclusively on a state's ability to counter external threats to its vital interests and core values.[34] Human security challenges this state-centric paradigm of security as it posits that decisions to intervene in a state could be human-centric.[35]

The ICRC has extended the activities provided for it in the Geneva Conventions I, II, III 1949 and the ICRC Statutes. Under Article 81(1) of Additional Protocol I, the ICRC may also 'carry out *any other humanitarian activities* in favour of these victims, subject to the consent of the Parties to the conflict concerned'. In terms of 'humanitarian initiative' the ICRC may be responding to the 'needs' of the people on the ground but it is walking a fine line in terms of its neutrality. At this moment in time, the ICRC appears to perform a grand balancing act between the two, but it is this aspect of its mandate that is most likely to see consent revoked by states. This chapter, taken with the empirical research and case study, shows that the ICRC has developed its practice far beyond that originally

[34] P Upadhyaya, 'Human Security, Humanitarian Intervention, and Third World Concerns' (2004–05) 33 *Denver Journal of International Law and Policy* 71, 72.

[35] A Collins (ed), *Contemporary Security Studies* (Oxford, Oxford University Press, 2007) 91–109.

envisaged in the Geneva Conventions in 1949. The extent to which this is to be wholly praised is examined in chapter 6 and the case study.

## A. The Process of Defining Human Security

The potential for a human security agenda was always present in the UN Charter, but it was not until the HDR 1994 that the UN embraced it. The UN Charter was created in a world where the greatest threat imagined to a state was external aggression by one state against another, but in recent decades far more people have been killed by NIACs, ethnic cleansing and acts of genocide than by inter-state armed conflicts.[36] Not only must humans become the referent objects of security, but while threats were once considered from an external sovereignty perspective, it is increasingly recognised that for people living in certain territories, the gravest threats may actually be from the state itself. During the Cold War, the Security Council defined threats to international peace and security as 'disputes between States that might or had become militarised, conflicts involving the great powers, and general menaces to global stability'.[37] It was not until the Cold War ended that the UN recognised that internal armed conflicts were putting entire populations at risk, creating mass flight and destabilising entire regions.[38]

In the meantime, the Brandt Commission 1981[39] and 1983,[40] the 1982 Palme Commission's report 'Common Security'[41] and the Stockholm Initiative on Global Security and Governance 1991[42] sought to broaden the definition of security threats to include HIV/AIDS, terrorism, environmental degradation and to deepen security considerations to include the security of individuals and groups. The Brandt Commission stated

[36] We the Peoples (n 28) 11.

[37] ND White, *Keeping the Peace* (Manchester, Manchester University Press, 1993) 34–38.

[38] M Barnett and TG Weiss, *Humanitarianism Contested: Where Angels Fear to Tread* (London, Routledge, 2011) 74.

[39] Institute of Development Studies Bulletin, 'The Brandt Commission Report 1981' (April 1981, Her Majesty's Stationery Office). This memorandum was prepared by the Foreign and Commonwealth Office for the Overseas Development Sub-Committee of the Foreign Affairs Committee.

[40] The Brandt Commission 1983, 'Common Crisis—North–South: Co-operation for World Recovery (1st draft from scanned book, 14 March 2002) files.globalmarshallplan.org/inhalt/coc_2.pdf.

[41] Swedish Prime Minister Olaf Palme, 'Report of the Independent Commission on Disarmament and Security Issues-Common Security: A Blueprint for Survival' (1982). This is known as the Palme Commission; J Galtung, 'The Palme Commission Report on Disarmament and Security: A Critical Comment' (1983) 14(2) *Bulletin of Peace Proposals* 147, 147–51.

[42] 'Common Responsibility in the 1990s: The Stockholm Initiative on Global Security and Governance' (22 April 1991, Prime Minister's Office, London).

that 'world hunger, mass misery and alarming disparities between living conditions of rich and poor' were threats to human security.[43] The Palme Commission declared that security must rest on a commitment to joint survival rather than a threat of mutual destruction.[44] It argued that the real security concerns of the world were whether the political, social and economic needs of all people were being met. Finally, the Stockholm Initiative stated that threats from 'failures in development, environmental degradation, excessive population growth and movement, and a lack of progress towards democracy' should be taken into account.[45]

In 1992, the Security Council Summit Statement declared that the 'non-military sources of instability in the economic, social, humanitarian and ecological fields have become threats to peace and security'.[46] The Security Council began to define a threat based on the 'the magnitude of human tragedy',[47] deteriorating civil war situations,[48] genocide[49] and humanitarian crises.[50] As Slaughter later argued:

> We need not be guaranteed prosperity but at least the health and education necessary to strive for it. We cannot be guaranteed long lives, but at least that our government will not try to murder us and will do its upmost to prevent our fellow citizens from doing so.[51]

The Security Council also recognised that the 'trans boundary affects' of human rights violations, such as the plight of refugees, allowed it to sidestep the legal commitment to non-intervention.[52] The Security Council continues to recognise that violations and abuses of human rights and IHL amount to a threat to the peace, for example in Syria.[53] The Security Council has also determined that complex humanitarian emergencies, which are a 'conflict related humanitarian disaster involving a high degree of breakdown and social dislocation and, reflecting this condition, a system wide aid response from the international community', amount to a threat to international peace and security.[54]

[43] Brandt Commission in Banakar (n 33) 254.
[44] ibid.
[45] Stockholm Initiative in Banakar (n 33) 254.
[46] Security Council, 'Summit Statement Concerning the Councils Responsibility in the Maintenance of International Peace and Security' (31 January 1992) S/23500.
[47] UNSC Res 794 (3 December 1992) Somalia, preamble.
[48] UNSC Res 788 (19 November 1992) Liberia.
[49] UNSC Res 955 (8 November 1994) Rwanda.
[50] UNSC Res 841 (16 June 1993) Haiti.
[51] Slaughter (n 14) 619.
[52] Note by the President of the Security Council (26 February 1993) S/25344; M Odello and S Cavandoli (eds), *Emerging Areas of Human Rights in the Twenty-first Century: The Role of the Universal Declaration on Human Rights* (London, Routledge, 2011) 28.
[53] UNSC Res 2139 (22 February 2014) Syria: Humanitarian Assistance.
[54] Barnett and Weiss (n 38) 76.

The HDR 1994 provided the first outline of what elements should be included under the umbrella of human security. Security can also refer to economic, food, health, environmental, personal, community and political security.[55] The HDR 1994 stated that security is 'a child who didn't die, a disease that did not spread, a job that wasn't cut, an ethnic tension that did not explode into violence, a dissident who was not silenced'.[56] Bilková argues that the HDR was evidence of a 'broader normative shift leading to the strengthening of the position of individual human beings at the international scene'.[57] The nature of threats to security outlined in the HDR 1994 definition recognises matters that the ICRC is already dealing with, under its mandates in the Geneva Conventions I, II, III and IV 1949 and the ICRC Statutes, in particular the importance of reconnecting families, delivering humanitarian aid, providing healthcare, and so on, are pertinent to definitions of human security and to the work of the ICRC. The importance, for this author, of the ICRC's potential contribution to human security for people's day-to-day lives is in its quiet determination to provide protection and assistance to people. Its principles, particularly confidentiality, neutrality and impartiality, means it finds favour within states and with the people on the ground.

Over a decade after the publication of the HDR 1994, in 2005 a World Summit was held from 14 to 16 September at the UN Headquarters in New York. It considered development, security, human rights and reform of the UN. In March 2005, Secretary-General Kofi Annan had set out proposals in this regard in his report, 'In Larger Freedom'.[58] The World Summit provided an opportunity to truly define and begin to implement human security. The 'Outcome Document 2005' was adopted following negotiations between states and organisations over the course of four days in September 2005.[59] It sought to enhance the system of collective security, following 'We the Peoples', by reviewing its progress and by making recommendations in areas of development, peace and security, human rights and institutional reform. The states at the World Summit welcomed 'In Larger Freedom' and it appeared at first that consensus would be reached

[55] UNDP, 'Human Development Report 1994' (UNDP, Oxford, Oxford University Press, 1994) (HDR 1994); See also FO Hampson, with J Daudelin, J Hay, H Reid and T Martin, *Madness in the Multitude: Human Security and World Disorder* (Oxford, Oxford University Press, 2001); D Hubert and RG McRae (eds), *Human Security and the New Diplomacy: Protecting People, Promoting Peace* (Canada, McGill University Press, 2001).

[56] HDR 1994 (n 55) 22; Eberhard (n 32) 112.

[57] Bilková in Ryngaert and Noortman (n 7) 30–31; See also A Amouyel, 'What Is Human Security?' (2006) 1 *Human Security Journal* 10, 10–23.

[58] Report of the Secretary-General, 'In Larger Freedom: Towards Development, Security and Human Rights for All' (21 March 2005) UN Doc A/59/2005 (In Larger Freedom) part V.

[59] UNGA, '2005 World Summit Outcome' (15 September 2005) A/60/L.1 (Outcome Document).

on the definition and implementation of human security.[60] However, by its conclusion, meagre progress had been made. States had merely agreed to continue to work towards a new security consensus.[61] In part, the World Summit highlighted many of the inequalities between states and between states and their citizens.

The broad security rhetoric and optimism of the HDR 1994, 'We the Peoples', the High-level Panel Report 2004 and 'In Larger Freedom' struggled to survive in the face of staunch criticism from many states when it actually came to adopting the ideas in some concrete form. Many states felt backed into a corner by states with political power and better financial resources.[62] The 'Outcome Document 2005' defined human security as 'the right of people to live in freedom and dignity, free from poverty and despair. We recognise that all individuals, in particular vulnerable people, are entitled to freedom from fear and freedom from want, with an equal opportunity to enjoy all their rights and fully develop their human potential.'[63] The 'Outcome Document 2005' was therefore criticised for failing to address the broad issues initially anticipated. It was also criticised for failing to provide specific, implementable action to achieve the Millennium Development Goals, disarmament, facilitating state struggles against terrorism and for failing to outline how all of the promises could be lived up to logistically and financially. Cuba stated, for example, that the failure clearly to address issues of the environment, trade and disarmament, amongst other issues, was an 'unforgiveable regression' and one which the United States and its closest allies had created.[64] Cuba also criticised the 700 amendments to the 'Outcome Document 2005' that 'diluted, distorted and jeopardised the unity which is essential to save the millions

[60] UNGA, 'Preparation for and Organization of the High-level Plenary Meeting of the General Assembly' (25 April 2005) Res 59/291, para 2.

[61] Outcome Document (n 59) para 143 states: 'We stress the right of people to live in freedom and dignity, free from poverty and despair. We recognise that all individuals, in particular vulnerable people, are entitled to freedom from fear and freedom from want, with an equal opportunity to enjoy all their rights and fully develop their human potential. To this end, we commit ourselves to discussing and defining the notion of human security in the General Assembly.'

[62] 'Revised Draft Outcome Document of the High-level Plenary Meeting of the General Assembly of September 2005 Submitted by the President of the General Assembly paragraph 120' (10 August 2005) UN Doc A/59/HLPM/CRP.1/Rev.2; 'Draft Resolution: 2005 World Summit Outcome' (*Cuba Video*, 16 September 2005) www.un.org/webcast/summit2005/statements.html; 'Draft Resolution: 2005 World Summit Outcome' (Venezuela video, 16 September 2005).

[63] HDR 1994 (n 5); See also UNGA, '2005 World Summit Outcome' (15 September 2005) A/60/L.1 (Outcome Document) para 143; Report of the Secretary General, 'Follow-up to General Assembly Resolution 66/290 on Human Security' (23 December 2012) UN Doc A/68/685 para 4.

[64] Cuba video (n 62).

and millions of lives that suffer from hunger, ill health'.[65] Nevertheless, during the World Summit, the General Assembly committed itself to discussing and defining the notion of human security and on 22 May 2008 it held a day-long thematic debate on the concept.[66] This ensured that human security remained on the policy agenda and entered the 'common international discourse'.[67] Moreover the 4th Vienna Workshop 2008 stated that: 'States can endanger both the international security and the security of their citizens.'[68]

The General Assembly 'Human Security Report 2010' takes account of the global financial and economic crisis; food prices and food insecurity; infectious diseases and other health threats; climate change; and the prevention of violent conflicts.[69] Roberts has argued that these are mass threats that kill or maim millions every year, but are quite preventable.[70] It is recognised that the threats included in broad human security discourse can potentially embrace any threat to human safety and therefore scholars find it difficult to prioritise different types of threats.[71] Within broad human security rhetoric, for example, Owen argued that: '[A]ny conceptualization of human security must have a response to genocide, the necessary consequence of which is a rethinking of sovereignty.'[72] Scholarly debates on human security in 2011 suggested that the theoretical and conceptual discussions on human security needed to end. It was questioned whether the idea of human security has any 'constructive impact on the behaviour or policies of States'?[73] The focus should be on how to increase the 'institutionalisation and operationalisation of the concept'.[74] However, the 'final' say on the definition of human security was in 2012.

The UN General Assembly has adopted a 'Common Understanding' of human security.[75] It echoes the 'freedom from' sentiments of earlier

[65] ibid.

[66] Outcome Document (n 59) para 143; HRH Prince El Hassan Bin Talal (General Assembly) 'Thematic Debate on Human Security' (22 May 2008).

[67] K Krause, 'Is Human Security More Than Just a Good Idea?' in M Rzoska and PJ Croll (eds), *Promoting Security: But How and For Whom?* (Bonn, Bonn International Center for Conversion, 2004) 43.

[68] Eberhard (n 32) 117.

[69] Report of the Secretary General, 'Human Security (8 March 2010) UN Doc A/64/70 (General Assembly Human Security Report 2010).

[70] D Roberts, *Global Governance and Bio Politics: Regulating Human Security* (London, Zed Books, 2010) 16.

[71] E Newman, 'Critical Human Security Studies' (2010) 36 *Review of International Studies* 77, 82.

[72] T Owen, 'Human Security—Conflict, Critique and Consensus: Colloquium Remarks and a Proposal for a Threshold-Based Definition' (2004) 35(3) *Security Dialogue* 373, 378.

[73] I Mgbeoji, 'The Civilised Self and the Barbaric Other: Imperial Delusions of Order and the Challenges of Human Security' (2006) 27(5) *Third World Quarterly* 855, 860.

[74] W Benedek, MC Ketteman and M Möstl (eds), *Mainstreaming Human Security in Peace Operations and Crisis Management: Policies, Problems, Potential* (London, Routledge, 2011) preface.

[75] Common Understanding (n 6): This report builds on General Assembly Human Security Report 2010 (n 69); Report of the Secretary General, 'Follow up to General Assembly

drafts.[76] It also 'calls for people-centred, comprehensive, context-specific and prevention-oriented responses that strengthen the protection and empowerment of all people and all communities' which supports this author's repeated contention that security must be human-centric. The 'Common Understanding Resolution' states that: '[H]uman security recognises the interlinkages between peace, development and human rights, and equally considers civil, political, economic, social and cultural rights.'[77] This reflects the sovereignty as responsibility concept and signifies the inherent human-centric normative underpinnings of the international community. It is not, however, a binding law. Critically, 'human security does not replace State security'.[78] The 'Common Understanding Resolution' shows acceptance by the international community of human security.[79]

The participation, commitment and determination of community members and civil society are considered a fundamental component of the progression of human security: '[V]ulnerability is both broad in nature and structurally dependent, and ... if we are to mitigate human insecurity, we must address not only the threats, but also society's ability to counter them.'[80] The role of civil society is more important today than ever before in advancing the goals of human security. Partnerships amongst civil society, the UN and the wider international community are a central component in promoting comprehensive policies and lasting solutions that can strengthen the triangle of development, freedom and peace.[81] The importance of local ownership of human security advancing projects and initiatives is therefore considered in chapter 6 and the case study.

On balance, therefore, human security can be seen as a 'post-Westphalian' framework; however, it is not about the abolition of a statist system, but rather the necessity to reformulate the concept of security to focus on individuals at the national and international level. It is about putting the vulnerabilities and needs of every person, everywhere as the focus of policy

Resolution 64/291 on Human Security' (5 April 2012) UN Doc A/66/763; UNGA, 'Follow-up to paragraph 143 on Human Security of the 2005 World Summit Outcome' (25 October 2012) Res 66/290; See also M Martin and T Owen, 'The Second Generation of Human Security: Lessons from the UN and EU Experience' (2010) 86 *International Affairs* 211.

[76] Common Understanding (n 6) para 4(a).

[77] ibid, para 4(c).

[78] ibid, para 4(e).

[79] ibid, para 4.

[80] FO Hampson and J Hay, 'Human Security: A Review of Scholarly Literature' (2002) paper presented to the annual meeting of the Canadian Consortium on Human Security, Ottawa, April in Owen (n 72) 376.

[81] OCHA (Human Security Unit), 'Human Security at the United Nations' (*Newsletter* (Issue 1), Fall 2007) https://docs.unocha.org/sites/dms/HSU/Publications%20and%20Products/Newsletters/Issue%201%20-%20Fall%202007%20Human%20Security%20Towards%20an%20Integrated%20Approach.pdf.

decisions on security.[82] The protection and assistance roles of the ICRC have always been human-centric and therefore this chapter shows that the expansion of its activities should be considered as contributing to the establishment of human security.[83]

The concept of human security understands threats as either narrow or broad. The key threats, in the narrow 'camp', are the use of force, armed conflicts and perhaps mass violations of human rights. The means to protect individuals from these threats are primarily militaristic responses; as such, the security should be provided by the state or, if unable/unwilling, the international community.[84] The narrow, or minimalist, theory of human security is enunciated most obviously in the Human Security Centre 'Human Security Report 2005', which abbreviated human security to the discourses of political violence, by a state or any other organised political actor.[85] The Human Security Centre maps trends in political violence, which includes 'torture; extrajudicial, arbitrary and summary executions; the "disappearance" of dissidents; the use of death squads; and incarceration without trial'.[86] The narrow approach focuses on violent threats, whereas the broad approach looks at insecurity independent of the source. Owen has argued that narrow proponents have to realise that security is about more than the mere absence of a violent threat and broad proponents have to see that not all development concerns constitute a threat to human security.[87]

The broad concept of human security includes 'safety from chronic threats such as hunger, disease and repression', along with 'protection from sudden and hurtful disruption in the patterns of daily life'.[88] Newman has argued that: '[T]hrough a broad human security lens, anything that presents a critical threat to life and livelihood is a security threat, whatever the source.'[89] In fact, the broad theory of human security is often criticised for its inability to define specific threats, as it aims to protect people from critical 'life-threatening dangers, regardless of whether the threats

[82] Roberts (n 70) 15.

[83] C Shucksmith, 'Building Human Security through Humanitarian Protection and Assistance: The Potential of the International Committee of the Red Cross' (2017) *Journal of Conflict Transformation and Security*.

[84] R Paris, 'Human Security: Paradigm Shift or Hot Air?' (2001) 26(2) *International Security* 93, 95.

[85] Human Security Centre, *Human Security Report 2005: War and Peace in the Twenty-first Century* (Oxford, Oxford University Press, 2005) 17–54 (Human Security Report 2005); Roberts (n 70) 18.

[86] Human Security Report 2005 (n 85) 64.

[87] Owen (n 72) 378.

[88] HDR 1994 (n 55) 23.

[89] E Newman, 'Critical Human Security Studies' (2010) 36 *Review of International Studies* 77, 82.

are rooted in anthropological activities or natural events, whether they lie within or outside States, and whether they are direct or structural'.[90] Krause strongly argues for the narrow conception, terming 'broad human security' as a 'shopping list', a 'loose synonym for "bad things that might happen", and then it loses all utility to policymakers'.[91] For Krause, therefore, human security ought to be about 'controlling the institutions of organised violence and evacuating force from political, economic and social life' and the 'struggle to establish legitimate and representative political institutions'.[92] In fact, the narrow conception of human security looks rather like the RtoP, which is considered later in this chapter. For this author, if human security is reduced to its narrow conception, it adds little to existing international law and policy. It is imperative that human security continues to be viewed in its broadest sense as, for the people on the ground, military threats are only one of a broad swathe of threats that limit security in their day-to-day lives.

Human security therefore joins together freedom from fear, freedom from want and freedom to live in dignity through people-centred, comprehensive, context-specific and preventive strategies of security.[93] The recognition of threats, beyond threats to national security, as relevant to the conceptualisation of human security did not automatically create a workable definition of human security. The realisation by the international community that a state can be a threat to its population, that the environment can be a threat or that food and healthcare are as important as a military to the security of the population was key to the international community developing an expanded understanding of security.

In terms of threats to human security, broadly defined, it is recognised that 'poverty, conflict and societal grievances can feed on one another in a vicious cycle',[94] as atrocities perpetuate poverty and set back development.[95] Unlike national security paradigms, however, human security does not rely upon the use of force to establish or maintain peace and security; rather it focuses on fostering government and local capacity to react to

[90] R Thakur and E Newman (eds), *Broadening Asia's Security and Discourse Agenda* (UN UP, Tokyo, 2004) 347.

[91] K Krause, 'The Key to a Powerful Agenda, If Properly Delimited' (2004) 35 *Security Dialogue* 367, 367–68.

[92] ibid.

[93] General Assembly Human Security Report 2010 (n 69) para 69; See also Report of the Secretary General, 'An Agenda for Development' (6 May 1994) UN Doc A/48/938 paras 16–20; Kofi Annan, 'Secretary-General Salutes International Workshop on Human Security in Mongolia', Two-day Session in Ulaanbaatar, Press Release, (8–10 May 2000) UN Doc SG/SM/7382; In Larger Freedom (n 58) para 14.

[94] General Assembly Human Security Report 2010 (n 69) para 10.

[95] In Larger Freedom (n 58) para 16.

threats.[96] The assistance and protection roles of the ICRC have an inherent human-centric underpinning and can act in response to threats to human security.

Imagine a village where different ethnic, religious and cultural communities live together under a central governmental authority. Over time rivalries and divides develop into tensions and eventually armed conflict. Then suppose an international organisation were to enter the conflict, identify the leaders of the warring factions and establish them as political groups, set up elections to choose one of those people to run the village and encourage all of the villagers to queue alongside recent rivals and vote for one of them. Is this truly addressing the root causes of the conflict? Is it likely to prevent the recurrence of hostilities?

The outcome of such elections would be an identifiable leader and a basis from which to build state institutions, but on the ground, within the community, but would there be any difference in feelings towards one another? The approach to post-conflict reconstruction outlined above is commonplace in the UN, in particular, as a peace-building strategy.[97] As a neutral, impartial and independent actor, the ICRC would not be directly involved in peace-building per se.[98] Anecdotally, this author was informed that, on the ground, the ICRC would, at a push, advocate for elections, as in the Central African Republic and Syria. It may also call for peace, as in Gaza in 2014 when it demanded that the killing be stopped.[99] This author does not pretend to have a solution to political approaches to conflict resolution, nor is this book aiming to find a solution to sustainable peace, but this book shows the increasing importance of the contribution made by humanitarian agencies, in this case the ICRC, to the humanity,

[96] General Assembly Human Security Report 2010 (n 69) para 23.

[97] L Brahimi (Chairman of the Panel on United Nations Peace Operations), 'Report of the Panel on United Nations Peace Operations' (21 August 2000) UN Doc A/55/305–S/2000/809 (Brahimi Report 2000); Report of the Secretary General, 'No Exit without Strategy: Security Council Decision-making and the Closure or Transition of United Nations Peacekeeping Operations' (20 April 2001) UN Doc S/2001/394 (No Exit Without Strategy); M Barnett, H Kim, M O'Donnell, and L Sitea, 'Peace Building: What Is in a Name?' (2007) 13(1) *Global Governance* 44; CT Call (ed), *Building States to Build Peace* (Boulder, CO, International Peace Institute/Lynne Rienner, 2008); V Chetail (ed), *Post-conflict Peace Building: A Lexicon* (Oxford, Oxford University Press, 2009); A Truger, 'Operationalisation through Training: Human Security Training and Education for Peace Building' in W Benedek, MC Ketteman and M Möstl (eds), *Mainstreaming Human Security in Peace Operations and Crisis Management: Policies, Problems, Potential* (London, Routledge, 2011); R Jenkins, *Peace Building: From Concept to Commission* (London, Routledge, 2013); See also J Galtung, *There Are Alternatives! Four Roads to Peace and Security* (Nottingham, Spokesman, 1984); See also JG Cockell, 'Conceptualising Peace Building: Human Security and Sustainable Peace' in M Pugh (ed), *Regeneration of War-Torn Societies* (London, Macmillan, 2000).

[98] This was clear from the interviews undertaken in Geneva 2014. Their key contribution to the book is included in chs 6 and the Case Study.

[99] J de Maio, 'Palestinians' Anger at Red Cross in Gaza is Misplaced but Understandable' (25 July 2014) www.theguardian.com/commentisfree/2014/jul/25/palestinian-anger-red-cross-gaza-humanitarian-icrc-conflict.

dignity and security of individuals and communities enduring and recovering from conflict.

The scenario outlined above focuses on state building after conflict, but human security is much broader. It encompasses economic, food, health, environmental, personal, community and political security.[100] Moreover, human security priorities, whether economic, community, health, and so on, must be context specific. Perhaps for some communities safe drinking water and food security is a priority; for others, a school where their children can be educated side by side, and perhaps grow up to be more tolerant; for others healthcare, especially mental health, for those suffering post-conflict trauma, would be the best use of resources and provide the best platform to address the root causes of conflict and prevent future recurrence of hostilities.

The threats to security contained in the concept of human security, as created by the HDR 1994 and now contained in General Assembly Resolution,[101] more aptly identify the corpus of humanitarian concerns facing individuals and communities nowadays, given the changed nature of conflict, which was considered in chapter 3. The international community has moved on from the binary distinction between war and peace, institutionalised by the UN and ICRC at the end of the Second World War, to adopt a concept, which, at its centre, reflects the principle of humanity. Human security is a human-centric reconceptualisation of traditional public international law principles, including state sovereignty and non-intervention. Its adoption at the General Assembly shows that the international community, at large, now recognises the importance of seeing human beings as a central concern in decision-making about intervention and protection. Critically, for this book, the ICRC is edging into the field of protection of and assistance in the creation of human security, as it is now coming to work 'in other situations of violence'. The ICRC is undertaking long-term projects beyond the cessation of hostilities, which have clear links with economic security, the specifics of which will be addressed in chapter 6 and the case study.

## IV. THE RELATIONSHIP BETWEEN HUMAN SECURITY, INTERNATIONAL HUMAN RIGHTS LAW AND INTERNATIONAL HUMANITARIAN LAW

Human security, IHRL and the assistance and protection mandate of the ICRC share common purposes.[102] This section builds on the analysis in

[100] HDR 1994 (n 55); See also UNGA, '2005 World Summit Outcome' (15 September 2005) A/60/L.1 (Outcome Document) para 143; Common Understanding (n 6) para 4.

[101] Common Understanding (n 6).

[102] Former UN Under-Secretary General for Legal Affairs (Hans Correll), 'Banquet Speech' from *Proceedings of the Annual Conference of the Canadian Council on International Law,*

chapter 3, which recognised the complementarity between IHRL and IHL. This section considers whether the protection and assistance activities of the ICRC could provide an additional 'layer' to the pursuit of human security. When IHRL and IHL laws are violated, can assistance and protection activities provide more security on the ground for the local population than existing legal and practical frameworks?

This section considers whether the 'minimum core' of economic, social and cultural rights has inherent links to the objectives of the establishment of human security. It postulates that should states be unwilling or unable to realise this standard, then ICRC assistance and protection work, which can reach individuals and communities at local, rather than state, level is able to bring substance to human security for the people on the ground. Some aspects of human security are uncontroversial for the ICRC, in particular food and health security. It is argued, however, that economic security is a contentious area for the ICRC to be working in, as it potentially conflicts with its fundamental principles and could damage its reputation should it be perceived as a partial or politically motivated organisation.

Noortman has argued that international law could be viewed as a regulatory instrument to achieve human security's goals of providing multi-dimensional security to all human beings.[103] This section tests whether IHRL or the protection and assistance activities of the ICRC can help to achieve human security. International Covenant on Civil and Political Rights (ICCPR) and the International Covenant on Economic, Social and Cultural Rights (ICESCR),[104] taken together, constitute an international bill of human rights. They are international treaties and are binding on state parties under international law. Indeed, the Vienna Declaration (1993) recognised civil and political rights and economic, social and cultural rights as 'indivisible, interdependent and interrelated'.[105] The reasoning is that both sets of rights are necessary to establish the integrity and dignity of the person. To this end, the principles of 'respect, protect and fulfil' permeate documents on IHRL.[106] 'Common Understanding Resolution' paragraph 4(c) states that: '[H]uman security recognises the interlinkages between

*'From Territorial Integrity to Human Security'* (The Hague, Kluwer, 2001) www.un.org/law/counsel/ottawa.htm.

[103] Noortman (n 7) 5.

[104] International Covenant on Economic, Social and Cultural Rights (adopted and opened for signature, ratification and accession by General Assembly resolution 2200A (XXI) of 16 December 1966 entry into force 3 January 1976, in accordance with Article 27).

[105] Office of the High Commissioner for Human Rights, 'Vienna Declaration and Programme of Action—Adopted by the World Conference on Human Rights in Vienna on 25 June 1993'.

[106] CESCR, 'General Comment 12: The Right to Adequate Food' (12 May 1999) UN Doc E/C.12/1999/5 para 15; CESCR, 'General Comment 14 on the Right to the Highest Attainable Standard of Health (art 12)' (11 August 2000) UN Doc E/C.12/2000/4, paras 33–37.

peace, development and human rights, and equally considers civil, political, economic, social and cultural rights.' They are legal frameworks that protect people in peacetime, during and after armed conflict, by limiting state action.

According to Noortman, 'a holistic approach to human security leaves little room for differentiating between political and civil rights, social, cultural and economic rights, and collective rights'.[107] In addition to the UN Charter and IHRL, there are a number of treaty laws that have been identified as examples of the 'intrinsic normative effects' of human security, including the 1997 Ottawa Treaty,[108] the 2008 Convention on Cluster Munitions,[109] the 1998 Rome Statute of the ICC,[110] the 2000 Protocols to the Convention on the Rights of the Child,[111] the 2000 Convention against Transnational Organized Crime and its Protocols[112] and the 2002 Protocol to the Convention against Torture.[113] There is also evidence that the Security Council has been systematically developing the human security agenda without calling it by that name, for example, with resolutions on protection of civilians, women and children.[114]

In order to reflect on the complementarity between IHRL, IHL and human security it is pertinent to restate the types of security included in the HDR 1994. They include economic, food, health, environmental, personal, community and political security. There are two key limitations to

[107] Noortman (n 7) 20.

[108] Convention on the Prohibition of the Use, Stockpiling, Production and Transfer of Anti-Personnel Mines and on their Destruction (adopted 18 September 1997, entered into force 1 March 1999) 2056 UNTS 211.

[109] Convention on Cluster Munitions (adopted 30 May 2008, entered into force 1 August 2010) 2688 UNTS.

[110] Rome Statute of the International Criminal Court (adopted 17 July 1998, entered into force 1 July 2002) 2187 UNTS 3.

[111] Optional Protocol to the Convention on the Rights of the Child on the Sale of Children, Child Prostitution and Child Pornography (adopted 25 May 2000, entered into force 18 January 2002) 2171 UNTS 227.

[112] UN (Office on Drugs and Crime), 'United Nations Convention Against Transnational Organized Crime and the Protocols thereto' (UN, New York 2004) www.unodc.org/documents/treaties/UNTOC/Publications/TOC%20Convention/TOCebook-e.pdf.

[113] Optional Protocol to the Convention against Torture and Other Cruel, Inhuman or Degrading Treatment or Punishment (adopted 18 December 2002, entered into force 22 June 2006) 2375 UNTS 237; See also G Oberleitner, 'Human Security: A Challenge to International Law?' (2005) 11 *Global Governance* 185, 195; Eberhard (n 32) 127; Benedek (n 74) 16.

[114] Protection of Civilians in Armed Conflict UNSC Res 1265 (17 September 1999); UNSC Res 1296 (19 April 2000); UNSC Res 1674 (28 April 2006); UNSC Res 1738 (23 December 2006) and UNSC Res 1894 (11 November 2009); 'Report of the Secretary General to the Security Council on the Protection of Civilians in Armed Conflict' (8 September 1999) S/1999/957 para 61; Protection of Children in Armed Conflict UNSC Res 1261 (30 August 1999); UNSC Res 1314 (11 August 2000); UNSC Res 1882 (4 August 2009); UNSC Res 1998 (12 July 2011); Women and Peace and Security UNSC Res 1325 (31 October 2000); UNSC Res 1820 (19 June 2008); UNSC Res 1960 (16 December 2010); UNSC Res 1888 (30 September 2009) Violence against Women and Children in Armed Conflict; UNSC Res 1706 (31 August 2006) Situation in the Sudan.

economic, social and cultural rights: firstly, that the obligation on states is 'progressive realisation'; and secondly, that such obligations are limited to realisation of a 'minimum core'. This is evidenced most clearly in Reports of the Committee on Economic, Social and Cultural Rights (CESCR), which will be relied on throughout this section to provide more information on the UN's expectations of states in terms of their ICESCR obligations.

Under Article 2(1) ICESCR governments are required to 'take steps, to the *maximum of available resources*, with a view to achieving *progressively* the full realisation of the rights recognised in the present Covenant by all appropriate means'.[115] According to Minkler: '[E]conomic and social rights enable each and every individual to claim sufficient resources to live a dignified life no matter what a country's average income or distribution might be.'[116] Moreover, Article 2(2) provides that states are also required to 'guarantee that the rights will be exercised without discrimination of any kind' and, finally, Article 3 provides that states must 'ensure the equal right of men and women to the enjoyment of all economic, social and cultural rights'.

CESCR General Comment 3 (1990) states that the 'minimum essential levels' of each of the rights is incumbent on every state party.[117] It provides that: '[A] State party in which any number of individuals is deprived of essential foodstuffs, of essential primary healthcare, of basic shelter or housing, or of the most basic form of education is, *prima facie*, failing to discharge its obligations under the Covenant.'[118] The 'minimum core' therefore provides a baseline for the realisation of economic, social and cultural rights; failure to meet this is unacceptable, even in post-conflict situations.[119] If states fail to meet these requirements they must 'demonstrate that every effort has been made to use all resources that are at its disposition in an effort to satisfy, as a matter of priority, those minimum obligations'.[120]

Modern-day armed conflicts have forced the ICRC to develop its practice on the ground to increase its protection and assistance activities in light of the protracted nature of conflicts, particularly NIACs. From prisoners of war, to wounded soldiers, to civilians, everyone affected by armed conflict needs access to food, health and economic stability. A lack

[115] Emphasis added.

[116] L Minkler (ed), *The State of Economic and Social Rights: A Global Overview* (Cambridge, Cambridge University Press, 2013) 2.

[117] CESCR, 'General Comment 3 on the Nature of States Parties' Obligations (art 2 para 1 of the Covenant)' (14 December 1990) UN Doc E/1991/23/ E/C.12/1990/8 para 10.

[118] ibid.

[119] A Chapman and S Russell (eds), *Core Obligations: Building a Framework for Economic, Social and Cultural Rights* (Oxford, Intersentia, 2002) 8–10.

[120] General Comment 3 (n 117) para 10.

of any of these can create security threats to the individual and the communities in which they live. There are also threats to personal, community, political and environmental security. Critically, the principle of humanity, once restricted to IHL and Red Cross work, now permeates the international stage and is reflected at the normative level in human security. The ICRC has continued to focus on its traditional mission whilst constantly adapting to new situations of armed conflict, new actors in those conflicts and the changing needs of the civilian population. The ICRC has worked to develop the law and its activities to reflect the humanitarian needs of people on the ground. The ICRC is well placed to understand the dynamics behind violence and why some actors choose to ignore IHL.

## V. CONCLUSION

This chapter has shown that the concept of security has changed. Whilst state sovereignty, that is, the Westphalian model of the international legal order, remains relevant, the type of threats to these states and the people living within them has expanded. Security discourse nowadays includes recognition that a government is a potential threat to its people. As such, the sovereignty as responsibility concept provided a turning point in the progressive inclusion of humanitarian concerns in a historically state-centric international legal order. It showed that states have a responsibility to their own people.

The ICRC has always recognised the centrality of human beings and has built upon its historical experiences with soldiers, prisoners of war and the shipwrecked to look after, provide for and assist the victims of conflict. It has been necessary for the ICRC to increase its protection and assistance activities in light of the protracted nature of conflicts, particularly NIACs. These types of conflicts create situations whereby the needs of the civilian population are ongoing and the threats to security include those to food, health and the economy. There are also threats to personal, community, and political and environmental security. ICRC protection and assistance roles have expanded to include economic security, provision of food and healthcare, interacting and building dialogue with communities, and helping individual families get back on their feet. There are clear parallels between the human security agenda and the original mandate of the ICRC, and there are also synergies between broad human security and the newer ICRC projects that we see today. The extent of this is examined in the empirical research undertaken for chapter 6 and the case study.

Fortunately, human security has links, in a human-centric sense, to existing legal frameworks including IHRL and IHL. Moreover, it has links to development, as threats to security are recognised as needing longer-terms solutions, in particular, economic growth. If human security is to have any real meaning for people on the ground, we have to look past state sovereignty and territorial integrity. We cannot do so in a legal vacuum otherwise human security is reduced to rhetoric only. To this end, it was shown that economic, social and cultural rights are increasingly relevant to analysis of the real-life impact of human security. By drawing analogies between the different legal frameworks, this part of the book has shown that the ICRC has the potential to be a legitimate actor in the establishment of human security, as its humanitarian protection and assistance activities overlap with human rights—however, this might be beyond its mandate, which is the issue to be considered in chapter 6 and the case study.

# 6

# *Interviews with the ICRC*

## I. INTRODUCTION

HUMAN RIGHTS, HUMAN security and humanitarian principles are firmly entrenched in the international legal order through the proliferation of human rights courts and institutions. The qualitative research in this book was designed to find out whether the ICRC's changing role may go beyond or overreach a strict interpretation of its protection and assistance mandate. Mindful of its guiding principles, this chapter and the case study show the protection and assistance roles of the ICRC on the ground nowadays and question whether states or NSAs, with whom the ICRC has built a dialogue, may revoke their consent if the organisation's activities become politicised or seemingly stray outside of its mandate. This chapter brings to the forefront the findings derived from semi-structured nterviews undertaken in April 2014 and April 2016 with ICRC delegates in its Geneva-based headquarters. The interviewees were long-standing ICRC delegates with experience in the Geneva headquarters and the field. The interviewees had worked for the ICRC for between five and twenty-five years, and included national Head of Mission staff, programme coordinators and legal advisors.

In one interview this author was told that the ICRC tries to avoid the perception that it is an organisation 'stuck in a certain mandate' because its ultimate focus is to tend to 'people facing challenges in their daily lives'.[1] To this end, the interviewee stated, the ICRC will work to address this need even if people say 'this is not your mandate'.[2] The same interviewee admitted that it is necessary 'not to try to put every action of every organisation in a certain box because people who are living on the ground, they don't care about the box, they care about the problems and the way they will be able to feed their families'.[3] The ICRC cannot turn away from victims and say, 'I'm sorry but you're not in the legal frame.'[4] This perspective is important when thinking about the ICRC's mandate

[1] Interview 001.
[2] Interview 001.
[3] Interview 001.
[4] Interview 001.

and practice, as the ICRC must be able to respond adequately to situations on the ground.

Times have changed since Dunant's vision at Solferino of volunteers ready to help injured soldiers: the ICRC has evolved into an organisation ready to assist anyone adversely affected by the scourge of war and other situations of violence. Its principles keep it grounded and set the ICRC apart from inherently political organisations, such as the UN, that also undertake humanitarian work. Its sui generis status allows the ICRC to adapt at both the Swiss and international level. In addition, the governance of the ICRC allows it to set its own agenda. The Assembly, for example, drafts the agenda for the International Conference. Critically, as an international legal person, the ICRC can act with legal effect, as it exercises and enjoys functions and rights that can be explained by the possession of international legal personality, such as its ability to make claims, negotiate agreements, and exercise privileges and immunities. It also has its own specific rights and duties for humanitarian protection and assistance which are contained in the Geneva Conventions I, II, III and IV 1949, Additional Protocols I and II 1977, and the Statutes of the IRCRCM, the latter being considered internal to the organisation rather than a treaty.[5] The ICRC may also have roles determined in its specific Headquarters Agreements with states. To this end, the ICRC performs a myriad of functions and exercises rights that aim to protect and assist those in need.

This chapter and the case study look at the breadth of interpretation the ICRC mandate now undergoes in Geneva and the field. This chapter shows that as conflicts and situations of violence have changed, so too has the role of the ICRC. Human insecurity permeates societies emerging from conflict, resulting in a lack of resources and threats to physical and economic security. This chapter considers the effects of protracted armed conflict on the ICRC, the necessity of local ownership of its projects, its early recovery agenda, economic security and, finally, prevention. It may seem strange to look at prevention last, but the ICRC learns from its work and can use lessons and best practice to strive to prevent similar situations. To this end, prevention is as much a part of 'post-conflict' situations as it is about preventing conflict ever occurring.

## II. REFLECTIONS BY DELEGATES ON THE MANDATE

Chapters 1–5 of this book have appraised the mandate of the ICRC from a theoretical and doctrinal perspective. Part of the interview methodology

[5] Vienna Convention on the Law of Treaties (adopted 23 May 1969, entered into force 27 January 1980) 1155 UNTS 331.

was to determine the perspective of the ICRC delegates on the mandate. Responses reflected on the breadth of the mandate and the necessity of the ability to interpret it in light of the situation on the ground. Interviewee 006 stated that:

> The legal mandate comes particularly from the spirit of the text of the Geneva Conventions. But to be more specific than that, I would view the mandate as being one of providing protection for people who are victims of conflict and don't have legal protection, ie are not in the armed forces or some other body and given legal protection. So for me, I would take a relatively broad view that there has to be violence or conflict and there has to be people who are victims of that who are in need of protection. What form the protection takes is very, very, very varied, but protection is the key word.

Interviewee 007 stated that:

> Very broadly, it's to provide assistance, protection to victims of armed conflict or situations of violence first and foremost. It could be a little bit more than that, depending on the context where we're present and if there are other things happening which require support from a humanitarian perspective, but that's pretty much it.

Interviewee 009 said:

> I think if you read it, you understand it quite well. The problem is how you translate it into actions in the field. … We have probably sixty-five or sixty-six delegations and you have sixty-five or sixty-six different ways of implementing this mandate because these are different, because the environment is different, because the culture is different, because of whatever. Okay, protection and assistance of victims in armed conflict or a situation of violence and sometimes a natural disaster is quite easy to understand as a concept. But when you put them into practice, it's a totally different ballgame because it's different to intervene in a rural area than in an urban area; it's different to intervene in Ukraine than in the Congo, and so on and so forth. … So the way you adapt, I mean the response, is always different. But the mandate, protection and assistance and, of course, the movement part, IHL, the simulation of IHL, is something which is quite easy to understand but difficult, again, to put on paper or to translate that into an integrated approach. … This is the ICRC. It's probably one of the only generalist organisations in the humanitarian sector, but with a mandate which is so broad that you can basically fit everything you want in it. … The ICRC mandate allows you to do more or less whatever you want to help the people maintain their dignity in a difficult situation. You have almost no restriction, and this is what I like in this mandate.

For this interviewee, in particular, the vagueness of the mandate was a strength, whereas for others, it was a natural consequence of trying to get states to agree to the Geneva Conventions I, II, III, IV 1949. Interviewee 010 stated that they thought that: '[T]he mandate comes from the state, through the Geneva Conventions. I mean, we have a role to play that has been agreed by the states. Our mission is to protect and assist people in need who are affected by armed conflict and situations of violence.'[6] When asked whether the mandate is still fit for purpose, this author was not surprised at the responses, which tended to focus on the unlikely renegotiation of the Geneva Conventions. The interviewees were pragmatic about making the Geneva Conventions work in the protracted armed conflicts seen today. Interviewee 007 argued, for example, that:

> I think they're still a set of standards which make sense. Even though they are violated in many occasions, they still make sense. They should be improved if possible, but that's a bit complicated, particularly in today's world. So I think we can certainly live with them. We have in them what is needed, I think, still today for making sure that conflicts or violence are not hitting too much on those not taking part thereof.[7]

Interviewee 006, similarly, stated that:

> In an ideal world, of course you would wish for a much stronger, much more robust protection framework, but because the Geneva Conventions are a universal treaty, perhaps one is dealing with the real politics of the world and what we have from the revised Geneva Conventions of 1949 and the additional protocols. If they didn't exist, we'd never be able to negotiate them as an international community today. We just wouldn't be able because the state wouldn't agree. But if you take another view of it, you would say that they are inadequate to deal with, particularly, the bigger issue. The biggest issue is compliance, but in specific reference to non-international conflict.
>
> So yeah, if you ask me are they fit for purpose, they do have a job because they give me a sufficiently robust set of rules and procedures and commitment that I can then use to negotiate. Because actually—I may be getting off your point here—it's not so much about what the Conventions say or what protections they offer, it's how you negotiate that and how you establish a negotiation with states that actually matters. It's certainly the strength of the ICRC that they have a mandate. It's a relatively straightforward one but it really depends on how it is negotiated. In the end, everything is about the delegate who is negotiating the respect for the implementation of the mandate. If that's done well, generally we have good operations. When that doesn't work, generally our operations are going to run into difficulties.[8]

Much of the response as to whether the mandate was fit for purpose framed their answers around the Geneva Conventions I, II, III, IV 1949. The primary mandate comes from the Geneva Conventions and there is a secondary mandate from the Statutes of the movement. Interviewee 007 also considered the 'secondary mandate' of the ICRC. They stated that:

> The right is the *right of initiative*, which comes from Statutes of the Movement. But also, in general, in a context where you have epidemics or an earthquake or

6 Interview 010.
7 Interview 007.
8 Interview 006.

> whatever, then we can provide assistance because we are there, we have some means, etc, etc. That's certainly something we will consider and we will do, even though it's not our primary mandate.[9]

Interviewee 007 also considered the Headquarters Agreements as forming part of the mandate

> I know there is some sort of a template, if you wish, for a headquarters agreement, which I guess is quite broad and then it's negotiated on a case-by-case basis, depending upon what the authorities are okay with us doing, but also in terms of privileges, etc, etc, that they are okay to give us.[10]

What these responses show is the breadth of interpretation even within a small number of ICRC delegates. We cannot provide a general understanding of the mandate from the sample but it can be said that the interviewees show a pragmatism and a prioritisation of the needs of the population when considering the mandate. In light of such responses, this author drew on conclusions presented in chapter 3 of this book and asked about the influence and utility of human rights law in the law and practice of the ICRC. The responses were varied and showed that human rights law usage depends on the role of the delegate and the person whom they are working with. Interviewee 006 stated, for example, that:

> Personally, I [tended] away from human rights legislation because I don't think it is our mandate. I think we should stick with the violence and the conflict. But there are others who believe that we should engage a little bit more with human rights legislation, and then the states all have their own opinion on whether we should or shouldn't.[11]

For example, interviewee 008 stated that:

> In detention we will refer to human rights law, I think. Working in detention, we will more refer on human rights law than in the community. I think in the community we will more present those things according to humanitarian needs than to human rights law … will not put this in front because, as we said before, for some states, they don't really like—They are a bit afraid of organisations whose mandate is human rights law.[12]

Interviewee 008 went on to state that:

> Even if I go to Geneva and say, 'Hey, I work for an organisation which promotes and monitors respect for international humanitarian law,' people will say, 'What? Humanitarian what? What is it about?' I say, 'Okay. Do you know what are your rights if there is a war? In other words, the duty of the …' Nobody

[9] Interview 007.
[10] Interview 007.
[11] Interview 006.
[12] Interview 008.

> knows. So the only way you can, again, look at this concept is to explain what you will do for them, and how.[13]

Likewise, interviewee 009 recalled that:

> People understand that there is something or that they have some rights, without you saying, okay, this is IHL and so on. This being said, we do a lot of disseminations of this IHL, but mainly to military politicians, military and civilian authorities. But the population, honestly, we just focus on their needs.[14]

In light of this practical approach on the ground and the utility of the International Conference to keep IHL on the table: '[I]t's about keeping international humanitarian law live and adapted to the new way of warfare. For that, it's important that the states can gather and talk about it from time to time.'[15] What comes through in the interviews is the willingness and ability of ICRC delegates to adapt to specific situations and audiences and use the language that will best get the ICRC's message across as regards its humanitarian mandate. In light of this, this author went on to ask interviewees about the principles of the IRCRCM and how they feature in the practice of the ICRC. Candidly, interviewee 006 relayed that:

> I don't always talk about an applied legal framework, which my lawyers in Geneva don't like, but for me and my job in the field it's to take the legal framework intervention and apply it. That means looking for where the Geneva Conventions can be interpreted in, for example, Belfast or Washington or wherever …, the principles and particularly the one is humanity is absolutely central and dominating because it's the kind of overarching humanitarian principle. … In a negotiation with a government, if you're referring to the need to protect civilians or wounded soldiers, you're doing it on the basis of humanity just as much as you're doing it on the basis of what the Geneva Conventions oblige them to do. Now, lawyers will tell you, no, no, it's an obligation on the state to respect IHL, but that's okay as long as everybody realises that applies. But generally there isn't an agreement around that, so it means you're having to use both arguments.[16]

Taking into account the necessary pragmatism of the ICRC approach to varied situations on the ground, the interviews question delegates on the consequences when states feel that the ICRC has overstepped its mandate. In asking this question, this author was mindful of the situation in Sudan and of the argument presented in chapter 2 that the ICRC be recognised as an international legal person on the international stage. 'When we are expelled by a country from an area, or from the country, it's rare.

[13] Interview 008.
[14] Interview 009.
[15] Interview 009.
[16] Interview 006.

But where, basically, our presence in the field is reduced to the capital, which happens in some countries today, nobody will help us.'[17]

Interviewee 009 elaborated on the potential consequences of ICRC overreach:

> Either you are convoked through the Minister of Foreign Affairs and they tell you that you should stop this and that. This is the first warning. The second warning, they just block you. They just expel the people. Usually in such countries you will have to ask for travel permits; you will not get it any more. For flight clearances, you won't get them.... You will not receive visas for your staff coming in. I mean there are many ways a state can make you understand that you are stepping over a certain line.

The interviewee also reflected on the desire for some states to see the ICRC act more through the national societies. Interviewee 009 stated that:

> I understand also this approach because we have always a short-sighted vision of the local capacities and how we can use them in the field because the people don't stay much longer than nine, twelve, fifteen months in one place and then rotate. It's often difficult for us to help.... We've been expelled three times, I think, from the Tigray region in Ethiopia, and we always went back. It took sometimes ten years, sometimes five years, and so on, but we are still there. For how long, I don't know. One day the Ethiopian government will say 'go out' again. We'll go out and we'll come back. We just wait for the political environment to be right to go back and make a proposal. But if you want to force your way in, then you have a security issue, I think.[18]

What the interviews show, which cannot be fully understood from reading the Geneva Conventions I, II, III and IV 1949, the IRCRCM Statutes or Headquarters Agreements is the fragility of situations on the ground and the inevitable negotiations that go into planning a mission and carrying out protection and assistance work. The ICRC has to be responsive and useful, using its broad mandate to be a useful humanitarian organisation. Interviewee 006 noted that the ICRC 'recently opened our office in Budapest because of migration, but because we've had a previous delegation there in the past, they were very familiar with the process that is required to establish an ICRC presence'.[19] The mandate may also be adapted to respond to urban violence.[20]

As we can see, the mandate of the ICRC is taken from a number of sources, interpreted by a number of delegates and implemented by the ICRC and national societies. To this end, no two missions are the same. The flexibility of the mandate, in this regard, is a positive for the people

[17] Interview 009.
[18] Interview 009.
[19] Interview 006.
[20] Interview 007.

on the ground but it may be a double-edged sword for ICRC delegates who must walk a fine line between observing the wishes of states who consented to the Geneva Conventions I, II, III and IV 1949, and responding to unique and changing situations on the ground.

Having reflected on the mandate, the interviews turned to the question of protracted armed conflict and how it has impacted upon the interpretation and utility of the ICRC mandate. Critically, protracted armed conflict means that for the delegates on the ground, 'it was not only a question of hit and run operations, even in situations of conflict [the ICRC] began to think about the long-term consequences, especially in situations where [it was] present for years and decades'.[21] There was a need to 'inject more sustainability' and so:

> Sometimes [the ICRC] goes towards more development activities but it's at the borderline. [The ICRC] also continue to have some activities in post-conflict situations and when [it has] activities in non-conflict situations, like 'other situations of violence', sometimes, yes, it's at the borderline of development. [The ICRC has] these reflections regularly on where to draw the line. What are [its] limits in terms of competence?[22]

The changing nature of armed conflicts, in particular their protracted nature, has pushed the ICRC to work for extended periods of time in certain states and to develop its protection and assistance roles to include longer-term activities. It cannot be known, for sure, to what extent the ICRC truly 'reflects' on where to draw the line between its mandate and its focus on addressing the needs of people on the ground. It appears that the humanitarian needs usurp the need to reconcile action with the specific activities contained in the Geneva Conventions I, II, III and IV 1949 and the ICRC Statutes. For example, Interviewee 006 stated that for the continuation of ICRC presence:

> The threshold is relatively high, but it probably has changed. We did a five-year project in the Favelas in Rio. We have an operation in Northern Ireland. We've continued to work in the Balkans. These are not typical ICRC contexts and the institution is supportive of them, obviously, because it does them, but not nearly as enthusiastic as it is about international conflict. So we would say that it hasn't really changed, but it probably has a bit. If you take the Balkans, there isn't conflict in the Balkans but there are missing people and I think our operation in the Balkans is really limited to try to sort, to help support the patient of the dead bodies of the missing. That would have been unheard of twenty years ago, that we keep an office open just for that.[23]

[21] Interview 001.
[22] Interview 001.
[23] Interview 006.

Interviewee 009 stated that:

> If I look at East Africa, all these conflicts, almost all of them started between' 89 and' 92. So it was the Berlin wall, the end of the Cold War and so on, and they've been going on since then. So, yes, it's over thirty years in each and every country. So it's definitely protracted conflicts and I'm really happy that the donors, or the governments, are giving more attention to these situations. We'll see how concretely they will do that, but it's a good move.[24]

It was recognised by interviewees that this development of ICRC activities was enough to raise questions about its competences, but for the ICRC delegates, they are first and foremost humanitarians.[25] One interview stated that:

> I think we provide hope. I think we provide hope because we're there. If I think of my operational background, it obviously depends from place to place, but if it's open conflict, the fact that you are present in the midst of an open conflict when normally the diplomatic communities are gone, the foreigners are gone, the UN is gone, the NGOs are gone, the fact that you're there gives them hope that they haven't just landed in hell, although they have landed in hell, because you're there and you give them a little bit of hope.[26]

During the interviews, this author asked the interviewees whether they considered the changes in the roles of the ICRC to be 'progression' within the organisation, or rather, a move away from the armed-conflict-specific activities of the ICRC, as identified in the Geneva Conventions I, II, III and IV 1949 and ICRC Statutes. It was asked whether such changes are risky for the sustainability of the guiding principles of the ICRC. The interviewees considered that 'needs' were the relevant consideration to an assessment of appropriate action; one interviewee stated that:

> I don't see that there's a risk as long as you target the right needs and then as long as you have identified the needs, the whole issue is how you address these needs and do you address the needs with a short term or long term solution.[27]

The interviewees provided examples of ongoing ICRC projects, which, unlike past protection and assistance activities, require longer-term thinking. The nature of armed conflict is constantly changing: battlefields, soldiers and weapons have been replaced by cyber warfare, NIACs, non-state armed groups, sexual violence used as a weapon, and so on. Unlike in the traditional armed conflict paradigm, the ICRC cannot identify an immediate need, 'fix it' and leave. Nowadays, conflicts are a long cycle

24 Interview 009.
25 Interview 001; Interview 002; Interview 003; Interview 004; Interview 005.
26 Interview 006.
27 Interview 001.

of violence that can have times of armed conflict and times of near peace. In any situation, the consequences for the population are still extremely important, as people will face the same lack of services, usually associated with armed conflicts, and periods where the system collapses completely.

Recovery from conflict takes a very long time. In some instances, protracted armed conflict can go on for years and even decades. The ICRC is being forced to adapt its preparations to these needs and be as flexible as possible to address particular issues. In some areas, again, this will only be by feeding people, bringing medicine, operating on the wounded, but in others, where the ICRC can engage with the local authorities, for example on primary healthcare, then it will develop a longer-term strategy. For one interviewee, these kinds of developments by the ICRC are

> [p]robably quite close to what the UN is doing [in peace building], I don't see that as incompatible. When you are working in conflict-affected areas, in countries like the DRC, the needs are so huge that there is space for all to work.[28]

This response to questions about the more long-term projects, including economic projects, was par for the course during the interviews. It appears, therefore, that humanitarian needs trump any real analysis of the legitimacy of action or whether it buys into broader concepts of peace and security.

In conclusion, by engaging with early recovery and economic security projects, the ICRC work bridges the nexus between security, development and human rights. To this end, the ICRC may increasingly overstep the functions, established in the Geneva Conventions I, II, III and IV 1949 and the ICRC Statutes, which keeps it as a neutral and independent actor. This trend raises an important question, however: if the ICRC continues to develop its economic security activities, perhaps attracting funding from development donors rather than humanitarian donors, will this push states to deny access?[29]

## III. EARLY RECOVERY

Since 1949 the ICRC has developed its specific mandate to include action to ensure economic security, health, water and habitat, landmine clearance, diplomacy and communication, and in its 2011–14 strategy it included these under the term 'Early Recovery'.[30] More recent reports by the ICRC

[28] Interview 001.

[29] A list of donors, both individuals and companies, can be found in the Annual Report 2015. This is the most recent annual report at the time of writing.

[30] ICRC, 'ICRC Strategy 2011–14: Achieving Significant Results for People in Need' (Geneva, ICRC, 2010) 5.

note that: 'IHL does not use the distinctions made in international policy of relief, early recovery and development; instead, it focuses on meeting basic needs.'[31] In practice, however, the meeting of basic needs includes not only immediate relief but also engaging with communities on a structural level, which many interviewees reflected on. The presence of the ICRC, particularly in protracted armed conflict, necessitates the ongoing provision of humanitarian protection and assistance, which eventually must tip into the realms of development. The long-term resilience of communities, should the ICRC leave, relies on ICRC delegates planning ahead. Indeed, in its 2016 report, the ICRC notes that it is 'increasingly unconvinced by simple distinctions between relief and development programming and financing. Relief and development serve more as bureaucratic funding distinctions than a genuine reflection of a needs-based approach.'[32] The official justification for these developments in its scope of action is 'to meet the needs of people affected by armed conflict and other situations of violence'.[33] The phase known as 'early recovery' describes the 'grey area' between war and peace, before development activities fully begin and whilst the situation on the ground remains fragile. Early recovery sits on the conflict to post-conflict continuum or between emergency relief and development and it 'encompasses the restoration of basic services, livelihoods, shelter, governance, security and rule of law, environment and social dimensions, including the reintegration of displaced populations'.[34] According to the United Nations Development Programme: '[E]arly recovery is the term used to describe the application of development principles to humanitarian situations.'[35] To what extent, therefore, has ICRC protection and assistance progressed into early recovery?

Early recovery should help the population get back on its feet. Practical initiatives include

> increasing the availability of resources or distribution of seeds directly to the community, in order they can restart farming when they come back from displacement [and] working with associations including basic help such as printing manuals to try and restart associations. Sometimes [the ICRC] organise[s] fairs in very remote areas, where [it] brings sellers from different parts to increase the level of available goods in the community. [It is] now starting to think of other forms of support, more linked to emergencies, they can be vouchers/cash

[31] ICRC, 'Protracted Conflict and Humanitarian Action: Some recent ICRC experiences' (Geneva, ICRC, 2016) 12.

[32] ibid, 20.

[33] ICRC, 'ICRC Strategy 2011–14' (n 30) 5.

[34] CWGER (in cooperation with the UNDG-ECHA Working Group on Transition), 'Guidance Note on Early Recovery' (April 2008) 6.

[35] UNDP (Bureau for Crisis Prevention and Recovery), 'UNDP Policy on Early Recovery' (February 2008) 5.

> transfers. Different ways of bringing, or trying to help communities cope, with the immediate effects of the conflict.[36]

The last examples are part of longer-term strategies and show the expansion of ICRC activities into early recovery.

The Cluster Working Group on Early Recovery describes early recovery as:

> Humanitarian and development agencies working together on recovery as early as possible within the humanitarian phase—assessing, planning, mobilizing resources, implementing and monitoring activities; supporting spontaneous recovery initiatives of affected populations; supporting capacity of national actors to manage and implement the recovery process; influencing the way humanitarian assistance is provided to avoid dependencies; capitalizing on opportunities to reduce risk; and establishing strong foundations for recovery and sustainable development.[37]

The ICRC early recovery operations are not intended to create a culture of dependency; rather, the 'aim is to promote the resilience and self-sufficiency of affected people or communities, and to protect their dignity in a way that food or other emergency relief alone cannot'.[38] Significantly the ICRC's 2011–14 strategy shows that the heart of the ICRC mission remains the same, that is, protection and assistance of those in need.[39] However, the ICRC acknowledges its encroachment into the early recovery phase, which includes 'medical, economic security, and water and habitat'. It will 'prepare to withdraw once the entry strategies of development organizations have been clearly set out and followed by concrete actions'.[40]

## A. Food, Health, Shelter and Water[41]

The ICRC works at the intersection of human needs, state sovereignty and international organisations. It is grounded by its principles and has access to state officials and the local population. It has influence within states and on the international stage, particularly through the International Conference and its observer status at the UN General Assembly.[42]

[36] Interview 001.

[37] CWGER, 'Implementing Early Recovery' (July 2006) 1.

[38] J Kellenberger, 'Overview of the ICRC's Operations in 2012: Message from the President, Jakob Kellenberger' (8 December 2011) www.icrc.org/eng/resources/documents/report/appeals-2012-message-president-2011-12-08.htm.

[39] ICRC, 'ICRC Strategy 2011–14' (n 30).

[40] ibid 6.

[41] For key information on current ICRC budgets and expenditure in these areas see the ICRC Annual Reports.

[42] C Koenig, 'Observer Status for the International Committee of the Red Cross at the United Nations: A legal viewpoint' (1991) 280 *IRRC* 47.

We know from chapter 2 that the ICRC can act with legal effect and develop its competences on the international stage. Taken together, the current legal framework and humanitarian protection and assistance strategies allow the ICRC to provide food, healthcare, shelter and water to those in need. This section therefore combines doctrinal and empirical research to show how the ICRC fulfils its mandate and adapts its functions to respond to specific situations on the ground, taking account of local ownership, state sovereignty, law, financing and its principles.

Under Article 25 (1) UDHR 'everyone has the right to a standard of living adequate for the health and well-being of himself and of his family, including food'. This is codified in Article 11(1) ICESCR which declares that state parties 'will take appropriate steps to ensure the realization of this right, recognizing to this effect the essential importance of international co-operation based on free consent'. In addition, Article 18(2) Additional Protocol II states that:

> If the civilian population is suffering undue hardship owing to a lack of the supplies essential for its survival, such as foodstuffs and medical supplies, relief actions for the civilian population which are of an exclusively humanitarian and impartial nature and which are conducted without any adverse distinction shall be undertaken subject to the consent of the High Contracting Party concerned.

According to Sivakumaran, that the 'customary norm has been framed along different lines', namely that: 'The parties to the conflict must allow and facilitate rapid and unimpeded passage of humanitarian relief for civilians in need, which is impartial in character and conducted without any adverse distinction to their right of control.'[43] To this end, the ICRC must be allowed to reach civilians in need. The HDR 1994 stated that:

> Food security means that all people at all times have both physical and economic access to basic food. This requires not just enough food to go around, it requires that people have ready access to food—that they have an 'entitlement' to food, by growing it for themselves, by buying it or by taking advantage of a public food distribution system.[44]

The CESCR recognises that in the case of the right to food, the obligation is to 'take the necessary action to mitigate and alleviate hunger … even in times of natural or other disasters'.[45] To this end, the *minimum core* that must be reached is that states must ensure their citizens are 'free from

[43] S Sivakumaran, *The Law of Non-International Armed Conflict* (Oxford, Oxford University Press, 2012) 330.

[44] UNDP, 'Human Development Report 1994' (UNDP, Oxford, Oxford University Press, 1994) 27.

[45] CESCR, 'General Comment 12: The Right to Adequate Food' (12 May 1999) UN Doc E/C.12/1999/5 para 15.

hunger, aiming to prevent starvation'.[46] Likewise, the right to water provides that priority should also be given to the water resources required to prevent starvation and disease, as well as water required to meet the core obligations of each of the Covenant rights.[47]

Violations of the minimum core obligations as regards the right to food include 'hijacking of food convoys, demands for extortion, the holding up in customs of food intended for distribution to the civilian population, or any other form of harassment or restriction imposed on international agencies engaged in food or nutrition programmes'.[48]

For the ICRC, 'food security has to be considered primarily at the individual and household levels, since conflicts affect individuals and households before adversely affecting the whole country'.[49] In situations of food shortages, people will channel their resources into obtaining food and other essential items, including medicines, clothes and shelter. The ICRC therefore provides support for these coping mechanisms. It continues to be involved in distribution of food and non-food relief, establishing public kitchens and setting up emergency water and environmental health facilities. These roles have expanded to include activities such as agricultural, veterinary and fishery programmes; general food distribution as a backup until the next harvest; small-scale credit programmes; and 'food-and-cash-for-work programmes'.[50]

Interviewees reflected on how protection and assistance activities have expanded over the last decades. Interviewee 006 recalled that:

> I think the model of the intervention three decades ago was very much around emergency lifesaving assistance. So, food, water—water was new—healthcare, particularly surgery, and child healthcare in famine situations [and] conflict. That has all now become a very sophisticated analysis and assessment of economic security and health indicators and major water projects which look particularly on the health and water side. We look much more at the infrastructure of society and ways in which we can reinforce or develop health support in some of those infrastructures, like urban water supply or a family healthcare model.
>
> On the emergency food side, we still do all the emergency stuff but we also do much more sophisticated early interventions, like cash, like agriculture, like

[46] CESCR, 'General Comment 3 on the Nature of States Parties' Obligations (art 2 para 1 of the Covenant)' (14 December 1990) UN Doc E/1991/23/ E/C.12/1990/8 para 10.

[47] CESCR, 'General Comment 15: The Right to Water (Arts 11 and 12 of the International Covenant on Economic, Social and Cultural Rights)' (20 January 2003) UN Doc E/C.12/2002/11, para 6; See also World Summit on Sustainable Development, 'Plan of Implementation 2002' (4 September 2002) A/CONF.199/20, para 25(c).

[48] R Barber, 'Facilitating Humanitarian Assistance in International Humanitarian and Human Rights Law' (2009) 91 *IRRC* 371, 394.

[49] 'World Food Summit: Food Security in Armed Conflicts—The ICRC's Approach and Experience' www.icrc.org/eng/resources/documents/misc/57jncy.htm.

[50] ibid.

veterinary science, which are much more supportive of a community than free food. So that's on the assistance side.

On the protection side, well, still pretty much as we always did. I guess one of the big changes in protection is that we are becoming more effective about providing protection for the civilian population, which, of course, is politically very sensitive. But that's really where, I think, the main thrust of the work is over the last three decades. I mean, we used to focus really on the wounded, the prisoners—I mean, they were the big focus—but now we really try to look at the civilian population and what we can do to support the civilian population.[51]

Chapter 1 of this book briefly recalled the experiences of Henry Dunant in the aftermath of the Battle of Solferino and his desire to provide medical assistance and healthcare to wounded soldiers. Indeed, his experiences of the wounded soldiers inspired the establishment of the ICRC. Nowadays, the provisions in the Geneva Conventions I, II, III and IV 1949 provide the mandate for the ICRC to be involved in the provision of healthcare to those in need.[52] Health security is also recognised in the HDR 1994, Article 25 UDHR and Article 12 ICESCR.[53] Threats to health security include infectious diseases resulting from poor nutrition and an unsafe environment. These pose a greater risk to the poor, women and children. One interviewee noted that these situations require thinking about not only the building to provide primary healthcare but also the recruitment and salary of doctors and healthcare professionals; this requires a ministry of health and the provision of healthcare plans for entire communities.[54] A lack of available national healthcare facilities, especially primary care and mental health services, is an issue for many post-conflict states.[55] These consequences inspired the 'Health Care in Danger' project, which was an

[51] Interview 006.

[52] Geneva Convention IV, Arts 14–22; Additional Protocol I, Arts 8 and 12–15; Additional Protocol II, Arts 7, 8 and 11(1).

[53] CESCR, 'General Comment 14 on the Right to the Highest Attainable Standard of Health (art 12)' (11 August 2000) UN Doc E/C.12/2000/4 explored the core obligations as regards the right to health. They include: (a) to ensure the right of access to health facilities, goods and services on a non-discriminatory basis, especially for vulnerable or marginalised groups; (b) to ensure access to the minimum essential food which is nutritionally adequate and safe, to ensure freedom from hunger to everyone; (c) to ensure access to basic shelter, housing and sanitation, and an adequate supply of safe and potable water; (d) to provide essential drugs, as from time to time defined under the WHO Action Programme on Essential Drugs; and finally, (e) to ensure equitable distribution of all health facilities, goods and services.

[54] Interview 001.

[55] Concluding Observations of the Committee on Economic, Social and Cultural Rights: Croatia (5 December 2001) UN Doc E/C.12/1/Add.73, para 34; Serbia and Montenegro (23 June 2005) UN Doc E/C.12/1/Add.108, paras 33–36, 60–63; Cambodia (12 June 2009) UN Doc E/C.12/KHM/CO/1, paras 32–33; Democratic Republic of Congo (16 December 2009) UN Doc E/C.12/COD/CO/4, para 34; Afghanistan (7 June 2010) UN Doc E/C.12/AFG/CO/2–4, paras 40–42; CESCR, 'Concluding Observations on the Second to Fourth Periodic Report of Rwanda, adopted by the Committee at its Fiftieth Session (29 April–17 May 2013)' (10 June 2013) UN Doc E/C.12/RWA/CO/2–4, para 25.

ICRC-led project of the IRCRCM which ran from 2012 to 2015 and 'aimed at improving the efficiency and delivery of effective and impartial health care in armed conflict and other emergencies'.[56]

Overall, the provision of food, healthcare, shelter and water are clearly linked to the ICRC's traditional mandate, but as conflicts have become protracted, the role of the ICRC has been forced to adapt. The ICRC must provide immediate relief and longer-term sustainable strategies for the provision of healthcare and food, which may require the support of external partners. The custom, under IHL, is to 'allow rapid and unimpeded passage of humanitarian relief for civilians in need, which is impartial in character and conducted without any adverse distinction to their right of control'. The question is whether increasingly long presence and projects can be considered to impede a state's right of control and whether humanitarian protection and assistance be considered to be partial.

## IV. ECONOMIC SECURITY

A decade ago the ICRC Director of Operations, Pierre Krähenbühl, recognised the need for the ICRC to work in the 'full spectrum of conflict situations' and that it needed the 'capacity to sustain longer term commitments in chronic crises, early transitional phases or situations of violence which attract little or no attention' or are out of the spotlight.[57] In this role:

> Its activities range from emergency distributions of food and essential household items to programmes for sustainable food production and micro-economic initiatives. Needs covered include food, shelter, access to health care and education. Economic security activities are closely linked to health, water and habitat programmes. All these activities come within the ICRC's global mission to protect victims of conflict.[58]

The ICRC defines economic security programmes as 'designed to ensure that households and communities have access to the services and resources required to meet their essential economic needs, as defined by their physical

[56] In December 2011 Resolution 5 on healthcare in danger was adopted at the 31st International Conference; healthcare in danger was also a key topic at the 32nd International Conference in December 2015: healthcareindanger.org/hcid-project/; ICRC, 'Health Care in Danger' www.icrc.org/eng/what-we-do/safeguarding-health-care/solution/2013-04-26-hcid-health-care-in-danger-project.htm.

[57] P Krähenbühl, ICRC Director of Operations, 'Challenges for Humanitarian Action in Situations of Armed Conflict and Internal Violence: Statement Council of Delegates of the International Red Cross and Red Crescent Movement, Seoul, Republic of Korea, 16–18 November 2005', www.icrc.org/eng/resources/documents/statement/council-of-delegates-2005-statement-161105.htm.

[58] 'Ensuring Economic Security' (ICRC) www.icrc.org/eng/what-we-do/ensuring-economic-security/overview-economic-security.htm.

condition and social and cultural environment'.[59] In practice, this translates into three different types of intervention: relief, production and structural. Relief interventions are designed to protect lives and livelihoods by providing people in need with the goods and/or services essential for their survival when they can no longer obtain them through their own means. This includes stable access to adequate and nutritional food and household items. Relief also takes into account economic activities, markets, food aid and cultural standards. The ICRC relief interventions focus on shelter conditions, clothing, living conditions, hygiene, water storage, and cooking capacity.

Production interventions aim to protect or enhance a household or community's asset base—its means of production—so that it can maintain or recover its livelihood. This could mean increasing food production capacity, for example by increasing the availability of land, access to means of production such as land, seed, tools or animals, harvest, animal health, livestock management, training, market and consumption of own product. It may also entail the ICRC improving processes and institutional capacity. This may include looking at the existence of services, type of service, quality of services, appropriateness of services, deployment capacity, political will and security. Finally, structural support aims to improve processes and institutions that have a direct influence on a target population's lives and livelihoods, such as agricultural or livestock services.[60] For the ICRC, therefore, these types of intervention span the conflict to post-conflict timeline.

One interviewee was keen to emphasise the importance of including local populations in economic security projects on the ground.[61] The interviewee argued that a wholly top-down approach includes so many stakeholders that the average people on the ground rarely feel the benefits; in some cases, they do not even understand what is happening. The interviewee stated that: '[I]f there is not a sense of ownership within the community, then it is doomed to fail. I am pretty sure about that.'[62] However, another interviewee explained that the EcoSec Unit is more of an aid to the assistance department more broadly and that its work is the first to scale down and withdraw from a situation.[63] Nevertheless, it is important, in this period of time, to help people to get their heads above water, which is already good for the population as a whole.[64]

[59] ICRC, 'Annual Report 2013', https://www.icrc.org/eng/assets/files/annual-report/icrc-annual-report-2013.pdf.
[60] ibid 29.
[61] Interview 001.
[62] Interview 001.
[63] Interview 005.
[64] Interview 001.

The 'official line' from the ICRC is that its work to 'promote economic security aims to ensure that households and communities affected by conflict or armed violence can meet essential needs and maintain or restore sustainable livelihoods'.[65] It relies on its 'statutory right of initiative and on its assessment of the level of organization of the armed groups involved, the scale of humanitarian impact, the support it can provide to National Societies and its own added value'.[66]

Outside of the ICRC, economic security refers to an assured basic income, threats to which include unemployment, temporary work, precarious employment, self-employment, low and insecure income.[67] The CESCR is concerned with unemployment levels in many 'post-conflict' states, including Croatia, Serbia and Montenegro, Cambodia and Rwanda.[68] The inability to ensure economic security can also be linked to the need for education[69] and 'the right to live somewhere in security, peace and dignity'.[70] Moreover, the HDR 1994 crucially linked human security with development and stated that progress in one area leads to progress in the other. Human development is a process of widening the range of choices people have about the way they live their lives and the opportunities afforded to them. To this end, the Commission on Human Security argued that human security and human development 'look out on shared goals but with different scope'.[71] However a 'more secure world' is only possible if poor countries are given a real chance to develop. The High-level Panel Report 2004 recognised that extreme poverty and infectious diseases, for example, threaten many people directly, but also provide a fertile breeding-ground for other threats, including civil conflict.[72]

[65] 'Overview of the ICRC's work to promote economic security' (ICRC, 29 October 2010) www.icrc.org/eng/what-we-do/ensuring-economic-security/overview-economic-security.htm.

[66] ICRC, 'Overview of Operations 2012' (Geneva, ICRC, November 2011) 9.

[67] This is echoed in UDHR, Arts 17 (right to property), 23 (right to work), 24 (right to leisure), 26 (right to education); ICESCR, Arts 6 (right to work), 7 (just work conditions), 8 (right to form trade unions, strike), 9 (right to social security), 10 (protection of the family), 13–14 (right to education); see also CESCR, 'General Comment 13: The Right to Education' (8 December 1999) UN Doc E/C.12/1999/10, para 57.

[68] Croatia Report (n 55) paras 12, 23 and 32; Serbia and Montenegro Report (n 55) paras 16–17; DRC Report (n 55) para 21; Cambodia Report (n 55) paras 21 and 39; Rwanda Report (n 55) para 12.

[69] Under ICESCR, Art 13(2)(a) compulsory primary education shall be free of charge for all. See also CESCR, 'General Comment 11: Plans of Action for Primary Education' (10 May 1999) UN Doc E/C.12/1999/4 para **??**; General Comment 13 (n 67) para 57; DRC Report (n 55) para 35; Cambodia Report (n 55) para 34; Afghanistan Report (n 55) para 43.

[70] CESCR, 'General Comment No 4: The Right to Adequate Housing (Art 11(1) of the Covenant)' (13 December 1991) UN Doc E/1992/23, para 7.

[71] Commission on Human Security, *Human Security Now* (New York, UN Publications, 2003) 10.

[72] Report of the Secretary General's High-Level Panel on Threats, Challenges and Change, 'A More Secure World: Our Shared Responsibility' (2 December 2004) UN Doc A/59/565, viii.

In the days following the publication of 'In Larger Freedom', Kofi-Annan published an article in the *Financial Times* identifying what he saw as the crucial focus of the time as regards security, human rights and development. Annan argued that the UN founders knew that development could only occur under the umbrella of freedom and that political freedom is only available once people have a fair chance of reaching decent living standards. He also argued that the illustrious 'larger freedom' embraces freedom from war and violence and the realisation of one's fundamental rights and dignity in law.[73] To this end, human security recognises the conditions that preclude survival, the continuation of daily life and the dignity of human beings.[74]

The traditional understanding of development was that economic growth, that is, increases in gross national product, was alone sufficient to bring benefit to a population. Over time this assessment came to include socioeconomic indicators, such as employment. The OECD recognised that a myriad of deficiencies preclude socioeconomic development, including weak governance, bad policies, human rights abuses, conflicts, natural disasters and other external shocks. A number of factors compound socioeconomic deficiencies, including the spread of HIV/AIDS, the failure to address inequalities in income, education and access to healthcare, inequalities between men and women, and finally poverty.[75]

The progression from 'development' to 'human development' means that individuals are viewed as subjects, not just objects. Likewise, human security places 'people's well-being as the ultimate end goal and propose[s] that development was not for increasing capital but for advancing people[']s choices, to give them freedom'.[76] Development is about more than income; it is about greater access to knowledge, better nutrition and health services, more secure livelihoods, security against crime and physical violence, satisfying leisure hours, political and cultural freedoms, the sense of participation in community activities, and ultimately, self-respect and dignity. All of which echoes the sentiments of human security, IHRL and IHL. For the UN, therefore, 'the real test, to a growing global population demanding a life of dignity, is the degree to which they

[73] K Annan, 'An Aspiration to a Larger Freedom', op ed, *Financial Times, London*, 21 March 2005.

[74] Human Security Now (n 71) 10.

[75] OECD Development Assistance Committee, 'Shaping the Twenty-first Century: The Contribution of Development Co-operation' (May 1996) www.oecd.org/dac/2508761.pdf; see also UN, IMF, OECD/ Development Assistance Committee and World Bank Group, 'A Better World for All: Progress Towards the International Development Goals' (2000) www.imf.org/external/pubs/ft/jointpub/world/2000/eng/bwae.pdf; UNGA, '1986 Declaration on the Right to Development' (4 December 1986) Res 41/128.

[76] S Tadjbakhsh and AM Chenoy, *Human Security: Concepts and Implications* (London, Routledge, 2007) 104.

are able to enjoy freedom from fear and want, without discrimination',[77] and that 'development includes consideration of decent work, health care, adequate housing, a voice in public decisions, fair institutions of justice, and a sense of personal security'.[78]

Development requires the creation of an environment in which people can engage in ordinary activity. If we look, for example, at recent conflicts, it is likely that schools were either used militarily or that children were unable or unwilling to attend school.[79] This not only prevents children from advancing their education but also limits their learning of valuable life skills. In addition to the disruption of children's education, mass displacement is also a consequence of many armed conflicts. It can also lead to the marginalisation of entire communities and impacts on post-conflict reconstruction as hundreds and thousands of people are displaced and most likely living in poverty. Unfortunately, all of these difficulties facing individuals, families and communities are compounded by the impact of conflicts on the environment, land, natural resources, and access to safe and nutritious food and water.

Human security is therefore a key component in the vocabulary, thinking and practice of international development; in fact, poverty, socioeconomic inequality and violent conflict are closely linked.[80] Indeed, 'lack of economic growth and therefore economic opportunity is often one of the underlying causes of conflict'.[81] Finally, 'the economic impact of civil wars is massive and it has been borne disproportionately by the poorest countries'.[82] An Agenda for Peace in 1992 suggested that insecurity could be resolved by socioeconomic activities.[83] In its most obvious sense this entails employment generation and livelihoods for youth and demobilised former combatants. Socioeconomic development can also include the development of social services (health, education, water and sanitation); rehabilitation of basic infrastructure, such as, reconstruction of roads, bridges and railways; improving transportation; promoting

[77] Report to the Secretary General, 'UN Development Agenda, 'Realizing the Future We Want for All: Report of the UN System Task Team on the Post: 2015 UN Development Agenda' (New York, June 2012) 3.

[78] ibid, 4.

[79] 'UNWRA Strongly Condemns Israeli Shelling of its School in Gaza as a Serious Violation of International Law' (30 July 2014) www.unrwa.org/newsroom/official-statements/unrwa-strongly-condemns-israeli-shelling-its-school-gaza-serious.

[80] FO Hampson, with J Daudelin, J Hay, H Reid and T Martin, *Madness in the Multitude: Human Security and World Disorder* (Oxford, Oxford University Press, 2001) 150.

[81] T Gerstle and L Meissner, *Peace Building Essentials for Economic Development Practitioners: Practice Note 1: Market Development in Conflict-affected Contexts* (London, International Alert, 2009–10) 3.

[82] Hampson et al (n 80) 151.

[83] Report of the Secretary General, 'An Agenda for Peace: Preventive Diplomacy, Peacemaking and Peace-keeping' (17 June 1992) UN Doc A/47/277 -S/24111, paras 56–59 (An Agenda for Peace).

environmental awareness; return and reintegration of displaced persons and refugees; and transitional justice.[84] In addition, it is important that communities reconcile and that community dialogue is re-established or developed. Finally, it is necessary to provide psychological trauma counselling for war-affected groups.[85] The latter is significant as people feel war long after it ends and 'peace' has arrived.

Crucially, economic development can alleviate ethnic tensions, reduce black markets for illicit products and overturn elite capture of natural resources, bringing warring groups together for trade; ex-combatants can be trained for jobs so they are less likely to instigate conflicts and economic alternatives to the production of narcotics can be promotede.[86] Economic development can therefore be used to build relationships and trust between people, thus addressing the root causes of conflicts and, hopefully, preventing their recurrence. However, socioeconomic development may often be limited to states embarking on mutually beneficial economic and social development projects[87] or to reaching 'entrenched macroeconomic benchmarks for social progress at the global level that have been utilised since the founding of the UN'.[88] Such grandiose visions need not be the only efforts to establish socioeconomic development. It is important for communities recovering from armed conflict to see real progress in the socioeconomic development of their daily lives, which is where the economic security projects of the ICRC are so important.

Collier has argued that stagnant economies are likely to rely on primary commodities and post-conflict countries are likely to return to conflict within a year. The question therefore is whether economic recovery should come after relief operations or whether this just creates a culture of dependency.[89] When the ICRC actively engages in a country that has

[84] Department of Peacekeeping Operations and Department of Field Support, 'United Nations Peacekeeping Operations: Principles and Guidelines' (18 January 2008) 25; Report of the Secretary General, 'Peace Building in the Immediate Aftermath of Conflict' (11 June 2009) UN Doc A/63/881–S/2009/304, paras 17 and 54; see also S Lewarne and D Snelbecker, 'Economic Governance in War-torn Economies: Lessons Learned from the Marshall Plan to the Reconstruction of Iraq: Long Report' (2004) prepared for US AID Bureau for Policy and Program Coordination (US AID, Washington DC 2004) 5.

[85] Report of the Secretary General, 'No Exit without Strategy: Security Council Decision-making and the Closure or Transition of United Nations Peacekeeping Operations' (20 April 2001) UN Doc S/2001/394 (No Exit Without Strategy) para 21.

[86] J Banfield, C Gündüz and N Killick (eds), *Local Business, Local Peace: The Peace Building Potential of the Domestic Private Sector* (London, International Alert, 2006) in Gerstle and Meissner (n 81) 4.

[87] Agenda for Peace (n 83) para 56.

[88] J Moore, *Humanitarian Law in Action within Africa* (Oxford, Oxford University Press, 2012) 77; See also UNGA, 'United Nations Millennium Declaration' (8 September 2000) Res 55/2 (A/55/L.2) para 19.

[89] P Collier and A Hoeffler, 'On Economic Causes of Civil War' (1998) 50(4) *Oxford Economic Papers* 563, 563–73; See also P Collier, *The Bottom Billion: Why the Poorest Countries are Failing and What Can Be Done About It* (Oxford, Oxford University Press, 2008).

seen 'populations largely affected with loss of livelihoods' it will deploy its EcoSec Unit, which comes under the 'assistance' umbrella of ICRC activities.[90] One interviewee stated that: '[O]nce the political situation stabilises a bit then [the ICRC] might think of other types of activities … usually EcoSec is the first department to withdraw.'[91] Put another way:

> If the level of conflict and violence decreases and people have access to markets, to employment and to normal exchange mechanisms, we will end our work rather quickly. If, however, the presence of violence and conflict restricts the access of the civilian population to things like markets and work and they're forced to migrate or to be displaced, then we will continue the programmes. That's a bit of a crude differentiation to make, but that's broadly how it works.[92]

## V. LOCAL OWNERSHIP

The ICRC is in a unique position to gain access to communities because its promises of independence and neutrality find favour with states. In addition, the ICRC's national societies build ground-level links with communities and include many local volunteers. The ICRC is well placed to engage in capacity-building amongst the local population and to eventually pass projects onto the local community. The ICRC 'offers its expertise and practical experience of conflicts to help governments meet their responsibilities by passing legislation, training the armed forces and the police and promoting international humanitarian law at universities and among young people'.[93] It undertakes this role through its Advisory Service.

One of the most important aspects of the ICRC, therefore, is its ongoing presence in states during and after conflicts. Its Headquarters Agreements provide it with the ability to establish field offices, deploy staff, and develop humanitarian protection and assistance projects, all of which may continue when conflict ends. The amount of financing for the operation and the number of staff may fluctuate depending on circumstances but its presence can continue. It is therefore well placed, at all times, to learn from locals about the situation on the ground and respond accordingly. However, one interviewee noted that:

> [T]o get access is a bit more complicated in some regions than it was in the past. Now, whether we have more access to places of detention or that type of thing, it's not really easy to assess when you're not directly working on those. But overall, in terms of access, I think we have a number of contacts when the

[90] Interview 005.
[91] Interview 005.
[92] Interview 006.
[93] ICRC, 'Building Respect for the Law' (1 May 2011) https://www.icrc.org/eng/what-we-do/building-respect-ihl/overview-building-respect-ihl.htm.

> situations are difficult [we are] taking more precautions and being more cautious than we used to be and having to do much more networking, etc, than we used to do in the past.... It's probably a responsibility of everyone in the field and beyond to make sure that we can gather as much information as possible. But we have special delegates dedicated to that aspect of things to make sure that we can have those links and we build the relationships, be it through our detention activities, be it through other types of contacts that we can develop with local communities, with local leaders, with armed groups.[94]

Part of the ICRC's humanitarian diplomacy role

> [c]omprises developing a network of close bilateral or multilateral, official or informal relations with the protagonists of armed conflicts and disturbances, and with any other State, non-State actor or influential agent, in order to foster heightened awareness of the plight of victims of armed conflicts, support for the ICRC's humanitarian action and respect for humanitarian law. The ICRC's humanitarian diplomacy consists chiefly in making the voices of the victims of armed conflicts and disturbances heard, in negotiating humanitarian agreements with international or national players, in acting as a neutral intermediary between them and in helping to prepare and ensure respect for humanitarian law.[95]

In terms of making the voices of victims heard, the ICRC works to establish dialogue with local people who were present in the state before and after the conflict. Local people know the root causes of the conflict, can see whether tensions still run high, and know what actions could stop a conflict recurring. Security concerns differ from conflict to conflict and therefore local people can identify specific actions that will bring security.

Local ownership can be defined as a process where the solutions to a particular society's needs are developed in concert with the people who are going to live with, and uphold, these solutions in the long run.[96] Accordingly, peace must be built simultaneously from the top down, bottom up and middle out.[97] In situations following armed conflicts, local people develop their 'own strategies to cope with the debilitating circumstances of post-war spaces; living life at the level of the "everyday", local people have shaped peace through cooperative activity and enterprising

[94] Interview 007.

[95] M Harrof-Tavel, 'The Humanitarian Diplomacy of the International Committee of the Red Cross' https://www.icrc.org/eng/assets/files/other/humanitarian-diplomacy-icrc.pdf. The original of this article was published in French in (2005) 121 *Relations Internationales* 72–89.

[96] A Hansen and S Wiharta, 'The Transition to a Just Order: Establishing Local Ownership After Conflict, A Policy Report' (Stockholm, Folke Bernadotte Academy, 2007) x.

[97] JP Lederach, 'Civil Society and Reconciliation' in CA Crocker, FO Hampson and P Aall, *Turbulent Peace, The Challenges of Managing International Conflict* (Washington DC, Institute of Peace, 2001) 843.

endeavours involving significant degrees of agency often overlooked by external peace builders'.[98] Moreover, Pouligny argues that:

> Whatever is done, on the ground, locally, on the streets and in the apartment blocks and villages, some form of regularised social interaction will begin to emerge, whether imposed or not. This is community, not as utopian or communitarian goal, but community in reality.[99]

'Bottom-up approaches', which engage in dialogue and engagement with individual community members, understand 'identity, ideas, [and] knowledge' and can therefore deliver genuine human security.[100] Local ownership can and should be context specific, that is, 'determined by and tailored to the diversity of political, social, and economic factors'.[101] Oxfam reported, for example, that in Afghanistan 'land and water cause disputes. As do family and tribal affiliations and with arms widely available the disagreements can easily escalate and flare into violence.'[102] Indeed, the issue of the availability of arms in post-conflict situations is regularly referred to as an issue perpetuating local insecurity.[103] It is these context-specific dilemmas that require local knowledge from international organisation and NGOs, in addition to local ownership to create sustainable peace.

The local community incorporates civil society organisations, such as trade unions, business associations, faith-based organisations, issue-specific advocacy coalitions, and other organisational forms and domestic actors. All of which are essential for the establishment of sustainable peace. The idea of 'local' has many definitions, for Anderson and Olsen, there is a distinction between insiders and outsiders: They define as:

> [Insiders are t]hose vulnerable to the conflict, because they are from the area and living there, or people who in some other way must experience the conflict and live with its consequences personally. ... [Outsiders are those] who choose to become involved in a conflict [and who] have personally little to lose.[104]

[98] O Richmond, 'Resistance and Post-Liberal Peace' (2010) 38 *Millennium Journal of International Studies* 665, 665–92.

[99] B Pouligny, 'Local Ownership' in V Chetail (ed), *Post-conflict Peace Building: A Lexicon* (Oxford, Oxford University Press, 2009) 179–80.

[100] E Conteh-Morgan, 'Peace Building and Human Security: A Constructivist Perspective' (2005) 10(1) *International Journal of Peace Studies* 69, 72.

[101] W Boyce, M Koros and J Hodgson, 'Community Based Rehabilitation: A Strategy for Peace-building' (2002) *BMC International Health and Human Rights* 216 in Pouligny (n 99) 181.

[102] Oxfam, 'Local Peace Building Urgently Needed to Reduce Insecurity in Afghanistan' (27 February 2008).

[103] C McEvoy and R Murray, 'Gauging Fear and Insecurity: Perspectives on Armed Violence in Eastern Equatoria and Turkana North' (Geneva, Small Arms Survey, Graduate Institute of International and Development Studies, 2008) 22–28; OH Rolandsen, 'Land, Security and Peace Building in the Southern Sudan' (Oslo, PRIO Paper, International Peace Research Institute, December 2009) 2 and 13; See also M Waldman, 'Community Peace Building in Afghanistan: The Case for a National Strategy' (Oxfam International Research Report, February 2008).

[104] M Anderson and L Olsen, *Confronting War: Critical Lessons for Peace Practitioners* (Cambridge, The Collaborative for Development Action Inc, 2003) 32.

Lederach has argued that local people must not automatically be seen as the problem and the outsider as the answer.[105] It is possible that on initial intervention outsiders could actually exacerbate local insecurity. When international actors enter states, often in their hundreds and thousands, they occupy space no longer available to local actors. They may also often have a detrimental effect on local economies, as they create, 'large increases in salaries, prices in the stores, and house rents—impeding local organizations from functioning properly'.[106] The international actors work away from their 'normal' life and enter into an environment, rife with prejudices and insecurity. In these circumstances international actors may fail to ascertain, let alone address, grievances and problems and therefore long-term security remains elusive.[107]

The ICRC must overcome such limits to truly protect and assist local people. In fact, the emphasis should be on international actors making themselves aware of and working with people on the ground, including political, military, economic actors and members of the indigenous 'civil society'.[108] However, it is recognised that grass-root stakeholders are often excluded from efforts to recover from conflict, as they are 'consulted only as a predetermined template for reform, often mere observers of the process'.[109] This may be, in part, because of a lack of understanding of the situation by outsiders and an assumption that international intervention, in particular for the purposes of democratisation and the establishment of the rule of law, will ensure post-conflict peace and security. The concern is that outsiders, in particular the UN, only reflect their own principles, interests and priorities.[110] The priorities of the local community are different from those of international actors. The ICRC should, theoretically, be viewed in a different manner to the UN due to the ICRC's principles of independence and neutrality, which are embedded in the organisation to ensure a universal approach to all people during and after conflict.

[105] JP Lederach, *Preparing for Peace: Conflict Transformation Across Cultures* (New York, Syracuse University Press, 1995) 212.

[106] Pouligny (n 99) 182.

[107] A Truger, 'Operationalisation through Training: Human Security Training and Education for Peace Building' in W Benedek, MC Ketteman and M Möstl (eds), *Mainstreaming Human Security in Peace Operations and Crisis Management: Policies, Problems, Potential* (London, Routledge, 2011) 126.

[108] No Exit Without Strategy (n 85) paras 10–12; R Orr, 'Governing When Chaos Rules: Enhancing Governance and Participation' (2002) 25(4) *Washington Quarterly* 140, 140; T Keating and A Knight (eds), *Building Sustainable Peace* (UN UP, 2004) xxxi; N Lemay-Hebert, 'The "Empty-Shell" Approach: The Setup Process of International Administrations in Timor-Leste and Kosovo, its Consequences and Lessons' (2011) 12 *International Studies Perspectives* 190, 190–211.

[109] C Cubitt, *Local and Global Dynamics of Peace Building: Post-conflict Reconstruction in Sierra Leone* (Oxon, Routledge, 2011) 58; Pouligny (n 99) 176.

[110] Pouligny (n 99) 177; See also D Curtis, 'The International Peace Building Paradox: Power Sharing and Post-Conflict Governance in Burundi' (2012) *African Affairs* 72, 72–91.

Pouligny has argued that in rural villages and city neighbourhoods, disarmament, demobilisation and reintegration (DRR), that is, reintegration of former combatants into civil society, and return and reintegration of displaced people and refugees, are generally the top priorities in which local communities ask for empowerment, but so far, with very few exceptions, this has not been put into practice.[111] Furthermore, because outsiders intervene in an unknown, often still highly insecure environment, outsiders tend actually to collaborate with other outsiders, in a largely closed circle, partially isolated from the 'real world'.[112] Autesserre notes that international agencies tend to recruit staff on the basis of their technical expertise. There are many situations, therefore, when 'newly hired staff members benefit, at best, from a few days briefing on the country. Most interveners therefore lack reliable information on current events.'[113]

In light of the above analysis, this chapter now turns to consider the interview data collected, as regards local ownership established by ICRC involvement. When asked about the issue of lack of local knowledge, the interviewees were keen to convey that ICRC delegates are well prepared before they are deployed to conflict areas. When pushed on this matter, however, it was admitted that, because the ICRC has been present for many years in some conflicts, in particular the DRC, the training is rather brief as the assumption is that the ICRC delegate will understand the situation on the ground.[114]

The ICRC is 'trying to build an environment that is safer for the people'.[115] The first thing the ICRC does when it arrives in an area is to 'have a discussion with the community to understand what is their perception of the problem is'.[116] This is to ensure that projects are not wholly designed elsewhere, which is a mistake that the ICRC and others have made in the past.[117] If an organisation is offering to help a community in an area suffering conflict or in the post-conflict stage, then the community will say 'yes' to everything.[118] The ICRC has to think about the long-term sustainability of projects—for example, if it agrees with a community to restart agriculture in a volatile environment, then it has to consider that the farmers will quite likely flee should fighting restart.[119] The ICRC has to develop projects that can be adapted should the situation on the ground change.

[111] Pouligny (n 99) 177.

[112] B Pouligny, 'Civil Society and Post-Conflict Peace Building: Ambiguities of International Programmes Aimed at Building 'New Societies'' (2005) 36(4) *Security Dialogue* 495, 501.

[113] S Autesserre, 'Dangerous Tales: Dominant Narratives on the Congo and their Unintended Consequences' (2012) 111(443) *African Affairs* 202, 208.

[114] Interview 002.

[115] Interview 002.

[116] Interview 001.

[117] Interview 001.

[118] Interview 001.

[119] Interview 001.

The intention of the ICRC is 'to be as close as possible to the field ... to get its own understanding of what is going on'.[120] In order to understand the situation, the ICRC retains dialogue with actors on the ground. These issues affect where the ICRC works; it has purposely chosen, for example, not to be involved in internally displaced person (IDP) camps because as soon as there are settlements close to urban settings there are a huge number of organisations willing to work there.[121] Moreover, it is pertinent to retain contact with groups in need because if the ICRC reaches a community and decides to engage in programmes, then there are essential follow-up activities.[122]

Another interviewee gave the example of the ICRC's work in Columbia:

> When the ICRC works with gang leaders, which are responsible for some neighbourhoods, the ICRC tries to get them to be more careful with their own inhabitants and the ICRC can have a dialogue on their responsibility as the local authority there. Sometimes the situation improves for the people and [the ICRC] priority remains to be there.[123]

Interviewees recognised that:

> Probably all activities allowing more stability will in one way or another have an effect on the peace process ... but the aim of the ICRC is not to be involved in the peace process. We are working much more on the consequences of the conflict and their resolutions.[124]

> Sometimes, for example, ICRC activities can have an impact on the reconciliation between communities, which can, in turn, stabilise the situation, in particular when there are insufficient means to live.[125]

## A. ICRC and National Societies

If we return briefly to the analysis in chapter 1, the ICRC benefits from its relationship with other components of the IRCRCM. It is argued, in particular, that national societies greatly benefit the local impact of ICRC protection and assistance work, due to their proximity to armed conflict and issues pertaining to human insecurity. The ICRC works with national societies when re-establishing family links of people displaced during military operations. This can include 'repatriation, family reunification,

[120] Interview 001.
[121] Interview 001.
[122] Interview 001.
[123] Interview 002.
[124] Interview 003.
[125] Interview 004.

and sometimes cross border family reunification'.[126] Interviewees frequently referred to the relationship between the ICRC and the national societies, creating the impression that the national societies are frequently relied often.[127] One interviewee stated that the national societies' 'network and number of volunteers scattered throughout the country is huge and allows [them] to reach out [to] a lot of families… when it comes to cross border issues [the ICRC] will engage the National Societies on both sides'.[128] It also became apparent in an interview at the ICRC that the UN also engages with the national societies.[129] The ICRC therefore interacts and works with communities and individuals on the ground to try and bring protection and assistance to those in need. One interviewee highlighted that the ICRC is

> [c]onsulting with more National Societies… to push them to participate, to get ready, to contribute. But at the end of the day, it's still a question of resources. It's easier for the British Red Cross to put items on the agenda or to propose things than for a National Society, or whatever, in a poor country in Africa. That's obvious, because they don't have the resources, because it's far away from their daily business or their day-to-day interests. So it's still a bit unbalanced in the way it is organised, prepared, conducted, but the objective is really to make those meetings real movement meetings and not a few who are happy or not so happy organising and doing everything.[130]

> In the ICRC's perception of the world, that started more than ten years ago when we realised that, in fact, we needed more and we will continue needing more National Societies as our partners to conduct our operations. That's the bottom line, basically. The objective is not to be nice to our movement partners for the sake of it, but because we are convinced that we should be working together more closely to have a better impact on the populations we're mandated to assist.[131]

Another interviewee regarded national societies as 'operational partners'.[132] This interviewee noted that:

> The National Societies are less likely to be involved in detention visits and protection of civilians but in every other activity you would find volunteers from the Congolese Red Cross. I mean, it's amazing. For family links, the volunteers are the ones doing the last mile, basically, because we are going to centralise the Red Cross message or the request, but we will go to a central point and then it will be basically a volunteer taking a bicycle and going to the last mountain, the

[126] Interview 001.
[127] Interview 002; Interview 003; Interview 004.
[128] Interview 001.
[129] Interview 002.
[130] Interview 007.
[131] Interview 007
[132] Interview 010.

last trees. It's literally like that. I mean, they will go and look for the families, so the work that they are doing is absolutely amazing.[133]

## VI. PREVENTION OF CONFLICT

Finally, this chapter turns to the question of whether the ICRC mandate to protect and assist can contribute to efforts to prevent recurrence of hostilities

> Owing to the constraints imposed by the principle of neutrality, the ICRC cannot play a role in political negotiations aimed at averting an imminent armed conflict, but it can on occasion make a significant contribution through preventive humanitarian diplomacy, its good offices and creative use of its role as a neutral intermediary.[134]

Moreover, the ICRC can 'play an important part in the prevention of renewed conflict, by helping to establish conditions conducive to reconciliation and social reconstruction it helps to consolidate peace' and 'carry out vital work on a long-term basis'.[135] In terms of human security, the prevention of future hostilities is closely linked to the concepts of freedom from fear and freedom from want. If armed conflict can be prevented it precludes people from suffering during and after conflict. Pragmatically, as Brahimi argued, it also saves the international community money and resources as it need not launch military intervention, provide emergency humanitarian relief or facilitate reconstruction after the conflict.[136] Those who favour focusing on the underlying causes of conflicts argue that such crisis-related efforts often prove either too little or too late. Attempted earlier, however, diplomatic initiatives may be rebuffed by a government that does not see or will not acknowledge a looming problem, or that may itself be part of the problem. Thus, long-term preventive strategies are a necessary complement to short-term initiatives.[137]

Broadly speaking, prevention requires relationship building, prejudice reduction, power sharing, socioeconomic equality, education and preventive diplomacy, including communication, negotiation and mediation. The latter requires the establishment of person-to-person interactions that

133 Interview 010.

134 International Red Cross Red Crescent 'Preventive Action: Understanding the Concept and Defining the ICRC's role in Preventing Armed Conflicts: Guidelines' (2002) 84(846) *IRRC* 463, 465.

135 ibid 466.

136 L Brahimi (Chairman of the Panel on United Nations Peace Operations) 'Report of the Panel on United Nations Peace Operations'(21 August 2000) UN Doc A/55/305-S/2000/809 (Brahimi Report 2000) para 29.

137 ibid, para 16.

focus on increasing understanding and functional cooperation between groups or states embroiled in destructive conflict.[138] Prevention may be crisis oriented and endeavour to strengthen political settlements and to address the cause of conflict. In order to prevent the violent escalation of crisis as early as possible and to achieve sustainable results, this approach has to cover all stages of the conflict cycle: crisis prevention, crisis intervention and post-conflict rehabilitation.[139] If we look to peace-building, for example, the 'stabilisation' imperative of peace building is to prevent relapse into violence and de-escalation, protection of civilians and promotion of political processes.[140] If local people are to recover from violence, even structural violence that has not yet led to massive civil unrest, then it is necessary to create a secure environment where resort to violence and destruction does not occur.[141] The possibility of conflict must therefore be detected early. Truger suggests that detection could be undertaken using a 'standardised assessment matrix', which would classify crisis situations and determine when to take preventative measures or intervene.[142] However, in order to prove effective, such a mechanism would need to take into account the specific circumstances and conditions.[143]

Notwithstanding the complexities of protracted armed conflict, the ICRC recognises that megatrends, such as climate change, natural disasters, environmental degradation, migration, pandemics and rampant urbanisation, have led to 'more and new manifestations of organized armed violence, many of which will lie below the threshold at which IHL starts to apply'.[144] They include, for example, state repression or inter-community violence.[145] 'Organised armed violence' can include transnational organised crime, sudden onset crisis and state repression that may not amount to armed conflict.[146] There has been 'widespread proliferation of weapons by mass migration from rural to urban settings, resulting in sprawling urban centres in many developing countries'.[147] There is consequently a blurred distinction between political violence and criminality.

[138] RJ Fisher, 'The Potential for Peacebuilding: Forging a Bridge from Peacekeeping to Peacemaking' (1993) 18 *Peace and Change* 247, 252.

[139] Truger (n 107) 127.

[140] D Neubert, 'The "Peacemakers" Dilemma: The Role of NGOs in Processes of Peace-building in Decentralised Conflicts' in M-C Foblets and T von Trotha, *Healing the Wounds: Essays on the Reconstruction of Societies after War* (Oxford, Hart, 2004) 54; DJ Francis, (ed), *When War Ends: Building Peace in Divided Communities* (Farnham, Ashgate, 2012) 4.

[141] H-W Jeong, *Peace Building in Post Conflict Societies: Strategy and Process* (Boulder, CO, Lynne Rienner, 2005) 4.

[142] Truger (n 107) 124.

[143] ibid.

[144] ICRC Strategy 2011–14, 4.

[145] ibid, 6.

[146] ICRC, 'Overview of Operations 2006' (Geneva, ICRC, 2006) 2.

[147] ibid.

The ICRC's voyage into such protection and assistance roles, that is, before IHL starts to apply, shows its ability to venture into the realm of preventing the recurrence of hostilities. Of course, prevention of armed conflicts is inextricably linked to addressing the root causes of those conflicts. Broadly speaking, economic factors such as poverty and frustration of human needs, access to political and economic participation, and resource and other environmental issues (eg food insecurity) can be causes of conflict. Human rights violations can also create conflict, in particular, denial of cultural and religious expression.[148] Peck argues that these matters are best precluded and resolved at state level, as this will 'provide the greatest human security to their populations'.[149] In addition, local people require social and structural transformation during and after conflict to establish security. Social transformation looks at psychological, spiritual, social, economic, political and military changes. It is more than post-accord reconstruction.[150] According to Lederach: '[A] sustainable transformative approach suggests that the key lies in the relationship of the involved parties, with all that term encompasses at the psychological, spiritual, social, economic, political and military levels.'[151]

## VII. CONCLUSION

The mandated activities of the ICRC are contained in the Geneva Conventions I, II, III and IV 1949 and the ICRC Statutes but it has been shown that the ICRC has developed its role to deal with other situations of violence and nowadays longer-term assistance roles. The ICRC has traditionally interpreted its role under the Common Article 3 and Articles 9, 9, 9 and 10 Geneva Conventions I, II, III and IV 1949, respectively, to include visiting detainees, administering a tracing and messaging service, and providing healthcare to wounded and sick soldiers during armed conflict. The ICRC now undertakes roles in protracted armed conflict, including prevention work, early recovery and economic security. In this regard, this chapter has shown the connections between the current activities of the ICRC and human security. As some of these activities are not specifically

[148] Brahimi Report 2000 (n 137) para 24.

[149] C Peck, *Sustainable Peace: The Role of the United Nations and Regional Organizations in Preventing Conflict* (Oxford, Rowman & Little, 1998) ch 2.

[150] JP Lederach, 'Conflict Transformation in Protracted Internal Conflicts: The Case for a Comprehensive Framework' in K Rupesinghe (ed), *Conflict Transformation* (New York, Macmillan, 1995) 201–22.

[151] JP Lederach, *Building Peace: Sustainable Reconciliation in Divided Societies* (Washington DC, US Institute of Peace Press, 1997) 75.

identified in the articles listed above, the ICRC may be able to justify its activities under Article 81(1) Additional Protocol I 1977, which states that it may undertake '*any other humanitarian activities* in favour of these victims, subject to the consent of the Parties to the conflict concerned'. It is the 'consent' requirement of this provision that keeps this author wondering about the sustainability of economic security activities. Even if economic security can be subsumed under '*any other humanitarian activities*', consent may be revoked or denied if states see the ICRC as buying into politicised models of socioeconomic development.

The changes in protection and assistance roles show recognition by the ICRC of the changing needs of the local people, in particular civilians, during protracted armed conflict, and the relevance of a broader understanding of humanity to its role. The ICRC engages in practices that can support or encourage peace, in particular economic security. This chapter also considered the Cluster Working Group on Early Recovery definition of 'early recovery', which includes

> assessing, planning, mobilizing resources, implementing and monitoring activities; supporting spontaneous recovery initiatives of affected populations; supporting capacity of national actors to manage and implement the recovery process; influencing the way humanitarian assistance is provided to avoid dependencies; capitalizing on opportunities to reduce risk; and establishing strong foundations for recovery and sustainable development.[152]

The ICRC responds to these elements by entering into a dialogue with national societies and local communities when it is establishing projects for protection, assistance and economic security. The ICRC can also establish 'spontaneous recovery initiatives' when it is led by demand on the ground. It supports national actors through its relationships with national societies and works to avoid dependency by creating ongoing economic projects, which will be discussed in greater depth in the case study on the DRC. There are additional elements to socioeconomic development, for example, development of social services (health, education, water and sanitation), which will also be discussed in the case study.

In terms of the ICRC's ability to facilitate local ownership, the results showed that the ICRC, overall, is more concerned with reaching the needs of victims of conflict and other situations of violence than strictly sticking to the Geneva Conventions I, II, III and IV 1949 and ICRC Statutes description of its rights and duties, in part because, it is necessary to work with local people to determine which needs should be addressed and take priority. The first job for the ICRC on the ground is to meet with local communities and design with, not for, the needs of those people. The ICRC

[152] 'Implementing Early Recovery' (n 37) 1.

therefore recognises the advantages of a 'bottom-up approach', as local people understand the conflict, recognise escalating tensions and human insecurities, and provide context to the situations. The interviews showed that the ICRC works alongside national societies, supporting their local knowledge and continued presence. However, it was acknowledged that, for long-term projects, the support of the authorities in each area in which the ICRC works is also essential. The success, or otherwise, of ICRC activities will be considered in the case study.

# *Case Study: Accounts of ICRC Delegates on the Democratic Republic of Congo*[1]

For decades, the people of the Congo have been tormented by the chaos of wars, conflicts and corruption. And whilst Congolese soil is exceptionally fertile and rich in raw materials such as copper, cobalt, gold, diamonds, coltan and oil, its people do not really reap the benefits. Indeed, the vast majority live in abject poverty. In the east of the country, one of Africa's bloodiest conflicts has claimed the lives of millions and the region remains in turmoil to this day. With looting, rape and murder commonplace, people have no option but to escape. As for the human rights situation, it is quite simply catastrophic.[2]

## I. INTRODUCTION

THE CURRENT SITUATION in the DRC is a conflation of a myriad of armed conflicts that began in Burundi, Uganda and the Sudan during the 1990s.[3] Various peace agreements have attempted to bring peace to the region, but since the armed conflict consists of many sub-conflicts fuelled by private, social and economic interests, no resolution has been reached. The ICRC has had a permanent mission in DRC since 1978. It works to promote respect for IHL amongst warring factions, facilitate the treatment of civilians and detainees, and provide relief to civilians affected by the armed conflict. It also works to improve water supplies and sanitation, and strengthen healthcare for the wounded and sick, including victims of sexual violence.[4] It also continues to reunify families.[5] The significance of its long presence is that the ICRC has a number of projects and has adapted its humanitarian protection and assistance roles

[1] I would like to thank Emma Robson (University of Lincoln) for her research assistance on this chapter in summer 2016.

[2] 'Between Frontlines: ICRC Delegates at Work' (ICRC, DRC) icrc.srf.ch/en/kongo#/introduction.

[3] G Prunier, *Africa's World War Congo, the Rwandan Genocide and the Making of a Continental Catastrophe* (Oxford, Oxford University Press, 2009) xxxi.

[4] 'The ICRC in DR Congo' (ICRC) www.icrc.org/eng/where-we-work/africa/congo-kinshasa/index.jsp.

[5] ibid.

on the ground in response to the fluidity of the conflict. It also means that, as the entire state has not been 'at war' for the entire period since 1978, the ICRC undertakes projects in situations not amounting to armed conflict.

In terms of its mandate the DRC is a microcosm of the ICRC mandate from the Geneva Conventions I, II, III and IV 1949 and the IRCRCM Statutes. That is, the DRC is, in some respects, an example of shifting trends in ICRC practice generally, for example towards more long-term humanitarian projects, such as Health Care in Danger.[6] On the other hand, the ICRC has adapted its mandate in the DRC to respond to the specific case of sexual violence and provide projects on the ground for victims of such, which will be considered in this case study.

In the DRC, the ICRC works to meet the emergency needs of those affected by armed conflict. The ICRC Annual Report 2013 identifies the organisation's role as follows:

> It meets the emergency needs of conflict-affected IDPs and residents, assists them in becoming self-sufficient and helps ensure that the wounded and sick receive adequate medical/surgical care, including psychological support. It visits detainees, helps restore contact between separated relatives, reunites children with their families and supports the Red Cross Society of the Democratic Republic of the Congo's development. It also promotes knowledge of and respect for IHL and international human rights law among the authorities.[7]

In 2009 the ICRC undertook research in eight countries, including the DRC, to 'develop a better understanding of people's needs and expectations, to gather views and opinions, and to give a voice to those who had been adversely affected by armed conflict and other situations of armed conflict'.[8] The research identified two 'priority actions' that the respondents in the DRC wanted to communicate to the rest of the world:

> The international community should use its power to force the local and neighboring governments to find a peaceful settlement and despite the fact that the armed conflict has continued for so long, civilians still need the most basic assistance to help them survive and rebuild their lives.[9]

This case study will examine, therefore, whether the humanitarian mission of the ICRC is having positive effects in communities and regions of the DRC, bringing stabilisation and human security to pockets of a country overwhelmed by conflict and insecurity. This case study focuses on the

[6] Health Care in Danger, healthcareindanger.org/hcid-project/.

[7] ICRC, 'Annual Report 2013' https://www.icrc.org/eng/assets/files/annual-report/icrc-annual-report-2013.pdf, 135–41.

[8] ICRC, 'Democratic Republic of the Congo: Opinion Survey and In-depth Research, 2009' (Geneva, December 2009) 1.

[9] ibid, 10.

experiences of the people on the ground throughout these difficult times by building on conclusions drawn in the preceding chapters of this book. To this end, this case study will test whether the role of the ICRC, in practice, goes beyond the roles prescribed in the Geneva Conventions I, II, III and IV 1949 and the ICRC Statutes, and whether there is evidence of the ICRC undertaking human security activities. The case study continues the analysis of interviews undertaken at the ICRC Headquarters, Geneva, in April 2014.

## II. THE CONGO WARS IN BRIEF: 1994–2016

This brief outline provides a timeline of major events in the DRC over the last twenty years. Its purpose is simply to provide context to the analysis of the protection and assistance work of the ICRC in the region. There are excellent texts by Stearns and Autesserre that provide a more comprehensive overview of the conflicts.[10]

The situation in the DRC is the 'largest conflict Africa has seen since independence'.[11] The First Congo War took place during the aftermath of the Rwandan genocide and ended with toppling of President Mobutu in May 1997.[12] Mobutu had seized power from Patrice Lumumba in 1965, just five years after the Congo became an independent state.[13] In fact, Mobutu had been Chief-of-Staff to Prime Minister Lumumba. Mobutu's rule lasted for thirty-two years, 'during which time the Republic of Congo's economic infrastructure was completely dismantled—at times literally being sold for scrap—gaining it an infamous repute for excessive corruption'.[14] Chapter 5 above considered the concept of sovereignty of responsibility and its connection to human security. In the context of the DRC, the idea that leaders of states can no longer shun the outside world and use state territory for their own gains or use sovereignty as a shield against the acts committed against the people is critically important. The independence

[10] JK Stearns, *Dancing in the Glory of Monsters: The Collapse of the Congo and the Great War of Africa* (New York, Public Affairs, 2011); S Autesserre, *The Trouble with the Congo: Local Violence and the Failure of International Peacebuilding* (Cambridge, Cambridge Studies in International Relations, 2010).

[11] T Carayannis, 'The Democratic Republic of the Congo, 1996–2012' in J Boulden (ed), *Responding to Conflict in Africa: The United Nations and Regional Organisations* (Basingstoke, Palgrave Macmillan, 2013) 177.

[12] Stearns (n 10) 153–62.

[13] G Kreijen, *State Failure, Sovereignty and Effectiveness: Legal Lessons from the Decolonisation of Sub-Saharan Africa (Developments in International Law)* (Leiden, Martinus Nijhoff, 2004) 74; Stearns (n 10) 61–64.

[14] Kreijen (n 13).

of the DRC in the 1960s did not protect the people from acts of brutality against them, which had been the situation under Belgian rule.[15]

When the Tutsi-led Rwandan Patriotic Front (RPF), led by Paul Kagame, seized power in Rwanda in 1994, two million Hutus fled to North Sivu and South Kivu, provinces situated in the east of the DRC.[16] Congolese of Rwandan descent allied with the new Rwandan government.[17] The groups of people who are indigenous to the DRC allied themselves into militias called Mai-Mai, eventually supporting defeated Rwandan Hutu rebels and the Congolese government.[18] The decline and collapse of the Zairian/Congolese state permitted the Hutu to continue their struggle against the RPF from Congo. During the Rwandan genocide and the period afterwards, the ICRC was helping protect and assist displaced people and providing food aid. The ICRC also supported health facilities.[19] The RPF responded to Hutu attacks.[20] The result of the violence in the region was that, in 1996, a regional coalition led by Angola, Uganda and Rwanda formed to overthrow Mobutu.[21] In April 1997, the DRC saw the fall of Lubumbashi and Kikwit, and by May of the same year, Kinshasa fell.[22] Following a failed attempt at peace talks, Laurent Kabila was sworn in as president on 16 May 1997 and, very quickly, Mobutu fled into exile.[23]

Unfortunately for the Congolese people, the new president, Laurent Kabila, fell out with his Rwandan and Ugandan allies, which sparked the Second Congo War.[24] The DRC, Angola, Namibia, Zimbabwe, Sudan and Chad fought against, Rwanda, Uganda and Burundi. There were also around thirty local militias involved in the war.[25] This second conflict lasted until the Final Act of the Inter-Congolese Dialogue on 2 April 2003.[26] The process leading up to this Act was rather complex and is therefore discussed below.

[15] A Hochschild, *King Leopold's Ghost: A Story of Greed, Terror, and Heroism in Colonial Africa* (Boston, MA, Houghton Mifflin Harcourt, 1999).

[16] L Arimatsu, 'The Democratic Republic of the Congo 1993–2010' in E Wilmshurst (ed), *International Law and the Classification of Conflicts* (Oxford, Oxford University Press, 2012) 148–50.

[17] Autesserre (n 10) 7.

[18] ibid, 161–68.

[19] ICRC, *ICRC Activities in Zaire/Democratic Republic of Congo: 1994–3 February 1999* (Geneva, International Committee of the Red Cross).

[20] T Turner, *The Congo Wars: Conflict, Myth and Reality* (New York, Zed Books, 2007) 150.

[21] Autesserre (n 10) 47; F Reyntjens, *The Great African War: Congo and Regional Geopolitics, 1996–2006* (Cambridge, Cambridge University Press, 2009) 194–231.

[22] ibid.

[23] United Kingdom Home Office, 'UK Home Office Immigration and Nationality Directorate Country Assessment—Democratic Republic of Congo' (1 April 2002) 3.13, www.refworld.org/docid/3c2b4e090.html.

[24] Arimatsu (n 16) 158–59.

[25] 'Between Frontlines: ICRC Delegates at Work' (ICRC, DRC) icrc.srf.ch/en/kongo#/introduction.

[26] The Final Act, 2 April 2003, reliefweb.int/report/democratic-republic-congo/inter-congolese-political-negotiations-final-act.

During the Second Congo War, on 10 July 1999 the Lusaka Ceasefire Agreement was signed, which aimed to bring a ceasefire to the DRC.[27] It called for the immediate cessation of hostilities within twenty-four hours of its signing.[28] This was to include an end to hostile action, including military movements and reinforcements and hostile propaganda,[29] disarmament of militia groups,[30] and exchange of hostages and prisoners of war.[31] It also called for peacekeeping, peace enforcement and Security Council authorisation of coercive force to disarm various armed groups.[32] Importantly, the Lusaka Ceasefire Agreement also stated that:

> The Parties shall allow immediate and unhindered access to the ICRC and Red Crescent for the purpose of arranging the release of prisoners of war and other persons detained as a result of the war as well as the recovery of the dead and the treatment of the wounded.[33]

In anticipation of forming an interim government, the Lusaka Ceasefire Agreement called for an 'all-inclusive' process to produce a new political order for the Congo, in which 'all parties in the inter-Congolese political dialogue shall enjoy equal status'.[34] Unfortunately, the peace agreement failed and the armed conflict disintegrated into a myriad of privatised, socially and economically motivated sub-conflicts.[35] To give an idea of the complexity of the conflict of the DRC, in 1998 the conflict consisted of: Kabila, with some elements of the Forces Armées Congolaises (FAC)/Armed Forces of Zimbabwe (ZDF)/Angolan Armed Forces (FAA)/Namibia (NDF), Chad's Armée Nationale Tchadienne (ANT) and Sudan against the military wing of the Rally for Congolese Democracy (RCD), the Armée Nationale Congolaise (ANC), the Movement for the Liberation of the Congo (MLC)/Armée de Libération du Congo (ALC), the Rwandan Patriotic Army (RPA), Uganda's People's Defence Force (UPDF) and the Forces Armées Burundaises (FAB). In May 1999 the RCD split into the pro-Rwandan wing (RCD-Goma) and the pro-Ugandan wing (RCD-ML).[36] In addition, Laurent-Désiré Kabila was killed by his bodyguard in Kinshasa on 16 January 2001, during the Second Congo War, and his son,

[27] 'Letter Dated 23 July 1999 From the Permanent Representative of Zambia to the United Nations Addressed to the President of the Security Council-Annex: Ceasefire Agreement' (23 July 1999) UN Doc S/1999/815.

[28] ibid, 'The Cease-fire', Art 1, para 2(c).

[29] ibid, Art 1, para 2(b).

[30] ibid, Art III 'Principles of the Agreement', para 22.

[31] ibid, Art III 'Principles of the Agreement', para 8.

[32] Carayannis (n 11) 186–87.

[33] Ceasefire Agreement (n 27) Art III 'Principles of the Agreement', para 9.

[34] ibid, 5.2(b).

[35] G Prunier, *Africa's World War Congo, the Rwandan Genocide and the Making of a Continental Catastrophe* (Oxford, Oxford University Press, 2009) 225, 235–37.

[36] Autesserre (n 10) 48–49; Kreijen (n 13) 75–77.

Joseph Kabila, swiftly took his place.[37] Shortly afterwards, Security Council Resolution 1341, of 22 February 2001, demanded that Ugandan and Rwandan forces and all other forces withdraw from the Congo.[38]

This complicated timeline and multitude of actors is symptomatic of a shift in the nature of armed conflict away from traditional battlefield scenarios. The throng of states, armed groups, international organisations and individuals involved in and affected by the conflict seems insurmountable by traditional peacekeeping or humanitarian activities. Chapter 3 considered the shifting nature of conflict and concurred with Ruti Teitel's concept of 'humanity's law', in so far as it shows that IHL, IHRL and international criminal law converge nowadays. The fluidity of war and peace; state armed forces, non-state armed groups and individual combatants; humanitarian aid, protection and assistance and so on is evidence that strict delineation of applicable armed conflicts is no longer possible. The DRC provides clear verification of the argument that conventional approaches to humanitarian protection and assistance would not be adequate to address the needs of civilians on the ground. The complexity of the situation in the DRC requires the ICRC to use its mandate in traditional and novel ways, the particulars of which are considered below.

On the 15 October 2001, more than two years after the signing of the Lusaka Ceasefire Agreement, the Inter-Congolese Dialogue officially opened in Addis Ababa.[39] The Dialogue was intended to allow for the liberation of the Congolese from external occupation and intervention. In December 2002 the Global and All-inclusive Agreement on Transition in the DRC was signed between the government; the MLC; the RCD; political opposition; civil society; factions of the RCD, including the RCD-ML (renamed Forces for Renewal) and the RCD-National; and the Mai-Mai.[40] It called for the establishment of a transitional government by the following summer. It reflected a deal between the principal warlords as to how they would share power at the governmental level during the twenty-four-month transition period, at the end of which elections should be held.[41] However, 'fighting continued in the east involving the Mai-Mai, dissident factions of the RCD-Goma and the Democratic Forces for the Liberation of Rwanda (FDLR)'.[42] Trouble in the north-eastern district of

[37] Autesserre (n 10) 51.

[38] UNSCR 1341 (22 February 2001) Situation in the Democratic Republic of Congo paras 2, 4, 6, 19–20.

[39] Institute for Security Studies, *The Peace Process in the DRC: A Reader* (a publication of the African Security Analysis Programme at the ISS, funded by the governments of Sweden and Switzerland).

[40] 'Global and All-inclusive Agreement on Transition in the DRC' (Pretoria, Republic of South Africa, 16 December 2002) reliefweb.int/report/democratic-republic-congo/global-and-inclusive-agreement-transition-dr-congo-inter-congolese.

[41] ibid, part IV.

[42] Arimatsu (n 16) 171.

Ituri was threatening the process and in 2003 massacres in Ituri put the whole national peace process at risk.[43] Nevertheless, the final session of the Inter-Congolese Dialogue was held in Sun City on 1–2 April 2003, during which the Final Act was signed. It endorsed all agreements approved until then.[44]

The period between 2003 and 2006 is considered to be the 'Transitional Period', that is, the period of transition to a democratic government. During 2005–06 the first 'free elections' took place, which saw the election of Kabila.[45] Presidential elections were then held in 2011, between Kabila and Etienne Tshisekedi, and saw Kabila triumph over his opponent.[46] Tshisekedi and international observers questioned Kabila's win.[47] Moreover, the result of the 2011 election sparked renewed violence.[48]

In recent years, the composition of armed groups in the DRC has continually changed. The National Congress for the Defence of the People (CNDP), for example, was integrated into the Forces Armées de la République Démocratique du Congo (FARDC).[49] In addition, perhaps most significantly, a number of ex-CNDP soldiers formed the 'March 23 Rebel Movement' (M23).[50] Its activities sought to destabilise the region and have had a 'negative impact on the deteriorating security and humanitarian situation in South Kivu and Katanga'.[51] In addition, the M23 committed

[43] S Hellmüller, 'The Power of Perceptions: Localizing International Peace Building Approaches' (2013) 20(2) *International Peacekeeping* 219, 220.

[44] The Lusaka Ceasefire Agreement (10 July 1999); Sub-plans for Disengagement and Redeployment (DR) of Forces in Accordance with the DR Plan Signed at Kampala on 8 April 2000 (18 November 2000); Memorandum of Understanding between the Governments of the Democratic Republic of Congo and Rwanda on the Withdrawal of the Rwandan Troops from the Territory of the DRC and the Dismantling of the Ex-FAR and Interahamwe Forces in the DRC (30 July 2002): Agreement between the Governments of the Democratic Republic of the Congo and the Republic of Uganda on Withdrawal of Ugandan Troops from the Democratic Republic of the Congo, Cooperation and Normalisation of Relations between the Two Countries (6 September 2002); Global and Inclusive Agreement on Transition in the Democratic Republic of the Congo (17 December 2002); Amendment of the Agreement Signed Between the Democratic Republic of Congo and Uganda (10 February 2003); Draft Constitution of the Transition (31 March 2003) and The Final Act (2 April 2003). These agreements are printed in full in the Institute for Security Studies (n 39).

[45] Autesserre (n 10) 3–5.

[46] ICRC, 'The Democratic Republic of Congo: The Cycle of Violence', icrc.srf.ch/en/kongo#/introduction.

[47] ibid.

[48] ibid.

[49] MONUSCO, 'Report of the United Nations Joint Human Rights Office on Human Rights Violations Perpetrated by Soldiers of the Congolese Armed Forces and Combatants of the M23 in Goma and Sake, North Kivu Province, and In and Around Minova, South Kivu Province, from 15 November to 2 December 2012' (May 2013) www.ohchr.org/Documents/Countries/CD/UNJHROMay2013_en.pdf.

[50] J Stearns, J Luff, T Kiepe and J Nash, *From CNDP to M23: The Evolution of an Armed Movement in Eastern Congo (Usalama Project)* (London, Rift Valley Institute, 2012).

[51] UNSC Res 2098 (28 March 2013) Democratic Republic of Congo, preamble.

'serious violations of IHL and abuses of human rights'.[52] In 2013 the UN Intervention Brigade against M23 was established, 'consisting inter alia of three infantry battalions, one artillery and one Special force and Reconnaissance Company with headquarters in Goma, under direct command of the United Nations Organization Stabilization Mission in the Democratic Republic of the Congo (MONUSCO) Force Commander'.[53] It has the 'responsibility of neutralizing armed groups' and 'the objective of contributing to reducing the threat posed by armed groups to state authority and civilian security in eastern DRC and to make space for stabilization activities'.[54] Its mandate was renewed on 30 March 2015, and again on 30 March 2016.[55] There has since been a renewed sanctions regime and Group of Experts mandate.[56]

It is outside the scope of this book to consider UN involvement in the conflicts in the DRC, but, needless to say, this particular development speaks volumes about the severity of the situation on the ground in the DRC. Indeed, local conditions, including the insecurity of vulnerable populations, continue to thwart outside attempts to bring peace and security to the region. Unfortunately, the FDLR, the Mai-Mai and the Lord's Resistance Army continue to fight and commit atrocities against civilians and the humanitarian situation remains fraught.[57] To this end, human insecurity continues to permeate the DRC.

Elections were scheduled for 2016 but on 28 September 2015 the Constitutional Court in the DRC ruled elections impossible.[58] They have been delayed until early 2018, an announcement that has resulted in seventeen deaths and protests against Kabila. In 2016, the FARDC and MONUSCO

[52] ibid; see also 'Special Report of the Secretary-General on the Democratic Republic of the Congo and the Great Lakes Region' (27 February 2013) UN Doc S/2013/119.

[53] UNSC Res 2098 (28 March 2013) Democratic Republic of Congo, para 9; See also SS Kayode, 'Intervention Brigade for the Congo: A Precedent for UN Peace Enforcement' (2014) 10 *Review of International Law and Politics* 88–118; D Whittle, 'Peacekeeping in Conflict: The Intervention Brigade, MONUSCO, and the application of international humanitarian law to United Nations forces' (2015) 46 *Georgetown Journal of International Law* 837–76.

[54] UNSC Res 2098 (28 March 2013) Democratic Republic of Congo, para 9.

[55] UNSC Res 2277 (30 March 2016) Democratic Republic of Congo; UNSC Res 2211 (30 March 2015) Democratic Republic of Congo; UNSC Res 2147 (28 March 2014) Democratic Republic of Congo, para 1.

[56] UNSC Res 2293 (23 June 2016) The situation concerning the Democratic Republic of the Congo.

[57] Statement by the President of the Security Council (8 January 2015) S/PRST/2015/1; Statement by the President of the Security Council (9 November 2015) S/PRST/2015/20; Statement by the President of the Security Council (5 November 2014) S/PRST/2014/22; MONUSCO 'Press Releases 2014' monusco.unmissions.org/Default.aspx?tabid=11469&language=en-US.

[58] Report of the Secretary-General on the United Nations Organization Stabilization Mission in the Democratic Republic of the Congo (28 September 2015) S/2015/741; Report of the Secretary-General on the United Nations Organization Stabilization Mission in the Democratic Republic of the Congo (24 December 2015) S/2015/1031.

have continued to work in the region.[59] Interviewee 008 talked about ICRC preparations for the elections:

> The presidential election was planned for November 2016 … for example, for this year for the health, I have increased the budget on first aid and the response for weapon wounded.… In such kind of country, it's better to be on the safe side and say, okay, I'll increase a bit my budgets to respond with the first aid, with war wounded kit, because maybe the number of weapon wounded could increase … maybe there will be nothing.… But I'm not sure because it could be a difficult situation if the election goes on and the population are not happy with the result. Or if the election won't be done and it will be postponed, I think it will also be a mess because the population will not be happy because it means that Kabila postpone all the process and they don't want it because he tried already to change the constitution to be able to do a certain mandate. And really, the population went out and they went on the street and it was quite … tense in January 2015 when he tried to change the constitution.
>
> So the idea, for sure, is we will stay in the DRC, but a bigger or smaller presence and budget. It depends, but more or less, I think it will stay the same because the situation, even if there is no problem related to the election, the situation is not getting better for the time being. Maybe it will change, but—it's long-term. Yeah, we started there, I think, and as you said, in the seventies with a big team, but from my personal point of view, I don't think that will be reduced a lot for years, or if it changes drastically if they have a new President committed to his country and starts to change things.[60]

This brief 'timeline' up to late 2016 shows the ongoing nature of the conflict in the DRC. In addition, it shows that multiple actors and stakeholders are affected by and involved in the conflict and violence. This case study will now, in the context of the work of the ICRC, reflect on the conclusions drawn earlier in the book.

## III. THE ICRC IN THE DEMOCRATIC REPUBLIC OF CONGO

The cycles of violence in the DRC make any kind of sustainable project very difficult:

> The level of involvement of the authorities is so poor because they don't have means and then sometimes it's difficult to say, 'oh they are all corrupt'. You have to put your feet in their shoes and realise that when you don't have means, when the money is not there, when you have to run services without money and budget, it is very difficult to provide services for the community.[61]

[59] Report on the United Nations Organization Stabilization Mission in the Democratic Republic of the Congo (9 March 2016) S/2016/233; Report on the implementation of the Peace, Security and Cooperation Framework for the Democratic Republic of the Congo and the Region (9 March 2016) S/2016/232.

[60] Interview 008.

[61] Interview 001.

In terms of an overall picture, the ICRC

> [h]ave been in the DRC for a long time as well, unfortunately for them. We have, in the DRC, a partnership with the National Society which is very diverse. Probably one of the most diverse around the world. Not very sophisticated because, well, they are at a certain level of development as an institution, so they don't necessarily have procedures in place. They are not a strong National Society, if you wish, but still they have lots of capacities in terms of first response, in terms of numbers of volunteers they can mobilise.
>
> So, all in all, almost every department of the ICRC delegation works, one way or another, with the National Societies, with their branches, their volunteers, or their staff in headquarters or elsewhere. So that's obviously for restoring family links, that's obvious, but we're doing a lot of things in terms of EcoSec. They take part in our distribution, at the very least, but also they have their own little assessments and distributions, which we support.
>
> In terms of communication, we're trying to slowly help them build their communication departments and have some joint whatever, press release or radio broadcast or different things. In terms of water and sanitation, we're trying to help them build their capacities and develop some programmes—well, not programmes, but projects here and there—building wells or whatever can be developed. We're also working in terms of protection of childhood, which is a bit special, not a programme that exists everywhere. As well, we're working on sexual violence with them. I haven't a clue how you say that in English. It's basically houses where victims of sexual violence, women or men, mostly women but it's open to everyone—actually, it's not only sexual violence, but it's every type of traumatic experience—can go and talk to someone and get some support or be referred to a proper hospital or medical facility when that's needed.[62]

Interview 010 also summarised the protection and assistance work of the ICRC in the DRC:

> We do detention, family links, protection of the civilian population (PCP), and we have some pilot programmes that were actually developed in DRC because of the specific needs and because of the context that allows us to work. Because we have a very large access despite everything, we are well accepted, we can work in the field, we can reach the population. So this is something very particular which makes it a very—sorry again to be cynical—nice context to work in because we have this access that we don't have in other countries.
>
> So, in protection, we've developed child protection programmes, targeting actually children that are associated with armed forces and armed groups, for instance. So this is something that does not exist, as such, in other countries. And we had also a quite important programme to help to assist victims of sexual violence. Now it's getting a bit mainstreamed in other contexts, of course, but I think it really started to gain importance in DRC. So this makes it really important.

[62] Interview 007.

> Then if it's responding to emergencies or development, I think what's great with ICRC is we try to really adapt to the needs. I mean it's a needs-based approach. So we are going to do emergency assistance when there are massive displacements in the region because it's a coping mechanism for the communities. So we will go with the …, the typical humanitarian assistance, go and try to deliver NFI kits and so on, food, whatever, and then you have more like long-term/mid-term assistance with the agriculture programmes. We do, like, fishing farms, we are doing seed distribution, but also helping communities and associations to basically farm better.[63]

Interviewee 008 reflected on the perceptions of the ICRC in a situation where so many international organisations are present and active:

> They know that we are not part of the conflict and that we are the Red Cross. The UN is a bit complicated in the DRC because you have the Monusco and they have a special mandate and they can be part of the conflict.… But after, when you go to the communities, it's true that when they see some big land cruiser, even if you are the Red Cross, they will cry MONUC MONUC MONUC. It was the former name of MONUSCO. So, for sure, the little children, and even the adult sometimes, will shout, 'Oh, MONUC, MONUC' and we say, 'No, we are not MONUSCO. We are the ICRC.' I think for the authorities and for the health staff, they know that we are the Red Cross and we are not Unicef or we're not— But for the community or the population, most of the time they mix it.[64]

Interviewee 010 also considered how the ICRC is perceived by the local population:

> The perception in North Kivu in particular, you have a very—It's basically a humanitarian hub, so there are many, many humanitarian actors, a large UN component, you have a peacekeeping mission—well it's not really peacekeeping actually. So you have the MONUSCO and in particular you have one MONUSCO [component] the FIB, which has an offensive mandate. So of course, I mean, the UN usually has a political mandate. In that specific context, you have also a force that has to basically get rid of armed groups. So for your Congolese that you see in the street, I mean we are all like white people trying to help but also taking advantage. You know, in these kinds of big hubs, it's kind of an issue. So of course what we want is to be perceived as different from the UN and the other organisations because we have a specific mandate and a specific mission. So of course we need to be distinct from the others because we don't work the same as they do. We go to areas where they don't go. We have another way to talk to access areas. I mean we are unarmed and so on, so of course communication has also this objective to ensure the security, I mean at some point of our teams.… The ICRC has had a massive operation in the country for years, with good reasons, because there was armed conflict. Now there is a peace deal, so, of course, I mean what is the role of the ICRC in this? Should we stay? Should we reduce? Should we leave completely? This ultimately depends on the needs.

[63] Interview 010.

[64] Interview 008.

> I mean, if there is still armed violence, whether it's from an armed conflict or another situation of violence, we'll intervene. Also, the needs after the conflict do exist.[65]

The interviews reflect the complexity and fluidity of humanitarian needs in the DRC.

## A. Traditional Roles: Dissemination and Detention

The first chapter of this book introduced a quote from Peter Maurer, President of the ICRC. He stated in 2012 that:

> The motivation behind our work has not changed since the final pages of Henry Dunant's ground-breaking book 'A Memory of Solferino'. What changes, however, is how the organization adapts its response to difference patterns of conflict and different contexts.[66]

The interviews conducted with ICRC delegates, in Geneva in April 2014, reinforce this proposition. The humanitarian activities currently being undertaken in the DRC are the broadest operations in terms of both protection and assistance.[67] In a protracted armed conflict, where warring factions can change, it is crucial that the ICRC maintains its reputation as a neutral organisation.

The key role of the ICRC, as guardian of the Geneva Conventions 1949, has always been the dissemination of IHL.[68] Indeed, 'in practice, armed opposition groups have frequently allowed the ICRC to disseminate international humanitarian law to civilians living in areas they controlled'.[69] In the DRC, the ICRC has a sustained dialogue with the FARDC and armed groups operating at ground level. Critically, however, it also works with MONUSCO, which is considered to be a party to the conflict.[70] This is, in part, because the UN Force Intervention Brigade under MONUSCO has a defensive mandate to carry out operations against active armed groups.[71]

The ICRC continues to provide protection and assistance in other traditional areas of practice such as detention and healthcare. The Annual Report 2013 stated that:

> Nine health centres serving some 83,000 people regularly benefited from drugs/medical supplies, staff training, monitoring of care, and infrastructure

[65] Interview 010.
[66] 'Interview with Peter Maurer' (Winter 2012) 94 (888) *IRRC* 1, 2.
[67] Interview 001.
[68] IRCRCM Statutes, Art 5; ICRC Statutes, Art 4.
[69] ICRC, 'Rule 143 Customary IHL: Dissemination of International Humanitarian Law among the Civilian Population', www.icrc.org/customary-ihl/eng/docs/v1_rul_rule143.
[70] Interview 001.
[71] Interview 001.

> upgrades. At these facilities: destitute patients had their treatment costs covered; 2,768 patients were referred to secondary care; some 19,800 vaccinations were performed out of a total of over 82,400, of which 96% were for children, as part of ICRC-supported national immunization campaigns; and women received mosquito nets after learning about malaria prevention at antenatal-health consultations.[72]

In the period January–May 2014, for example, the ICRC estimated that it visited or helped 17,000 detainees in the DRC.[73] This included the provision of medical and nutritional support, distribution of hygiene items, and the carrying out of renovation work in some facilities that helped improve living conditions.[74] The ICRC also believes that 'some detainees are facing protection issues in terms of ill treatment and possibility of disappearance in detention'.[75] The ICRC, therefore, provides individual case follow-ups and also provides water, sanitation and health programmes in detention facilities in the DRC.[76] It also works to establish nutritional programmes in detention facilities. The concern for the ICRC is that budgets for food do not always actually reach the detainees.[77]

## IV. ICRC AND HEALTH

In terms of health, more broadly:

> The ICRC works to address the whole chain of care. When people are first wounded they need first aid and stabilisation and then they need to be referred to a medical facility. In some cases, this leads to necessary referral to a secondary health facility where they can be treated and then some people might need rehabilitation and prosthetics.

Moreover, the ICRC is supporting small-scale rehabilitation and orthopaedic centres in the Kivus.[78] Healthcare in the DRC 'means first aid, hospital projects, primary healthcare projects, rehabilitation, a physical rehabilitation programme and health in detention'.[79] The ICRC has developed its role over time. In terms of its core activity:

> We start to speak about war wounded or weapon wounded and first aid. We started with this and after we built other activities because you have the

[72] Annual Report 2013 (n 7) 137.
[73] 'ICRC in the DRC: Facts and Figures', www.icrc.org/eng/where-we-work/africa/congo-kinshasa/index.jsp.
[74] ibid.
[75] Interview 001.
[76] Interview 001; Annual Report 2013 (n 7) 138.
[77] Interview 001.
[78] Interview 001.
[79] Interview 008.

> wounded, the first aid, and this is linked, but after you have the other populations who have no access to health. So we turn to the Geneva Conventions, I think, to the responsibility of the state to keep the access to health for all the population.
>
> So we work on this so that, for example, when you have the conflict, okay, you have the wounded, but you have also destruction or maybe not functioning health structure, so you deprive all the population, the civilian population, for healthcare. So I think it is in the Geneva Conventions that they should preserve or they should allow access to the healthcare for the population. So in fact it's—It's a natural—But it's true that the health activity started with surgical work on the war wounded and the first aid because the first aid is really the base of the Red Cross movement. And then it's true that we started to have some PHC, primary healthcare projects, and rehabilitation is also part of the war wounded, physical rehabilitation projects.[80]

It is clear, therefore, that some activities, such as visiting detainees and providing healthcare, are common to many operations but there are also projects specific to the DRC, such as child protection. This book has not focused on the human insecurity of children during armed conflict but it is interesting and reassuring to note that the ICRC in the DRC gives children specific attention. The ICRC specifically tries to sensitise communities and armed groups in order to prevent recruitment, or re-recruitment of children into armed groups, which something not commonly found in other delegations. It is a pilot programme to try and address this particular vulnerability.[81] Another protection role specific to the ICRC is that dealing with the trauma of children recruited to the Lord's Resistance Army, which is restricted to one province of the DRC.[82] It came to an end at the end of 2014 at which point the ICRC intended to pass the programme to the community.[83] This is significant as chapter 6 highlighted the importance,

[80] Interview 008.
[81] Interview 001.
[82] Interview 001.
[83] Interview 001; ICRC 'DR Congo: Invisible Wounds and Local Paths to Recovery' (10 October 2012) https://www.icrc.org/eng/resources/documents/feature/2012/congo-kinshasa-drc-mental-health-feature-2012-10-10.htm: 'Since September 2011, the ICRC's psychosocial team has trained over 150 Congolese Red Cross volunteers, teachers, and religious and spiritual leaders in the villages of Doruma, Banda and Dakwa, to better understand psychological and emotional symptoms and integrate this kind of care into their normal work. Two counsellors from each community were also trained to provide more specialized support. After the successes of this work in creating more "fertile" ground for children's recovery, the ICRC plans to launch similar programmes in other villages.' For additional information on the ICRC working with former child soldiers, see ICRC, 'Democratic Republic of the Congo: 152 Demobilized Children Reunited with Families', https://www.icrc.org/en/document/democratic-republic-congo-152-former-child-soldiers-reunited-families#.VQRZdEJZFNO; ICRC, 'Democratic Republic of the Congo: Tackling Child Recruitment by Armed Groups', https://www.icrc.org/en/document/democratic-republic-congo-tackling-child-recruitment#.vqrzj0jzfnm.

indeed necessity, of local ownership of humanitarian protection and assistance projects. The work of the ICRC for the protection and assistance of children appears to be in sync with this proposition. This case study provides a more specific analysis of local ownership below.

Interviewee 008 shared insights into and experiences of how the provision of healthcare is currently designed and delivered by the ICRC in the DRC.

> Normally, for example, for a hospital you have often a team, a surgical team, a mobile person, expatriate, and you have also some resident positions, ICRC local person, and you have often the national people working with you because you are in the hospital. You cannot put everybody under ICRC contracts, so you have the normal people working in the hospital that work with us and sometimes we give some, like, say, top-up or incentive to try to get them to work with us, but the hospital is run under a private contract, as for example, in Goma, we worked in a hospital that we decided to support the surgical part for the wounded or weapon wounded persons. So in fact we were in charge of this, but the other part of the hospital—maternity, paediatric—was run by the hospital. They were the landlord of the structure and we were paying some running costs to be in the hospital for the infrastructure, and we had our staff but also the staff of the hospital helping us. …
>
> In Kinshasa, in fact you have the management of the delegation, ICRC delegation, and the coordination, but after, our team were really in the field. So you have most of our activity deployed in the east of Congo. So Goma, Bukavu but also in the Katanga, former Katanga because it's now it's dividing. So, in Lubumbashi, then in the province [Orientale Bunia] and Kisangani. So really, Kinshasa is, let's say, the management and the coordination, but after the work and the implementation are done in the provinces—so, in the east, in the north, south Kivu, Katanga and Province Oriental.[84]

The protracted armed conflict in the DRC has impacted on the provision of healthcare locally, one interviewee stated that:

> Because of the situation and the context, the quality of the education is very low. So you had in the past good doctors or nurses, trained by the Belgians or going outside to be trained, and they have really a good level of university and this has … completely collapsed. So in fact, the level of the younger doctors or nurses is very low.

The interviewee went on to state that:

> In the past, for example, the University in Kinshasa where we are famous and people from West Africa, for example, the Senegalese—I was in Senegal before—it was common to go to Kinshasa to be trained and to do their specialisation of surgery or—it was a very famous one a long time ago, and it's the opposite.

[84] Interview 008.

> If the Congolese want to do some good training or specialisation, they go to Dakar, to the Senegal.[85]

To try and assist with this situation, and to embed a more long-term solution to this training deficit, the ICRC has developed a specific project.

> There is only one project now that we have started to work, the war surgery seminar. In each country we work, normally we organise some war surgery seminars. So it's a one-week seminar for surgeons, for nurses, how to deal with war wounded patients. And now we have an agreement with—it's in the west part of Africa—the curriculum of the university to include in all surgery specialisation—So for example, for a medical doctor who would like to be a surgical obstetrician, he has to do two years of training and, inside this training, you will have the module of the war wounded seminar.
>
> So in fact, yes, for West Africa, French-speaking countries where we've done this, we succeeded to put our war surgery training in the curriculum of the surgeons.... I think it started four years ago but, yeah, it's like a revolution because we try to focus on the curriculum of the surgeons, for example, or the training.[86]

### A. Sexual Violence and Psychosocial Support

Of course, no analysis of humanitarian protection and assistance in the DRC could fail to consider sexual violence. For a time, it seemed, from academics and the media, that sexual violence was the main problem to be solved in the DRC.[87] Autesserre articulates why the world was so ready to give sexual violence prominence. Firstly, sexual violence carries an emotional impact for outsiders; secondly, victims are often tortured and subject to social stigma after the event; and finally, sexual violence continued after the 2006 election, which was evidence to the outside world that the DRC remained in conflict.[88] This book does not focus on sexual violence, as the impact of conflict on local populations reaches far beyond sexual violence. This is not meant to reduce the horror of sexual violence for its victims, but rather, to accept Autesserre's contention that sexual violence cannot be the only narrative of the DRC conflicts. In fact, Autesserre emphasises that: '[I]nternational focus has also led to unintentionally counterproductive results, namely discrimination against other vulnerable populations

[85] Interview 008.

[86] Interview 008.

[87] See SP Tunamsifu, 'The Right to Justice: A Challenge for Survivors of Conflict-related Sexual Violence in the Eastern Congo' (2015) 15(2) *African Human Rights Law Journal* 473–95; J Trenholm et al, 'The Global, the Ethic and the Gendered War: Women and rape in Eastern Democratic Republic of Congo' (2016) 23(4) *Gender, Place and Culture: A Journal of Feminist Geography* 484–502.

[88] S Autesserre, 'Dangerous Tales: Dominant Narratives on the Congo and their Unintended Consequences' (2012) 111(443) *African Affairs* 202, 215.

and, at times, an increase in the use of sexual abuse by combatants.'[89] Nevertheless, in addition to traditional protection and assistance activities, the ICRC has a specific focus in the DRC on sexual violence, which is a relatively new activity for the ICRC.[90] In these contexts, its psychosocial activities are probably more developed than in other situations.[91] The ICRC takes both a physical and psychosocial approach to victims whilst documenting and approaching alleged perpetrators.[92] This includes trying to establish a dialogue with the perpetrators, whilst in no way having any involvement in the judicial process or prosecution at all.[93]

The ICRC, as described in chapter 1, must remain very remote from any kind of judicial activities, as it must not be perceived as documenting violations in order to feed prosecutions.[94] One interviewee highlighted that in contexts such as that found in the DRC, where the ICC is very active, perpetrators of violence know which of their colleagues are already in The Hague. It is crucial, therefore, for the continuing work of the ICRC that the perpetrators of violence understand that the ICRC is not collaborating with the ICC.[95] If suspicions were raised of such a situation, then the dialogue that the ICRC has established on the ground would be ruined. This would have repercussions, not only from the perspective of dissemination of IHL to those involved in conflict, but also for the people relying on the protection and assistance of the ICRC.

Interviewee 001 described the ICRC support for sexual-violence-related counselling services.[96] Interviewee 008 also noted that:

> The project started in 2005—so, more than ten years—but it's more or less the first project and the big one. But it has opened our eyes regarding this psychosocial support, that we need to go to other contexts and to improve. So now we

[89] ibid.

[90] In addition to the interview data, there are resources available on the ICRC sexual violence projects. See, eg, UN Human Rights Council (Statement by the ICRC) 'High Level Dialogue in Combatting Sexual Violence in the Democratic Republic of the Congo' (24 March 2014); ICRC, 'Sexual violence in the Democratic Republic of the Congo: Telling the Story and Overcoming the Trauma: Interview with Caroline Marquer' (4 June 2014) https://www.icrc.org/eng/resources/documents/audiovisuals/video/2014/06-04-sexual-violence-drc.htm; Sarah Cotton and Charlotte Nicol, 'The ICRC's Response to Sexual Violence in Armed Conflict and other Situations of Violence' (Humanitarian Practice Network).

[91] Interview 005.

[92] Interview 005; ICRC Annual Report 2013 (n 7) official numbers. The ICRC Annual Report 2013 accounts for the provision of psychosocial support for 4,544 victims of sexual violence in North and South Kivu. Of these, 2,205 were referred to nearby ICRC-supported health facilities for treatment. Another 2,077 people suffering from trauma linked to the conflict in North and South Kivu and to LRA-related attacks in five areas in Bas and Haut Uélé in Province Orientale also received psychological support from trained community counsellors.

[93] Interview 002; Interview 003; Interview 004; Interview 005.

[94] Interview 002.

[95] Interview 002.

[96] Interview 001.

> are—I don't know—we are present in twenty/thirty contexts with psychosocial projects.[97]

The ICRC aims to work with communities to provide additional support to existing programmes for victims of sexual violence.[98] This includes training counsellors to listen to women who have been attacked and also works to refer those women as quickly as possible to primary healthcare. The aim is for the women to be treated within the first seventy-two hours to prevent other medical issues. For the ICRC, the sexual violence initiatives can also be linked to projects that address economic vulnerabilities. It might offer small donations to help women restore their livelihoods, for example. The interviewee who described this project was keen to emphasise that this is a new project for the ICRC, and hence it cannot be predicted to what extent the results will be positive.[99]

Although the ICRC is able to adapt its mandate to respond to the humanitarian needs of victims of armed conflicts, ultimately local and national authorities must change the status quo. Sexual violence is a crime against humanity and, as was considered in chapter 4, it can be punished through judicial mechanism. However, in the meantime, it is critical that the ICRC, as an invaluable humanitarian actor, is able to respond to the needs on the ground. The effectiveness of the ICRC action can be said to be in its utility for victims of sexual violence. The adaptation of its mandate to provide specific assistance to victims of sexual violence is an invaluable asset; having said that, sexual violence continues to be used as a weapon of war. To this end, the protection and assistance activities of the ICRC are having a positive impact in terms of the recovery of victims, in particular women, but the ICRC cannot prevent the recurrence of such IHL offences. In terms of the concept of 'humanity's law', therefore, it is suggested that although in theory and in academic literature there may be evidence of a shift in thinking, it is difficult to transpose such ideals onto the ground. In particular, it is very difficult to change the practices of the state and non-state armed groups in protracted and violent armed conflicts. The ICRC, therefore, is still responding to the immediate effects of armed conflicts on the ground; it is just that the victims and types of conflict are changing.

## V. FOOD SECURITY AND WATER

In 2013, the ICRC reported that in the DRC 'over 1 million people had access to safe drinking water as a result of coordinated action by local

[97] Interview 008.
[98] Interview 001.
[99] Interview 001.

water authorities, communities, the DRC Red Cross and the ICRC'.[100] In addition, the ICRC provided food commodities to 253,295 beneficiaries.[101] The ICRC's work on food security concerns mainly trying to bring food and non-food items to those who have been displaced.[102] Military operations and activities of armed groups create situations where people are displaced for a short period of time. People living in rural communities may, for example, regularly flee into jungle areas to hide for a number of days before returning to their homes.[103] The ICRC tries to address their immediate needs through donation of food or non-food items to last a few weeks.[104] One interviewee estimated that the ICRC provides food to around 50,000 families per year. This amounts to roughly 220,000 individuals, which is evidence of the 'logistical quagmire' and insecurity of the DRC.[105] The interviewee stated that: '[I]t is quite remarkable that [the ICRC] manages to provide such an amount of food and non-food items.'[106]

The ICRC also works to reconnect or establish water supplies in the DRC. In urban areas such as Goma and Bukavu it is now rehabilitating water networks alongside another organisation, Merlin, which runs a huge programme.[107] The ICRC is working on the production side, including pumping stations, lakes, water treatment and transmission to the network, which is looked after by Merlin. The ICRC is also working on several other rural projects throughout the Kivus and Katanga, where it is rehabilitating smaller networks. The ICRC usually works within priority areas, defined, of course, according to the conflict zones. Within these priority areas it looks at the needs of the populations and then tries as much as possible to apply a multidisciplinary approach to address problems in a more holistic manner. 'Usually you will never help people fully recover because the other problem being unaddressed will weigh a lot on the community.'[108]

The work of the ICRC to ensure food security and reconnect water supplies is an ongoing project. These projects are logical expansions of the more traditional role of bringing food and water to wounded soldiers. Food security and clean, running water is necessary, not only during the conduct of hostilities, but is also essential for the creation of broad human security. The space constraints of this book do not permit exploration of

[100] ICRC Annual Report 2013 (n 7) 137.
[101] ibid 135.
[102] Interview 001; Interview 003; Interview 004.
[103] Interview 003; Interview 004.
[104] Interview 003.
[105] Interview 001.
[106] Interview 001.
[107] Interview 001.
[108] Interview 001.

the specific effects of lack of resources on armed conflicts but it is important to note the importance of access to food and water to prevent recurrence of hostilities. In some cases, lack of food and water could be a root cause of the conflict. The ICRC provides help for those affected by conflict to survive and become self-sufficient. Its efforts to improve healthcare and, as a related activity, provide access to water and decent sanitation are crucial to post-conflict recovery and the ability of local people to overcome the effects of conflict.

Interviewee 007 reflected on the relationship between food security and economic security in their consideration of the protection and assistance roles of the ICRC:

> You have some aspects which are kind of humanitarian or live-saving when you're getting people starving to death, bringing food. You have other types of EcoSec interventions which are a bit longer term. All that relates to vaccinations of cattle or of certain things which takes at least a couple of years to have some effect. Obviously we're trying in many cases also not only to distribute food but to help the populations grow their own seeds or whatever, foods, so that, at the end of the day, they become less dependent on international aid than they are today. So that also has some longer term developmental implications. So I think, first and foremost, the objective is to help today and tomorrow and not necessarily to play that developmental role, but whether we like it or not, that is the case in some instances. And if it makes sense, that's perfectly fine for us. I mean, we shouldn't constrain ourselves too much by terminology.[109]

## VI. ECONOMIC SECURITY

This book has shown that economic security is tied into both the establishment of human security and socioeconomic development. Trefon has written on the economic insecurity of people in Kinshasa:

> Sacrifice is omnipresent in contemporary Kinshasa. The term here pertains to the hard reality of doing without. People do without food, they do without fuel wood, they do without primary health services and they do without safe drinking water. They also do without political participation, security, leisure or the ability to organize their time as they would like.[110]

For people living in Kinshasa economic security does not mean a secure, salaried job in the formal economy. The economic crisis and poverty is endemic and, as a consequence, the ability of people to establish or find economic security is incredibly difficult. It should be noted that much of the ICRC's work focuses on the east of the DRC, in particular North and

[109] Interview 007.

[110] T Trefon (ed), *Reinventing Order in the Congo: How People Respond to State Failure in Kinshasa* (London, Zed Books, 2004) 4.

South Kivu, and as such its economic security projects, when discussed in the interviews, are referring to the eastern regions. The quote from Trefon provides context to the type of economic insecurity faced in the DRC, which is somewhat different to economic insecurity in the UK, by example.

Trefon argues that the generations born and raised during the reign of Mobutu's Le Mouvement Populaire de la Révolution (MPR) lack individual initiative because Mobutu claimed to be responsible for all Zaireans from cradle to grave.[111] The overall feeling during this time was that 'individual interests supplant[ed] collective ones; corruption, theft, extortion, collusion, embezzlement, fraud, counterfeiting and prostitution' were all means of survival'.[112] Moreover, massive nationalisation of large and small foreign-owned companies launched a 'fend for yourself culture'.[113] Alternative means of income included accosting boats on the Congo River and doing deals over the produce aboard, also known as 'Les Mamans Manouvres'.[114] Overall, during Mobutu's reign, in the DRC, the foundations of a legitimate nation state were eroded by economic mismanagement. The people were

> [l]eft to live by their wits, residents developed parallel networks of interdependence and revenue generation, ranging from the 'tax' demanded at the police roadblock to the 'little present' made to a hungry official. Donors and humanitarian organisations played along with the intellectual fiction that was Zaire.[115]

These circumstances precluded the realisation of socioeconomic development and economic security. In the DRC, the ICRC works to enable families affected by conflicts to meet their own basic needs.[116] In 2013 this necessitated providing 78,000 households with essential household items and food supplies to 88,200 people; 60,400 received seeds to grow produce to feed them and earn a living, 360 people received support to build fishponds, and 150 people benefited from a 'cash-for-work' project.[117] From the perspective of the ICRC delegates, the situation in the DRC changes over time and from place to place.[118] When situations are less violent communities might try to plant and grow food in the hope that the situation will remain stable until the crops are ready to harvest.[119] In terms of

[111] ibid, 21–23.
[112] ibid, 23.
[113] ibid, 21.
[114] ibid, 25ff.
[115] M Wrong, 'Congo Lesson: Africa's Colonial Borders are Dissolving', *International Herald Tribune*, Europe, 31 January 2001, 7.
[116] 'ICRC in the DRC: Facts and Figures', www.icrc.org/eng/where-we-work/africa/congo-kinshasa/index.jsp; See also Annual Report 2013 (n 7) 135.
[117] ibid.
[118] Interview 003; Interview 004; Interview 005.
[119] Interview 004.

distributing seeds or assisting with farming, 'every activity is based on a direct assessment of the needs of the people but also the environment and the perspectives of the people on the move who have been displaced for a long time and will probably remain displaced in a camp for a long time'.[120]

One interviewee identified that in eastern Congo displacement is usually short term, as people spend three to four days in the bush and come back to see what the situation is like and determine whether they can return.[121] In such volatile and changing environments it is difficult for the ICRC to establish the same kinds of activities that it can when people have been in a camp for months and it is likely that they will continue stay there for a long time.[122] The interviews show that the ICRC has to be adaptable and be able to adjust to constantly changing situations.[123] Finally, if we reflect on the arguments made for local ownership in chapter 6, interviewees argued that the conflict in the DRC is not countrywide so responses by the ICRC have to be heavily contextualised and work at a very local level.[124] The ICRC will work with local people by approaching a community, talking to individuals to understand the precise needs and then working on a response that includes as many people as possible because they are all affected by the same situation.

When interviewees were asked further questions about economic assistance, they were keen to explain that the initiatives undertaken by the ICRC are on a very small scale.[125] The ICRC works on giving a family the means to survive for the next three to six months.[126] The ICRC, stated the interviewee, is not involved in large economic impact projects.[127] To this end, the initial assessment undertaken by the ICRC will determine whether a particular community would benefit from agricultural support or whether the best the ICRC can do is provide food parcels.[128] In the DRC, the ICRC also works on very small projects with the Institute Internationale de Rochercher Monamique.[129]

In terms of economic security, the ICRC also facilitates microeconomic initiatives (MEIs) for farmers, which are 'an income-generating programme that is implemented through a bottom-up approach, whereby each beneficiary is involved in identifying and designing the assistance to

[120] Interview 004.
[121] Interview 004.
[122] Interview 004.
[123] Interview 001; Interview 002; Interview 003; Interview 004; Interview 005.
[124] Interview 004.
[125] Interview 002; Interview 003; Interview 004.
[126] Interview 004.
[127] Interview 005.
[128] Interview 004.
[129] Interview 005.

be received'.[130] The specific example of an MEI provided during an interview was of a project whereby the ICRC helped to develop seeds resistant to diseases prevalent in the DRC.[131] In the first year, the primary association of Congolese farmers affiliated to the project had a history of working together, and luckily in that year the seeds grew well. In the second year, however, the farmers involved in the project were more opportunistic. The interviewee stated that the second group of farmers only wanted the economic incentives provided by the ICRC. They did not, therefore, repeat the growing of seeds the second year.[132]

Interviewee 005 also noted that this problem was also seen with MEIs for women who were victims of sexual violence; many asked for money to start small shops or tailoring businesses, but the women who received the money really needed it for something else and the businesses were never started or closed very quickly. Interviewee 005 argued that the ICRC could not provide constant financial support to the women and the MEIs failed.[133] However, the interviewee argued that the ICRC is still keen to support 'social safety net' type economic projects but from lessons learnt have determined that money should be provided in stages.[134]

The interviews identified that the ICRC might also utilise economic projects to bring communities together. Such projects can work towards not only human security but also the prevention of future recurrence of hostilities. In the Kivus, for example, for a period of two to three years, the ICRC ran vaccination and animal treatment programmes separately in two communities, one of which was predominantly made up of people of Rwandan heritage and the other Congolese. The aims of the ICRC, stated an interviewee, were to try and benefit the two communities and at the same time improve attitudes between communities.[135]

Interviewee 001 recognised that the ICRC has to take the security of local communities into account when making the assessments as to the kinds of support that can be made available.[136] The ICRC will open a dialogue with armed groups and authorities in the region.[137] In fact, one interviewee stated that: '[T]he protection the ICRC can provide is more thanks to the contacts we can have with the different parties [that is] high ranking military officers on both sides.'[138]

[130] ICRC, *Micro-Economic Initatives: Handbook* (Geneva, ICRC, 2002) 11 www.icrc.org/eng/assets/files/other/icrc_002_0968.pdf.
[131] Interview 005.
[132] Interview 005.
[133] Interview 005.
[134] Interview 005.
[135] Interview 005.
[136] Interview 001.
[137] Interview 001; Interview 003; Interview 004.
[138] Interview 005.

Interviewee 003 stated that the establishment of a dialogue is always done with full transparency and the security of the beneficiaries is taken into account before providing assistance, as the ICRC does not want to exacerbate any problems on the ground.[139] Interviewee 004 commented that in terms of security, therefore, what is interesting is that the ICRC, in starting a dialogue with armed groups or those in authority, will not necessarily talk to them about the Geneva Conventions I, II, III and IV 1949 and their IHL obligations. They also noted that the ICRC is more pragmatic and talks about the impact of the groups' activities on the living situation of the people in an area.[140] The ICRC will opt to use such humanitarian arguments when it is apparent that talking about breaching specific laws will not make the group sensitive to the people around them.[141]

In this regard, dissemination has taken on a more practical approach. The humanitarian goals of the ICRC take priority over the dissemination of specific provisions. Accordingly, the activities of the ICRC have evolved. If we think back to the conclusions earlier in this book that IHL and IHRL are increasingly intertwined, based, in particular, on their synonymous 'human' core, it is logical that the ICRC can rely on discourse beyond strict dissemination of IHL.

An issue to keep in mind when considering the practicalities of the ICRC establishing a dialogue with key actors in the DRC is the sheer number of armed groups; the UN has recorded fifty-four armed groups in the Kivus. These armed groups are forming and reforming or gaining representation at the political level. Indeed Interviewees 003 and 004 commented that the means employed by the UN to establish dialogue with these groups varies from one to the other.[142] Interviewee 001 also suggested that when these groups are in control of particular areas it is very easy to promote and then to advocate for those in authority to take responsibility to provide basic services, to ensure that people can get food and water and then the ICRC is able to engage in a dialogue.[143]

Overall, therefore, the establishment of economic security in the DRC encounters a myriad of difficulties. The traditional protection and assistance models, such as dissemination, detention and healthcare, are coupled with economic support and initiatives to try and help people get back on their feet, but the majority of people in the DRC are nevertheless in survival mode. Interviewee 001 stated that when people are in survival mode and there are high levels of corruption, lack of basic infrastructure

[139] Interview 003.
[140] Interview 004.
[141] Interview 004.
[142] Interview 003; Interview 004.
[143] Interview 001.

and difficulties in sustaining ICRC action, then the initial aims of the ICRC have to be amended.[144]

## VII. ICRC AND THE CONGOLESE NATIONAL SOCIETY

Chapter 6 reflected on the positive outcomes of local ownership and national society engagement. Interviewee 007 provided insight into this in the DRC:

> In terms of communication, we're trying to slowly help them build their communication departments and have some joint whatever, press release or radio broadcast or different things. In terms of water and sanitation, we're trying to help them build their capacities and develop some programmes—well, not programmes, but projects here and there—building wells or whatever can be developed. We're also working in terms of protection of childhood, which is a bit special, not a programme that exists everywhere. As well, we're working on sexual violence with them. I haven't a clue how you say that in English. It's basically houses where victims of sexual violence, women or men, mostly women but it's open to everyone—actually, it's not only sexual violence, but it's every type of traumatic experience—can go and talk to someone and get some support or be referred to a proper hospital or medical facility when that's needed.[145]

Interviewee 008 also noted that:

> The DRC Red Cross, in fact, is everywhere. So you have a lot of volunteers everywhere, but after, it's really centralised. So everything you would like to do in the province has to go through the Kinshasa management, but after, in the field, for example, in north and south Kivu, you have quite strong branches and there are a lot of volunteers, so you are able to work with them and they are able to deliver some services to the community and the place where sometimes the ICRC cannot go, or other organisations cannot go. So it's quite a strong, I would say, National Society regarding the—how to say?—their visibility. They are everywhere and everybody knows the Red Cross and they respect, more or less, the Red Cross. It's well known. But after, regarding the quality of the service provided—This depends on the volunteers, but it depends on the support they get from their line manager, and sometimes it's not terribly well done. But what it shows is that, in DRC, everywhere you go, everywhere you will find some Red Cross volunteers. This is incredible … but in some instances, the ICRC is keen to use its mandate to show its limits so that the local population doesn't take advantage.[146]

144 Interview 001.
145 Interview 007.
146 Interview 008.

## VIII. CONCLUSION

It is almost impossible for academic literature to provide an overview of the conflict in the DRC, or convey the horrors of such a protracted armed conflict. This case study has shown the changing role of the ICRC in the DRC, its potential in terms of the establishment of human security, and its relationship with the local population. The motivation behind the establishment of the ICRC, to protect and assist victims of armed conflicts, continues to this day. The type of conflict seen in the DRC during the ICRC's thirty-eight-year presence there, however, is indicative of broader trends on the international stage towards protracted internal armed conflicts. This is very different from the situations anticipated by the ICRC following Solferino, the First World War and during the drafting of the Geneva Conventions I, II, III and IV 1949.

This case study has shown that what was missed in the decolonisation process, a voice still missing in recovery from armed conflict in many contexts, is a local voice—a voice that is able to articulate what is needed on the ground to make life positive and secure. The interviews showed that for the delegates of the ICRC it is important, in fact essential, to build a dialogue with people on the ground. For the ICRC, when working with armed groups, it is also pertinent to explain the requirements of humanity under IHL or IHRL. Overall, the ICRC delegates emphasise the humanitarian core of both legal frameworks. Pragmatically, therefore, it is about teaching the people involved in the conflict about their responsibilities towards those involved and not involved in conflict. The ICRC will, at the same time, work with local communities on projects to improve their daily lives. Creating projects with the involvement of local populations is the core strength of the ICRC. The ICRC can work from the bottom up for the creation of human security. This can be seen in food projects, MEIs, and the provision of healthcare for detainees and victims of sexual violence, and, finally, sustained dialogue with those involved in the conflict.

In the DRC multiple non-state armed groups have authority over certain areas and the leaders of the DRC, even when supposedly democratically elected, have inflicted suffering on the civilians and plundered resources to preclude true economic development. Somehow the ICRC has, in practice, maintained a trusted presence since 1978 and has forged links with local actors and the national society. Its proven record of confidentiality and neutrality in the DRC allowed it to build a dialogue and create context-specific protection and assistance projects for the people of the DRC. Sometimes the ICRC utilises IHRL, or human rights more generally, to convey the humanitarian message; the implications of human rights for the ICRC are discussed fully in the final chapter of this book.

As was shown in chapter 4, the security paradigm on the international stage has shifted. Whilst state sovereignty and territorial integrity remain, the Common Understanding Resolution shows that the international community has accepted human-centric security concerns. For the DRC, this progression to human-centric ideas is particularly interesting. Westphalian sovereignty is both external and internal sovereignty. If we recall from chapter 4, external sovereignty 'is about the relationship between States, as legal persons, whereas internal sovereignty is about the State and its relationship with NSA's within its territory'.[147] Although external sovereignty has become part of the DRC framework, internal sovereignty has never really been established in the DRC. Although the 'state' fulfils the Montevideo requirements and it is a member of the UN, it does not, in terms of security, provide its population with human security. The people of the DRC have always faced the challenges recognised by the UNDP in 1994; in fact, the types of human insecurity in the DRC closely resemble those included in the broad 'Freedom from Want' narrative of human security. To this end, political security, such as democratisation and the rule of law, championed by MONUC and MONUSCO, will not bring true security to the population of the DRC.

This case study has shown that the ICRC focus on food, water, health, sexual violence and economic insecurity reaches people at a local level. If the people relied on the realisation of human rights frameworks to establish the right to health or water and so on, it would be fruitless. There is not a 'state' to receive, adjudicate and provide remedies for human rights claims. Nor are there adequate resources to achieve even the 'minimum core' of economic, social and cultural rights. To this end, this case study has suggested that the ICRC dialogue with the state, non-state armed groups and local communities using 'humanitarian' language and projects are valuable currency for the realisation of human security on the ground. In addition, the ICRC's economic security projects on the ground in the DRC aim to help victims of armed conflict, in particular at the local level. The ICRC cannot be involved in peace building, as to do so would compromise its neutrality and impartiality. However, for people on the ground, reconciliation of different groups, economic stability of farming communities and improvements in health, sanitation and the availability of food all contribute to a more stable environment. That being said, this does not answer the question of whether these developments in its roles from the Geneva Conventions I, II, III and IV 1949 and the ICRC Statutes are legitimate? Can the ICRC argue 'humanitarianism' every time it undertakes an activity that is difficult to reconcile with any wording of the Geneva Conventions? Do its small-scale successes such as those shown in this case study preclude any real assessment of whether it can lawfully undertake these activities or projects? These issues are considered, taking into account all chapters of the book, in the concluding chapter.

[147] A Peters, 'Humanity as the A and Ω of Sovereignty' (2009) 20(3) *European Journal of International Law* 513, 514, 515–16.

# *Conclusion*

THE CURRENT SITUATION, as regards armed conflict, can be viewed in two ways. On the one hand, armed conflict continues, as the situations in the DRC, Syria and Ukraine show. The nature of armed conflict, however, continues to change; the 'front line' is a myriad of continually shifting lines, often spreading into areas populated by civilians. The gloom of war, therefore, continues to hang over states and the people within them. Moreover, the human cost of conflict increasingly affects those not taking part in hostilities. On the other hand, the significance of IHL continues to develop, as it is designed to protect people not directly participating in hostilities and limit the effects of armed conflicts. The drafting and ratification of the Geneva Conventions I, II, III and IV 1949 and Additional Protocols I and II 1977 and the drafting of the Customary Study on IHL are evidence of state acceptance of limitations on their actions during armed conflicts. In addition, it was shown in chapter 3 that other legal frameworks, including IHRL, apply during hostilities and echo the humanitarian principles of the ICRC.

Throughout the twentieth and twenty-first centuries, the ICRC continued to focus on its traditional mission and mandate whilst constantly adapting to new situations of armed conflict, new actors in those conflicts and the changing needs of civilian populations. The ICRC has worked to develop the law and its activities to reflect the humanitarian needs of people on the ground. Critically, the ICRC is well placed to understand the dynamics behind violence and why some actors choose to ignore IHL. The issue at hand in this book, however, was how far the ICRC can develop its mandate and practice and continue to remain true to the principles and purposes of the movement. To this end, this book has addressed the protection and assistance roles of the ICRC, both traditionally and currently.

In order to determine the authority of the ICRC, one of the purposes of this research was to consider what kind of international organisation the ICRC is, that is, whether it resembles an intergovernmental organisation with ILP, or whether it is more closely akin to an NGO, such as Amnesty International or Human Rights Watch. It was concluded that the ICRC is difficult to define in terms of its organisational 'type' and should, as such, be considered sui generis. Nevertheless, it does possess ILP.

The ICRC is a unique organisation within the most comprehensive humanitarian movement on earth. The three components of the IRCRM—the ICRC, the IFRC and 190 national societies—along with all of the High

Contracting Parties to the Geneva Conventions meet every four years at the International Conference to debate major humanitarian challenges.[1] Each component has its own mandate and, therefore, its own focus and priorities, from conflict, to disasters, and localised humanitarian protection and assistance concerns. The International Conference is the supreme deliberative body for the movement and facilitates dialogue and decision-making throughout the movement and state parties to the Geneva Conventions I, II, III and IV 1949. In terms of its humanitarian protection and assistance roles, under the Geneva Conventions the ICRC has the right to be active in international armed conflicts.[2] The right of initiative, in terms of NIACs is different; the ICRC can 'offer' its services.[3] The basis of its presence in either case will be the Headquarters Agreement that is negotiated with the state.[4] The Headquarters Agreements have minimum requirements, in particular the immunity of staff. Finally, in addition to the international mandate and Headquarters Agreements, the ICRC also has a mission statement, which is inspired by the mandate and which stems from an ICRC 'Doctrine/Policy' that is adopted by the Assembly, its supreme governing entity. The Assembly is the only body that can amend and adopt 'Doctrine/Policy'.[5]

Analysis of the ICRC as an organisation ultimately showed that the ICRC is a sui generis organisation with ILP. These conclusions provided the building blocks for the book to consider the development of the activities of the ICRC. Firstly, the International Conference provides states with the opportunity to develop the mandate of the ICRC; to this end, states continue to be involved in the overall direction of the ICRC. Thereafter, the delegates at headquarters and in the field undertake the day-to-day work of the ICRC. International legal persons cannot act outside their constitutional mandate; likewise, just because an entity does not have ILP does not mean that it cannot respond to situations as it sees fit—for example, an NGO adapting its activities in light of specific human needs. Nevertheless, owing to its ILP, the ICRC has the capacity for autonomous development of its rights and duties. It is clear, however, that the purposes of the ICRC are not as extensive as the UN, which was the focus of the *Reparations* case, and, therefore, it was shown that expansion of powers by the ICRC is more circumspect. The ICRC has been able to develop its legal framework and practice in response to the changing nature of conflict and security paradigms. Nevertheless, the ICRC must remain true to its object

1 International Conference, https://www.icrc.org/en/who-we-are/movement/international-conference.

2 Geneva Conventions I, II, III and IV 1949, Arts 9, 9, 9, 10.

3 See Geneva Conventions I, II, III and IV 1949, common Art 3; Additional Protocol, Art 18.

4 See analysis in ch 1.

5 'ICRC Strategy 2015–2018: Adopted by the ICRC Assembly on 18 June 2014', https://www.icrc.org/fre/assets/files/publications/icrc-002-4203.pdf.

and purposes, including its principles of humanity, neutrality, impartiality and independence. In addition, states must consent to the presence of the ICRC on their territory, which is not always the case with the UN. Accordingly, the ICRC continues to balance its willingness and ability to provide humanitarian protection and assistance with the necessity of remaining true to its fundamental principles.

The mandate of the ICRC and its practice was influenced, arguably, by the fact that the normative development of the *jus ad bellum* and *jus in bello*, following the end of the Second World War, took two distinct paths. The UN, keen to 'never again' witness a world war, sought to preclude the use of force on the international stage, except in specific and limited circumstances. The ICRC, on the other hand, arguably more pragmatic than the UN, recognised that hostilities and armed conflicts would continue. The ICRC therefore pursued the development of legal frameworks to limit the suffering of people not involved in conflicts. Chapter 3 showed that these two distinct, both commendable, approaches to armed conflict were ultimately thwarted by not only the continuation of inter-state conflicts but by the increase in the types of conflict commonly seen today, that is, protracted NIACs. Nowadays people within states fight one another, not just other states, and the reasons for armed conflict no longer reflect the concerns of states prior to 1945, that is, predominantly territorial gain. Today, lack of access to resources, religious disputes, more localised land disputes and political ideological clashes perpetuate conflict and strife in many countries. This book recognises the importance, therefore, of the protection and assistance work provided by the ICRC in such fragile circumstances. The governance of the ICRC allows it to respond and adapt to human needs. At times it can act autonomously by virtue of its ILP, but it can also get consent at the International Conference or Headquarters Agreements to forge ahead with bigger or more bespoke humanitarian protection and assistance projects.

The examination of the legal frameworks guiding the ICRC led this author to question where the ICRC sits in relation to other human-focused legal regimes, including *jus in bello* and IHRL. Ruti Teitel's 'humanity's law' echoes this author's argument that there is an inherent humanisation of international law. Chapter 3 built on existing literature, which shows the inherent links between IHL, IHRL and international criminal law. It examined how the concept of humanity's law can be reconciled with the mandate of the ICRC and showed that the principle of humanity as something to be protected during armed conflict has expanded into other situations of violence. To this end, chapter 4 undertook a doctrinal critique of the principles of humanity and neutrality and the limitations that they place on the ICRC. Chapter 4 also highlighted the suggestions in chapter 3 that 'humanity's law' is, in fact, in existence and relevant to the mandate of the ICRC.

In this regard, Peter Maurer, President of the ICRC, recognised in 2012 that: '[I]n situations where the government or international coalitions are unable to assert their control, the ICRC must be able to reach vulnerable groups in an effective manner.'[6] The ICRC acknowledges that: '[I]n many situations, conflicts have become entrenched, forcing assistance work to cover the longer term, to meet needs that are at once urgent and recurrent, or even chronic.'[7] The international response to current conflicts has been termed the 'new humanitarianism' as humanitarianism has expanded to include human rights, provision of medical aid, economic development, promotion of democracy, and even building responsible states.[8] The current roles of the ICRC include protecting civilians; visiting detainees; reuniting families; ensuring access to medical care, water, food and essential household items; and running programmes for sustainable food production and MEIs.[9] The ICRC is in a position to put people on the ground first, above political and, hopefully, economic considerations. In fact, the changing nature of conflict has forced the ICRC to recognise that the needs of people within states are part of the 'security' paradigm of armed conflict. Whereas, historically, the type of security linked to international armed conflict was primarily national security, which required military responses to aggression or intervention, nowadays the predominantly internal conflicts show that human security is of paramount importance, not only to states, but to the people, the civilians and victims, living within those states. The protection and assistance roles provided in the Geneva Conventions contain potential for the realisation of that human security, although interviewees were keen to distance the ICRC from human security as a UN concept. Nevertheless, the 'big picture' in this regard is that ultimately international law is shifting; it is moving away from resolute notions of sovereignty towards a model of sovereignty that incorporates human-centric norms, that is, sovereignty as responsibility. To this end, security can be measured not only by lack of military aggression, but also by security in the daily lives of the population. This includes food, economic, health, personal, political, community and environmental security, all of which are supported by the mandate of the ICRC.

The definition of humanity provided in the IRCRCM Statutes states that 'its purpose is to protect life and health and to ensure respect for the human

[6] ibid.

[7] 'ICRC Assistance Policy (Adopted by the Assembly of the International Committee of the Red Cross on 29 April 2004) Public Version' (ICRC) 677, www.icrc.org/eng/assets/files/other/irrc_855_policy_ang.pdf.

[8] M Duffield, J Macrae and D Curtis, 'Editorial: Politics and Humanitarian Aid' (2001) 25(4) *Disasters* 269; M Barnett, 'Humanitarianism Transformed' (2005) 3(4) *Perspectives on Politics* 723 in FK Abiew, 'Humanitarian Action under Fire: Reflections on the Role of NGOs in Conflict and Post-Conflict Situations' (2012) 19(2) *International Peacekeeping* 203, 213.

[9] Ban Ki-Moon, 'The ICRC and the Changing Humanitarian Landscape' (2012) 94 *IRRC* 1251, 1252.

being'. If we take the mandate of the ICRC, then its right to visit prisoners of war or to provide healthcare to wounded soldiers is clearly linked to this part of the principle of humanity. This book addressed whether 'protection' and 'assistance' have had to adapt to new types of conflict and broader humanitarian concerns. IHL, IHRL, humanitarian principles and human security all reinforce the same ideal, that is, the protection of human beings. The action taken by different organisations is premised on different aspects of these legal norms but, ultimately, the purpose is the same. It is therefore reasonable to consider how action taken on the ground under one legal framework may, intentionally or otherwise, advance the pursuit of another human-focused framework. The humanitarian protection and assistance of the ICRC can positively impact the human security of the people on the ground.

The ICRC is working beyond the specific humanitarian protection and assistance roles mandated to it in the Geneva Conventions I, II, III and IV 1949 and to what this author considers to be the peripheries of humanitarianism as it is more widely understood, that is, into human security, development and other long-term humanitarian projects. Nevertheless, the ICRC is more restricted than organisations than can be openly politically motivated, which works to its advantage when negotiating Headquarters Agreements and making contact with non-state armed groups. It was shown that the ICRC has adapted its practice on the ground to respond to broader humanitarian needs given the changing and protracted nature of armed conflict, and that in doing so it may have expanded its mandate.

Current practice indicates that the ICRC understands humanity in a broader sense. At the same time as ICRC practice shifted too, to broader and more long-term humanitarian protection and assistance activities, the principle of humanity, once restricted to IHL and Red Cross work, now permeates the international stage and is reflected in the concept of human security. This book showed that the concept of human security is reflective of a normative shift on the international stage whereby states, including within the UN and other groups, have recognised the central role that 'humanity' has during and after armed conflict. The threats to security contained in the concept of human security, as created by the UNDP and now contained in the Common Understanding Resolution, more aptly identify the corpus of humanitarian concerns facing individuals and communities nowadays, given the changed nature of conflict.

Overall, this book identified how the international community has moved on from the binary distinction between war and peace, institutionalised by the UN and ICRC at the end of the Second World War, to adopt a concept that, at its centre, reflects the principle of humanity. Human security is a human-centric reconceptualisation of traditional public international law principles, including state sovereignty and non-intervention. Its adoption at the General Assembly shows that the international community, at large, now recognises the importance of seeing human beings as a central concern. Whilst humanity underlies such developments, the ICRC is edging into a 'human security' interpretation of its mandate. The ICRC works 'in other situations of violence', it undertakes long-term projects which continue beyond the cessation of hostilities, and it has clear links to economic security—the specifics of which were explored in chapter 5 and the case study and will be concluded below. Therefore, the concept of humanity has driven the ICRC and other organisations to develop human-focused frameworks and activities. It also developed into newer concepts such as human security which the ICRC humanitarian protection and assistance roles can link into. The concept of humanity therefore permeates and drives a myriad of concepts and legal frameworks at the international level.

In terms of 'humanitarian initiative' the ICRC may be responding to the 'needs' of the people on the ground but it is walking a fine line in terms of its neutrality. It is this aspect of its mandate that is most likely to see consent revoked by states, more so than a broader understanding of humanity. The conclusions to chapter 5 therefore drew on the principles discussed throughout the book, the question of the usurpation of its mandate and whether there might be consequences for the ICRC, reflecting on the analysis of chapter 2.

The ICRC draws its rights and duties on the international stage from Articles 9, 9, 9 and 10 Geneva Conventions I, II, III and IV 1949. It has traditionally interpreted its protection and assistance mandates conferred by these articles to include the right to visit detainees, administer the central tracing and messaging service, and provide medical assistance to the sick and wounded. Under Additional Protocol I it 'may also carry out *any other humanitarian activities* in favour of these victims, subject to the consent of the Parties to the conflict concerned'.[10] Paragraph 4(2) of the ICRC Statutes states that: '[T]he ICRC may take *any humanitarian initiative* which comes within its role as a specifically neutral and independent institution and intermediary, and may consider any question requiring examination by such an institution.'[11] This broad power of initiative is also found in the IRCRCM Statutes.[12]

Increasingly, however, the ICRC's mandate and practice have come to involve newer activities, such as economic security. Legally speaking therefore, the ICRC can attempt to justify the expansion of its activities to include economic security by subsuming them under 'any other humanitarian activities' provided for in Additional Protocol I, which only applies

[10] Emphasis added.
[11] Emphasis added.
[12] IRCRCM Statutes, Art 5(2)(d) and 5(3); ICRC Statutes, Art 4(2).

during international armed conflicts. This is difficult to reconcile with the ICRC's current roles, as so many conflicts are now NIACs. Thus, even if the ICRC can explain its activities under 'any other humanitarian activity', this book has shown that there may come a time when it is found to have encroached into long-term projects which do not appear, to states, to be within the mandate provided in the Geneva Conventions or IRCRCM Statutes. If and when this happens states are likely to revoke their consent for the presence of the ICRC or they will deny it access in the first instance. In the latter scenario, its traditional roles and activities will also be stopped. The argument is, overall, that the ICRC has many legal provisions from which it can explain its practice, and some were drafted rather broadly, all of which states had to consent to, but this does not mean that states have to consent to every activity of the ICRC on their territory. States may consent to resolutions at the International Conference but this does not bind them to consent to everything that the ICRC does within its territory.

It was important to test the theoretical and doctrinal conclusions of this research by speaking to delegates of the ICRC. Chapter 6 and the case study of the book also considered whether, *if* the ICRC continued to work beyond a strict understanding of its humanitarian mandate, it would affect the willingness of states to allow the ICRC to enter. At the moment, the ICRC relies on its reputation of neutrality and independence and promises of confidentiality to ensure access to fulfil its protection and assistance roles. Traditionally the role of the ICRC ended with the end of the conflict, but nowadays the ICRC stays longer. The ICRC's principles of neutrality, independence and consent preclude it from engaging in politicised activities. The ICRC is, however, able to command the respect of states whilst utilising its proximity and national societies to reach the people on the ground. As was concluded earlier, this book explored to what extent the ICRC can contribute to human security. Critically, it also considered whether within its expanding protection and assistance role, the ICRC could provide a localised method to develop human security on the ground for the victims of armed conflict, in particular, protracted armed conflict. When the ICRC can get access to vulnerable groups who are out of reach of other organisations, whether because they are already present in an area at the outbreak of conflict or serious violence, then they might engage in basic humanitarian roles, such as feeding people. The problem for the ICRC is that if a particular community is linked to the current government, then it might look as if it is not being impartial. For the ICRC, potentially, the concern is not usurpation of its mandate by expanding its powers too far, but rather the risks posed by looking partial and too closely linked to the government. The ICRC, in these instances, continues to walk a fine line between assisting those in need and compromising its reputation.

The interviews conducted in Geneva were essential to the analysis of the ICRC's present roles. The conclusions drawn up to the point of interviewing were abstract theories based on laws, academic literature and theories behind humanitarian protection and assistance, international human rights law, *jus in bello, jus ad bellum* and human security. It was imperative, therefore, to test them with the people who work on the ground and to ask what they see their role as being and from where they take their mandate. The interviews provided unique insight into the governance, autonomy and mandate of the ICRC. The current literature on the ICRC is often drafted by ICRC delegates or is available in the *IRRC*. In terms of understanding and critiquing the mandate of the ICRC it proved useful to ask delegates how they interpret the mandate on the ground. In addition, the interviews were a unique and invaluable opportunity to gather first-hand knowledge of the situation on the ground of the DRC.

The interviews showed that the ICRC does not, in its protection and assistance roles, try to substitute the activities that governments traditionally take care of. The ICRC will try, first and foremost, to remind authorities of their responsibilities to the people in a state or in their region of control. This can include reminding authorities about provision of food and healthcare. The intervention of the ICRC into the provision of such services begins when the authorities are no longer in a position to provide them. The ICRC will then have to decide if it has the capacity to intervene and provide those services. It must, therefore, maintain a dialogue with local communities and parties to the conflict. This dialogue can help in maintaining the view of the ICRC as neutral and impartial.

For the ICRC perhaps the most telling statement came from an interview conducted in April 2014. An ICRC delegate stated that:

> We have to be very humble. I am always suspicious of those who believe that what they are doing is perfect and they have reached all the beneficiaries. And I would say that the level of difficulties that you can reach on the ground is incredible and it's remarkable that you can move on and you can acquire certain expertise that will help you to, or at least you can learn from past mistakes, which is always what we do when we are making projects. So of course with 150 years of past mistakes, I would say, we are quite knowledgeable, but we are now definitely in some operations we have gained certain expertise that will help us to reach out. But again when you talk about the conflict like the DRC, the level of needs is absolute.[13]

The case study also explored the conclusions drawn in the first six chapters of the book. In part, state sovereignty's traditional corollary, non-intervention, allowed the newly independent DRC to turn against its own population and commit mass atrocities against people unable to ensure

[13] Interview 001.

their own human security. When we look at the historical development of the conflict, it appears that actors have scant regard for the UN Charter or the Geneva Conventions I, II, III and IV 1949. Nevertheless, the ICRC and the UN have been present in the DRC for decades. With the emerging concept of sovereignty as responsibility, according to Kofi Annan's 1999 report, and the evolution of human security, the idea of a human-centric international agenda has prospered and could have offered people on the ground hope for a future resilient to the recurrence of conflict. The typical means to enforce the idea of sovereignty as responsibility has, however, remained military intervention or complete inaction on the part of the international community.

For the ICRC, therefore, it is concluded that it has the power to develop its capacities to respond to the needs on the ground. It is also, as an organisation, inextricably linked to other normative and legal frameworks including human security and IHRL. It can thus draw on these synergies when acting on the international stage, within states and local communities. Its human-centric origins, its relationship with national societies and its proximity to conflicts allows it actually to connect to the needs of people on the ground.

# *Appendix 1: Interview Guide 2016*

*Prospective Participant Information Sheet*

*Title: The International Red Cross and Red Crescent Movement and its Mandate to Protect and Assist: Law and Practice*

*Researcher: Dr Christy Shucksmith*

*Affiliation: Lincoln Law School, University of Lincoln, UK*

UNIVERSITY OF LINCOLN

*You are being asked to take part in a research project carried out by Dr Christy Shucksmith of the University of Lincoln* (http://staff.lincoln.ac.uk/cshucksmith). *Before you decide to take part, it is important for you to understand why the research is being done and what it will involve. Please take time to read the information carefully and decide whether or not you wish to take part.*

*Aims of Project*

*The research project is to support the theoretical and legal research undertaken for a monograph. Data from the proposed interviews may be used in subsequent research projects and publications.*

The purpose of the book is to consider the changing practice of the International Committee of the Red Cross (ICRC/ IFRC) and International Federation of the Red Cross (IFRC). It provides extensive legal analysis of the ICRC/ IFRC as organisations, legal persons, and humanitarian actors. It draws on the law of organisations, International Humanitarian Law, International Human Rights Law, and other relevant branches of international law in order to critically assess the mandate and practice of the ICRC/ IFRC on the ground. The book also draws on more abstract human-centric concepts, including sovereignty as responsibility and human security in order to assess the development of the concept of humanity for the mandate and practice of the ICRC/ IFRC.

Critically the book uses qualitative interviews with ICRC/ IFRC delegates to test the theoretical and doctrinal conclusions.

It should be said that this author finds that the work of the ICRC and IFRC is unparalleled on the international stage and its humanitarian mandate is a vital component for those embroiled in the undertaking and recovery from conflict.

***Objectives of Interviews***

***The research project is primarily desk-based, combining theoretical and doctrinal analysis with empirical analysis of ICRC/ IFRC practice. It draws on literature from other disciplines, such as politics and sociology.***

***The objectives of the proposed interviews are to supplement this theoretical analysis and to test the theoretical hypotheses, and where appropriate gain further insight into the interpretation of the mandate by ICRC/ IFRC delegates. In sum, its purpose is to strengthen the accuracy of the desk-based analysis and interpretation of the theory and practice.***

***Why have you been Approached?***

***You have been approached due to your experience working with the ICRC/ IFRC. You have been identified and selected due to your expertise and your ability to provide insight into the mandate and practice of the ICRC/ IFRC.***

***What will be Required of Participants?***

***Participants will be asked to participate in the aforementioned interviews. They are entitled to respond to questions as they see fit, and are entitled to decline a response to any question asked.***

***The researcher will ask if the participant is willing to have the interview recorded, however they are entitled to decline permission for recording, or to withdraw or suspend permission at any point during the interview.***

Where audio recording is not permitted by the participant, the researcher will take notes throughout the interview in order to ensure the accuracy of the researcher's data. After the interview, the researcher will write up the notes from the meeting and/or will take a written transcript of any audio recording, and will send it to the participant. All participants have the right to review and request the rectification of transcripts or notes made by the researcher within reasonable time, and no later than 1st July 2016. Participants will be entitled to make further observations upon the records of the meeting.

***Anonymity and Confidentiality***

The collection, storage and processing of data by the researcher will conform with the ethics requirements of the University of Lincoln.

All personal data of participants will be kept strictly confidential and will be obtained and stored in accordance with the Data Protection Act 1998. Only personal data pertinent to the research will be collected by the researcher.

Research data, that is records of the interviews (including recordings where appropriate, but also transcripts or notes taken by the researcher) emails or other communications between participants and the researcher will be anonymised and kept separately from the personal data. Statements from these communications may be used in publications arising from this research; however no information will be used or made public that could identify the participant.

Unless requested otherwise by the participant (see below, 'Right to withdraw from research'), data will be securely retained for a period of seven years from the date of any publication that may be based upon it. During this period, this data may be used in subsequent research outputs in addition to the monograph.

***Right to Withdraw from the Research***

All individuals have the right to refuse to participate in the research, and all individuals who agree to participate have the right to withdraw from the research at any time until the 1st November 2016, the date upon which the text of the researcher's monograph will be finalised for submission.

Until the 1st November 2016, all participants have the right to request that content from their interviews will not be used in any way in the researcher's outputs. The researcher will ensure that this request is acted upon.

At any point, any participant may request the deletion of their personal data and research data as a result of the interview(s) from the researcher's records.

After the 1st November 2016, the researcher will endeavour to accommodate requests to remove reference to the participant's interviews, however no guarantee can be made that this will be possible.

***Contact Details***

***Dr Christy Shucksmith***

***David Chiddick Building***

***University of Lincoln, Lincoln Law School***

***Brayford Pool***

***Lincoln***

***LN6 7TS***

cshucksmith@lincoln.ac.uk

***Lincoln Law School Director of Research and Ethics Coordinator***

***Professor Matthew Hall*** (mhall@lincoln.ac.uk)

***Respondent Consent Form***

***Title: The International Red Cross and Red Crescent Movement and its Mandate to Protect and Assist: Law and Practice***

***Researcher: Dr Christy Shucksmith***

***Affiliation: Lincoln Law School, University of Lincoln, UK***

***Please complete the following form having read the accompanying and attached 'Prospective Participant Information Sheet'.***

1. I confirm that I have read and understand the information sheet dated ................ explaining the above research project and I have had the opportunity to ask questions about the project. ☐

2. I understand that my participation is voluntary and that I am free to withdraw at any time without giving any reason and without there being any negative consequences. In addition, should I not wish to answer any particular question or questions, I am free to decline. ☐

3. I understand that my responses will be kept strictly confidential (<u>only if true</u>). I give permission for Dr Christy Shucksmith to have access to my anonymised responses. I understand that my name will not be linked with the research materials, and I will not be identified or identifiable in the report or reports that result from the research. ☐

4. I agree for the data collected from me to be used in future research. ☐

5. I agree to take part in the above research project. ☐

| ________________ | ________________ | ________________ |
|---|---|---|
| Name of Participant | Date | Signature |
| ________________ | ________________ | ________________ |
| Lead Researcher | Date | Signature |

*To be signed and dated in presence of the participant*

Copies:

*Once this has been signed by all parties the participant should receive a copy of the signed and dated participant consent form, the letter/pre-written script/information sheet and any other written information provided to the participants. A copy of the signed and dated consent form should be placed in the project's main record (e.g. a site file), which must be kept in a secure location.*

***Interview Schedule for ICRC/ IFRC Delegates***

***Preliminaries***

***How long have you worked for the IFRC?***

***What drew you to this work?***

***Please can you briefly describe your role within the organisation?***

***Key Questions***

***The mandate of the ICRC/ IFRC:***

***How do you understand the 'mandate' of the IFRC?***

***Do you think that the Geneva Conventions/ Additional Protocols are fit for purpose in terms of humanitarian protection and assistance to be provided by the IFRC today?***

***How have protection and assistance activities expanded in the last decade?***

***What, in your view, are the key roles of the IIFRC in armed conflict and disaster situations?***

***How would you describe the relationship between the IFRC and States? How do you negotiate access to vulnerable populations?***

***How has the mandate of the IFRC developed during your time at the organisation?***

***How is the agenda set for the International Conference?***

***What is the relationship between the ICRC and IFRC?***

***What is the relationship between the IFRC and National Societies?***

***The legal frameworks surrounding humanitarian protection and assistance:***

***Are there projects currently undertaken by the IFRC that draw on other legal frameworks (i.e. human rights law/ refugee law)?***

> ***What situations threaten the neutrality and independence of the IFRC?***
>
> ***How do the principles of the movement link to its legal framework?***

***Questions about field work:***

> ***What field operations have you worked in? What was your role?***
>
> ***How do civilians on the ground view you as an individual working for the IFRC?***
>
> ***What is a 'successful' IFRC role?***
>
> ***How are decisions taken to begin a mission and end a mission? What are the decision making processes within the organisation?***

*Follow-up Questions*

***Is there anything else that you would like to talk about in terms of your work or the mandate of the IFRC?***

***How do you view the role of the IFRC in the world today?***

***In your view, what's in store for the IFRC over the next 10 years?***

# *Appendix 2: Interview Guide 2014*

INFORMATION SHEET FOR INTERVIEWEES

**About me**

I am a final year law PhD student at the University of Nottingham and former volunteer with the British Red Cross and Armenian Red Cross Society. The ICRC has the right to provide humanitarian assistance during armed conflict. It has developed its role to include economic security, development and transitional justice. This thesis considers whether this expansion of powers is legitimate and whether it compromises the ICRC's neutrality and independence to the extent that its value as a humanitarian actor is challenged. It also considers whether the ICRC has a peacebuilding role and whether it can help to establish human security on the ground. The thesis uses a case study of the Democratic Republic of the Congo to consider the practice of the ICRC.

**Project**

PhD Thesis: 'The International Committee of the Red Cross, Human Security and Peacebuilding: Law and Practice'

**Instructions to the interviewer (opening statements)**

I will record this interview to facilitate note taking at a later date. I will be the only person privy to the tapes, which will be destroyed after they are transcribed. The transcriptions will be electronically stored with password access. The information provided may appear in the main body of my PhD thesis and in an Appendix. The transcripts will be anonymised. Thank you for agreeing to participate.

I have asked you to be part of the research for my PhD as you are an expert in your field and have a great deal to share on the current humanitarian assistance practice of the ICRC and its role in the DRC. The research project as a whole focuses on the ICRC in peacebuilding contexts and whether its practice can establish human security on the ground for people. This research has a particular interest in the conflict in the DRC. I am trying to learn about the extent of the development of 'humanitarian assistance' into realms beyond those envisaged by the drafters of the Geneva Conventions 1949/Additional Protocols 1977 and whether experts within the ICRC feel that these developments are legitimate, in law and practice.

**Consent Form**

**Project title**

'The International Committee of the Red Cross, Human Security and Peacebuilding: Law and Practice'

**Researcher's name:**

**Christy Shucksmith**

**Supervisor's name:**

**Professor Nigel White**

— I have read the Participant Information Sheet and the nature and purpose of the research project has been explained to me. I understand and agree to take part.
— I understand the purpose of the research project and my involvement in it.
— I understand that I may withdraw from the research project at any stage and that this will not affect my status now or in the future.
— I understand that while information gained during the study may be published, I will not be identified and my personal results will remain confidential.
— I understand that I will be audiotaped/videotaped during the interview.
— I understand that data will be stored electronically on a password protected home computer which only the interviewer has access to. Tapes will be destroyed after transcripts are made. A transcript of the interview is available to the interviewee on request.
— I understand that I may contact the researcher or supervisor if I require further information about the research, and that I may contact the Research Ethics Coordinator of the School of Law, University of Nottingham, if I wish to make a complaint relating to my involvement in the research.

**Signed** ………………………………………………..(research participant)

**Print name** ………………………………… **Date** ……………………..…

**Contact details**

Researcher:

*Christy Shucksmith*

*Llxcs13@nottingham.ac.uk*

*07739 845084*

Supervisor: nigel.white@nottingham.ac.uk

INTERVIEW PROTOCOL/PARTICIPANT INFORMATION SHEET

**Project**

PhD Thesis: 'The International Committee of the Red Cross, Human Security and Peacebuilding: Law and Practice'

**Instructions to the interviewer (opening statements)**

I will record this interview to facilitate note taking at a later date. I will be the only person privy to the tapes, which will be destroyed after they are transcribed. The transcriptions will be electronically stored with password access. The information provided may appear in the main body of my PhD thesis and in an Appendix. The transcripts will be anonymised. Thank you for agreeing to participate.

I have asked you to be part of the research for my PhD as you are an expert in your field and have a great deal to share on the current humanitarian assistance practice of the ICRC and its role in the DRC. The research project as a whole focuses on the International Committee of the Red Cross in peacebuilding contexts and whether its practice can establish human security on the ground for people. This research has a particular interest in the conflict in the DRC. I am trying to learn about the extent of the development of 'humanitarian assistance' into realms beyond those envisioned by the drafters of the Geneva Conventions 1949/Additional Protocols 1977 and whether experts within the ICRC feel that these developments are legitimate, in law and practice.

**Key research questions to be asked**

* What ICRC actions come under the umbrella of humanitarian assistance? What forms do humanitarian assiatance take in the DRC?

* Is the ICRC constrained by the mandate given to it in the Geneva Conventions or has it managed to adapt to the times and maintain legitimacy on the international stage?

* Do you think the development of humanitarian assistance to include economic security/transitional justice roles (ie humanitarian aspects of peace agreements), challenges the ICRC's neutrality and independence?

* Although the ICRC is careful to distance itself from the term peacebuilding, to what extent do you think economic security work fits into a peacebuilding legal framework?

* To what extent does the ICRC coordinate with the UN on the ground in the provision of aid, involvement in economic projects and rule of law?

* How does the ICRC engage with/include the civilian/local population in humanitarian assistance roles? Do you think the ICRC is better placed, than MONUSCO, to reach local people and create human security?

**My Comments and Reflective Notes**

# *Bibliography*

'(1949) ILC Yearbook 281 paragraph 18' in F Kalshoven, 'Reaffirmation and Development of International Humanitarian Law Applicable in Armed Conflicts: The Conference of Government Experts, 24 May–12 June 1971' (1971) 2 *Netherlands Yearbook of International Law* 68.

'After the Death of Georges Olivet: Delegate of the International Committee of the Red Cross' (1962) 2 *IRRC* 21.

'Agreement between the International Committee of the Red Cross and the Swiss Federal Council to Determine the Legal Status of the Committee in Switzerland' (1993) 293 *IRRC* 152.

'Agreement between the International Committee of the Red Cross and the Swiss Federal Council to Determine the Legal Status of the Committee in Switzerland' (1993) 293 *IRRC* 152.

'Following the Death of Georges Olivet: Delegate of the International Committee of the Red Cross' (1962) 2 *IRRC* 84.

'Guiding Principles on the Right to Humanitarian Assistance' (1993) 33 *IRRC* 519.

'Human Rights in Armed Conflicts' (1970) 10 *IRRC* 220.

'In Memory of an ICRC Delegate' (1967) 7(74) *IRRC* 271.

'Interview with Peter Maurer' (Winter 2012) 94 (888) *IRRC* 1.

'News Items' (June 1962) IRRC 295, 315.

Abbott, KW and Snidal, D, 'Why States Act through Formal International Organisations' (1998) 42(1) *Journal of Conflict Resolution* 3.

Abromeit, H and Hitzel-Cassagnes, T, 'Constitutional Changes and Contractual Revision: Principles and Procedures' (1999) 5 *European Law Journal* 23.

Aldrich, GH, 'New Life for the Laws of War' (1981) 75(4) *American Journal of International Law* 764.

Allott, P, *Eunomia: New Order for a New World* (Oxford, Oxford University Press, 1990).

Alvarez, JE, *International Organizations as Law-makers* (Oxford, Oxford University Press, 2005) 133.

Amerasinghe, CF, *Principles of the Institutional Law of International Organizations*, 2nd edn (Cambridge, Cambridge University Press, 2005).

Amouyel, A, 'What Is Human Security?' (2006) 1 *Human Security Journal* 10.

Anderson, K, 'Humanitarian Inviolability in Crisis: The Meaning of Impartiality and Neutrality for UN and NGO Agencies Following the 2003–2004 Afghanistan and Iraq Conflicts' (2004) 17 *Harvard Human Rights Journal* 41.

Anderson, M and Olsen, L, *Confronting War: Critical Lessons for Peace Practitioners* (Cambridge, The Collaborative for Development Action Inc, 2003).

Arimatsu, L, 'The Democratic Republic of the Congo 1993–2010' in E Wilmshurst (ed), *International Law and the Classification of Conflicts* (Oxford, Oxford University Press, 2012).

Aust, A, *Handbook of International Law*, 2nd edn (Cambridge, Cambridge University Press, 2010).

Autesserre, S, 'Dangerous Tales: Dominant Narratives on the Congo and their Unintended Consequences' (2012) 111/443 *African Affairs* 202.

Autesserre, S, *The Trouble with the Congo: Local Violence and the Failure of International Peacebuilding* (Cambridge, Cambridge Studies in International Relations, 2010).

Ban Ki-Moon, 'The ICRC and the Changing Humanitarian Landscape' (2012) 94 *IRRC* 1251.

Badescu, CB, *Humanitarian Intervention and the Responsibility to Protect: Security and Human Rights* (New York, Routledge, 2011).

Banakar, R (ed), *Rights in Context: Law and Justice in Late Modern Society* (Farnham, Ashgate, 2010).

Banfield, J, Gündüz, C and Killick, N (eds), *Local Business, Local Peace: The Peace Building Potential of the Domestic Private Sector* (London, International Alert, 2006).

Barbara, C, 'International Legal Personality: Panacea or Pandemonium? Theorizing about the Individual and the State in the Era of Globalization' (2008) 20(1) *Sri Lanka Journal of International Law* 243.

Barber, R, 'Facilitating Humanitarian Assistance in International Humanitarian and Human Rights Law' (2009) 91 *IRRC* 371.

Barnett, M, 'Humanitarianism Transformed' (2005) 3(4) *Perspectives on Politics* 723 in Abiew, FK, 'Humanitarian Action under Fire: Reflections on the Role of NGOs in Conflict and Post-Conflict Situations' (2012) 19(2) *International Peacekeeping* 203.

Barnett, M and Weiss, TG, *Humanitarianism Contested: Where Angels Fear to Tread* (London, Routledge, 2011).

Barnett, M, Kim, H, O'Donnell, M and Sitea, L, 'Peace Building: What Is in a Name?' (2007) 13(1) *Global Governance* 44.

Baxter, R, 'Human Rights in War' (1977) 31(2) *Bulletin of the American Academy of Arts and Sciences* 4.

Bedermann, DJ, 'The Souls of International Organizations: Legal Personality and the Lighthouse at Cape Spartel' (1996) 36 *Virginia Journal of International Law* 371.

Beigbeder, Y, *The Role and Status of International Humanitarian Volunteers and Organizations: The Right and Duty to Humanitarian Assistance* (Leiden, Martinus Nijhoff Publishers, 1991).

Benedek, W, Ketteman, MC and Möstl, M (eds), *Mainstreaming Human Security in Peace Operations and Crisis Management: Policies, Problems, Potential* (London, Routledge, 2011).

Bergsmo, M and Tianying, S (eds), *On the Proposed Crimes against Humanity Convention* (Brussels, Torkel Opsahl Academic E-Publisher, 2014).

Best, G, *Humanity in Warfare: The Modern History of the International Law of Armed Conflicts* (London, Weidenfeld & Nicolson, 1980).

Biersteker, TJ and Weber, C, *Sovereignty as a Social Construct* (Cambridge, Cambridge University Press, 1996).

Bilkovà, V, 'Ensuring Human Security in Armed Conflicts: The Role of Non-State Actors and it Reflection in Current International Humanitarian Law' in C Ryngaert and M Noortman, *Human Security and International Law: The Challenge of Non-State Actors* (Cambridge, Intersentia, 2014).

Bindschedler, RD, 'Red Cross' (1983) 5 *EPIL* 250.

Bisaz, C, *The Concept of Group Rights in International Law: Groups as Contested Right-Holders, Subjects and Legal Persons* (Leiden, Martinus Nijhoff, 2012).
Bond, J, 'International Conflict and Article 3 of the Geneva Conventions' (1971) 48 *Denver Law Journal* 266.
Bossier, P, *History of the International Committee of the Red Cross: From Solferino to Tsushima* (Geneva, Henri Dunant Institute, 1985).
Bothe, M, Patsch, KJ and Solf, WA, with Eaton, M, *New Rules for Victims of Armed Conflicts: A Commentary on the Two 1977 Protocols Additional to the Geneva Conventions of 1949* (The Hague, Martinus Nijhoff, 1982).
Boyce, W, Koros, M and Hodgson, J, 'Community Based Rehabilitation: A Strategy for Peace-building' (2002) *BMC International Health and Human Rights* 216.
Brölmann, C, *The Institutional Veil in Public International Law: International Organisations and the Law of Treaties* (Oxford, Hart Publishing, 2007).
Brownlie, I, *Principles of Public International Law*, 7th edn (Oxford, Oxford University Press, 2008).
Bryman, A, *Social Research Methods*, 3rd edn (Oxford, Oxford University Press, 2012).
Bugnion, F, 'Red Cross Law' (1995) 308 *IRRC* 491.
Buzo, A, *Pacific Union: The Story of the San Francisco-Forty Fivers* (Monash University of Melbourne, Currency Press, 1995).
Byrne, B, 'Qualitative Interviewing' in C Seale (ed), *Researching Society and Culture*, 2nd edn (London, Sage, 2004).
Call, CT, (ed), *Building States to Build Peace* (Boulder, CO, International Peace Institute and Lynne Rienner, 2008).
Calogeropoulos-Stratis, AS, 'The Humanitarian Dimension of War: Protection of the Individual, whether Military or Civilian' (1992) 32 *IRRC* 183.
Carayannis, T, 'The Democratic Republic of the Congo, 1996–2012' in J Boulden (ed), *Responding to Conflict in Africa: The United Nations and Regional Organisations* (Basingstoke, Palgrave Macmillan, 2013).
Casalin, D and Lamb, C, 'Participation of States in the International Conference of the Red Cross and Red Crescent and Assemblies of other International Organisations' (2009) 91 *IRRC* 733.
Cassese, A, *International Law in a Divided World* (Gloucestershire, Clarendon Press, 1986).
Cassese, A, *International Law*, 2nd edn (Oxford, Oxford University Press, 2004).
Chadwick, A, 'The Emerging Roles of NGOs in the UN System: From Article 71 to a People's Millennium Assembly' (2002) 8(1) *Global Governance* 93.
Chapman, A and Russell, S (eds), *Core Obligations: Building a Framework for Economic, Social and Cultural Rights* (Oxford, Intersentia, 2002).
Charnovitz, S, 'Two Centuries of Participation: NGOs and International Governance' (1997) 18 *Michigan Journal of International Law* 183.
Charnovitz, S, 'Nongovernmental Organizations and International Law' (2006) 100(2) *American Journal of International Law* 348, 348.
Chehtman, A, 'Contemporary Approaches to the Philosophy of Crimes Against Humanity' (2014) 14(4–5) *International Criminal Law Review* 813.
Chetail, V (ed), *Post-conflict Peace Building: A Lexicon* (Oxford, Oxford University Press, 2009).

Chimni, BS, 'Third World Approaches to International Law: A Manifesto' (2006) 8 *International Community Law Review* 3.
Cockell, JG, 'Conceptualising Peace Building: Human Security and Sustainable Peace' in M Pugh (ed), *Regeneration of War-Torn Societies* (London, Macmillan, 2000).
Coicaud, J-M, 'Deconstructing International Legitimacy' in H Charlesworth and J-M Coicaud (eds), *Fault Lines of International Legitimacy* (Cambridge, Cambridge University Press, 2010).
Collier, P, *The Bottom Billion: Why the Poorest Countries are Failing and What Can Be Done About It* (Oxford, Oxford University Press, 2008).
Collier, P and Hoeffler, A, 'On Economic Causes of Civil War' (1998) 50(4) *Oxford Economic Papers* 563.
Collier, PA and Söderbom, M, 'Working Paper Produced by the Centre for the Study of African Economics' (Department of Economics, Oxford University) WPS/2006-12, August 17 in Call, T and Cousens, EM, 'Ending Wars and Building Peace: International Responses to War Torn Societies' (2008) 9 *International Studies Perspectives* 1.
Collins, A (ed), *Contemporary Security Studies* (Oxford, Oxford University Press, 2007).
Collins, R, 'Modern-Positivism and the Problem of Institutional Autonomy in International Law' in R Collins and ND White, *International Organisations and the Idea of Autonomy: Institutional Independence in the International Legal Order* (London, Routledge, 2011).
Collins, R, 'Non-State, Inter-State or Supra-State? The Peculiar Identity of the Intergovernmental Organization' in J d'Aspremont (ed.) *Participants in the International Legal System* (Abingdon, Routledge, 2011).
Collins, R and White, ND, 'International Organizations and the Idea of Autonomy, Introduction and Overview' in R Collins and ND White, *International Organisations and the Idea of Autonomy: Institutional Independence in the International Legal Order* (London, Routledge, 2011).
Conforti, B and Focarelli, C, *The Law and Practice of the United Nations*, 4th edn (The Hague, Martinus Nijhoff, 2010).
Conteh-Morgan, E, 'Peace Building and Human Security: A Constructivist Perspective' (2005) 10(1) *International Journal of Peace Studies* 69.
Corbett, PE, 'World Order: An Agenda for Lawyers' (1943) 37(2) *American Journal of International Law* 207.
Cornell, D, 'Facing Our Humanity' (2003) 18(1) *Hypatia* 170.
Coupland, R, 'Humanity: What Is It and How Does It Influence in International Law' (2001) 83 *IRRC* 969.
Crossland, J, *Britain and the International Committee of the Red Cross 1939-1945* (London, Palgrave Macmillan, 2014).
Cubitt, C, *Local and Global Dynamics of Peace Building: Post-Conflict Reconstruction in Sierra Leone* (Oxon, Routledge, 2011).
Curtis, D, 'The International Peace Building Paradox: Power Sharing and Post-Conflict Governance in Burundi' (2012) *African Affairs* 72.
Deng, FM, Kimaro, S, Lyons, T, Rothchild, D and Zartman, W (eds), *Sovereignty as Responsibility: Conflict Management in Africa* (Washington DC, Brookings Institution, 1996).

Denzin, NK and Lincoln, YS, *Handbook of Qualitative Research* (Thousand Oaks, CA, Sage, 2005) 1–32 in Sarantakos, S, *Social Research* (Basingstoke, Palgrave Macmillan, 2013).

Dominicé, C, 'La Personalité Juridique International du CICR' in C Swinarski (ed), *Studies and Essays on International Humanitarian Law and Red Cross Principles in Honour of Jean Pictet* (The Hague, Martinus Nijhoff, 1984).

Doswald-Beck, L and Vité, S, 'International Humanitarian Law and Human Rights Law' (1993) 293 *IRRC* 94.

Draper, GIAD, 'The Relationship between the Human Rights Regime and the Law of Armed Conflict' (1971) 1 *Israel Yearbook on Human Rights* 205.

Droege, C, 'The Interplay between International Humanitarian Law and International Human Rights Law in Situations of Armed Conflict' (2007) 40 *Israel Law Review* 310.

Droege, C, 'Elective Affinities? Human Rights and Humanitarian Law' (2008) 90 *IRRC* 501.

Duffield, M, Macrae, J and Curtis, D, 'Editorial: Politics and Humanitarian Aid' (2001) 25(4) *Disasters* 269.

Dunant, H, *A Memory of Solferino* (Geneva, ICRC, 1986).

Durand, A, *The International Committee of the Red Cross: From Sarajevo to Hiroshima* (Geneva, ICRC, 1981).

Eberhard, H, Lachmayer, K, Ribarov, G and Thallinger, G (eds), *Constitutional Limits to Security: Proceedings of the 4th Vienna Workshop on International Constitutional Law* (Bergasse, Facultas Verlags, 2009).

Eide, A, 'International Law, Dominance, and the Use of Force' (1974) 11(1) *Journal of Peace Research* 1.

Elrod, RB, 'The Concert of Europe: A Fresh Look at the International System' (1970) 28(2) *World Politics* 159.

Falk, R, 'Revisiting Westphalia, Discovering Post-Westphalia' (2002) 6(4) *Journal of Ethics* 311.

Fidler, DP, 'The Return of the Standard of Civilisation' (2001) 2 *Chicago Journal of International Law* 140.

Fidler, DP, 'Revolt Against or from Within the West? TWAIL, the Developing World, and the Future Direction of International Law' (2003) 2 *Chinese Journal of International Law* 29.

Fisher, RJ, 'The Potential for Peacebuilding: Forging a Bridge from Peacekeeping to Peacemaking' (1993) 18 *Peace and Change* 247.

Fleck, D, *The Handbook of International Humanitarian Law*, 2nd edn (Oxford, Oxford University Press, 2008).

Forsythe, DP, *The Humanitarians: The International Committee of the Red Cross* (Cambridge, Cambridge University Press, 2005).

Forsythe, DP and Rieffer-Flanagan, BAJ, *The International Committee of the Red Cross—A Neutral Humanitarian Actor* (London, Routledge, 2007).

Francis, DJ (ed), *When War Ends: Building Peace in Divided Communities* (Farnham, Ashgate, 2012).

Franck, T, 'United Nations Based Prospects for a New Global Order' (1990) 22 *New York University Journal of International Law and Politics* 601.

Galtung, J, 'The Palme Commission Report on Disarmament and Security: A Critical Comment' (1983) 14(2) *Bulletin of Peace Proposals* 147.

Galtung, J, *There Are Alternatives! Four Roads to Peace and Security* (Nottingham, Spokesman, 1984).

Gasser, H-P, 'International Non-International Armed Conflict: Case Studies of Afghanistan, Kampuchea, and Lebanon' (1982) 31 *American University Law Review* 911.

Gasser, H-P, 'International Humanitarian Law' in H Haug, *Humanity for All, the International Red Cross and Red Crescent Movement* (Geneva, Henry Dunant Institute, 1993).

Gasser, H-P, 'Protection of the Civilian Population' in D Fleck (ed), *The Handbook of International Humanitarian Law*, 2nd edn (Oxford, Oxford University Press, 2008).

Gasser, H-P, 'International Committee of the Red Cross (ICRC)' in R Wolfrum (ed), *The Max Planck Encyclopedia of Public International Law* (Oxford, Oxford University Press, 2009).

Gautier, P, 'The Reparation for Injuries Case Revisited: The Personality of the European Union' (2000) 4 *Max Planck Yearbook of United Nations Law* 331.

Gazzini, T (ILA Committee on Non-State Actors), 'A Unique Non-State Actor: The International Committee of the Red Cross' (Provisional Draft) (26–28 March 2009).

Gazzini, T, 'The Relationship between International Legal Personality and the Autonomy of International Organizations' in R Collins and ND White, *International Organisations and the Idea of Autonomy: Institutional Independence in the International Legal Order* (London, Routledge, 2011).

Gerstle, T and Meissner, L, 'Peace Building Essentials for Economic Development Practitioners: Practice Note 1: Market Development in Conflict-affected Contexts' (International Alert, 2009–10).

Gheciu, A, 'Divided Partners: The Challenges of NATO–NGO Cooperation in Peace building Operations' (2011) 17(1) *Global Governance* 95.

Gill, T, 'Chivalry? A Principle of the Law of Armed Conflict' in M Matthee, B Toebes and M Brus, (eds), *Armed Conflict and International Law: In Search of the Human Face* (The Hague, TMC Asser Press, 2013).

Green, F, 'Fragmentation in Two Dimensions: The ICJ's Flawed Approach to Non-State Actors and International Legal Personality' (2008) 9(1) *Melbourne Journal of International Law* 47.

Greenwood, C, 'Historical Development and Legal Basis' in D Fleck, *The Handbook of International Humanitarian Law*, 3rd edn (Oxford, Oxford University Press, 2013).

Gutteridge, JAC, 'The Geneva Conventions of 1949' (1949) 26 *British YB Intl L* 300.

Hampson, FO, with Daudelin, J, Hay, J, Reid, H and Martin, T, *Madness in the Multitude: Human Security and World Disorder* (Oxford, Oxford University Press, 2001).

Hansen, A and Wiharta, S, 'The Transition to a Just Order: Establishing Local Ownership After Conflict, A Policy Report' (Stockholm, Folke Bernadotte Academy, 2007).

Harding, C and Lim, CL, *Renegotiating Westphalia: Essays and Commentary on the European and Conceptual Foundations of Modern International Law* (The Hague, Martinus Nijhoff, 1999).

Harroff-Tavel, M, 'Neutrality and Impartiality—The Importance of these Principles for the International Red Cross and Red Crescent Movement and the Difficulties Involved in Applying Them' (1989) 29(273) *IRRC* 536.

Hartwig, M, *Die Haftung der Mitgliedstaaten* (Berlin, Springer Verlag, 1993).

Haufler, V, 'Private Sector International Regimes' in RA Higgot, GRD Underhill and A Bieler (eds), *Non-State Actors and Authority in the Global System* (London, Routledge, 2000).

Haug, H, 'Neutrality as a Fundamental Principle of the Red Cross' (1996) 36(315) *IRRC* 627.

Haug, H, *Humanity for All: The International Red Cross and Red Crescent Movement* (Vienna, Henry Dunant Institute/Paul Haupt, 1993).

Heike Spieker, AP, 'Twenty-Five Years after the Adoption of Additional Protocol II: Breakthrough or Failure of Humanitarian Legal Protection?' (2001) 4 *Yearbook of International Humanitarian Law* 129.

Hellmüller, S, 'The Power of Perceptions: Localizing International Peace Building Approaches' (2013) 20(2) *International Peacekeeping* 219.

Henckaerts, J-M, 'Reports and Documents-Bringing the Commentaries on the Geneva Conventions and their Additional Protocols into the Twenty-first Century' (Winter 2012) 94 *IRRC* 1551.

Henckaerts, J-M and Doswald-Beck, L, *Customary International Humanitarian Law: Volume 1 Rules* (Cambridge, Cambridge University Press, 2005).

Henckaerts, J-M and Doswald-Beck, L, *Customary International Humanitarian Law: Volume 1 Rules* (Cambridge, Cambridge University Press, 2005).

Hernández, GI, 'Non-State Actors from the Perspective of the International Court of Justice' in J d'Aspremont (ed), *Participants in the International Legal System: Multiple Perspectives on Non-State Actors in International Law* (London, Routledge, 2011).

Hilderbrand, RC, *Dumbarton Oaks: The Origins of the United Nations and the Search for Post War Security* (Durham, University of North Carolina Press, 1990).

Hobe, S, 'Global Challenges to Statehood: The Increasingly Important Role of Nongovernmental Organizations' (1997–98) 5 *Global Legal Studies J* 191.

Hochschild, A, *King Leopold's Ghost: A Story of Greed, Terror, and Heroism in Colonial Africa* (Boston, MA, Houghton Mifflin Harcourt, 1999).

Hubert, D and McRae, RG, (eds), *Human Security and the New Diplomacy: Protecting People, Promoting Peace* (Montreal, McGill University Press, 2001).

Human Security Centre, *Human Security Report 2005: War and Peace in the Twenty-first Century* (Oxford, Oxford University Press, 2005).

Humanitarian Practice Network, 'Operational Security Management in Violent Environments' (London, Overseas Development Institute, 2010).

ICRC, *The Fundamental Principles of the Red Cross and Red Crescent* (Geneva, ICRC, 1996).

Ignatieff, M, *Human rights as Politics and Idolatry* (Princeton, Princeton University Press, 2001).

ILA, *Briand-Kellogg Pact of Paris (August 27, 1928): Articles of Interpretation as adopted by the Budapest Conference, 1934, together with the report of the relevant proceedings* (London, Sweet & Maxwell, 1934).

International Red Cross Red Crescent, 'Preventive Action: Understanding the Concept and Defining the ICRC's Role in Preventing Armed Conflicts: Guidelines' (2002) 84(846) *IRRC* 463.
Jacobsen, T, Sampford, C and Thakur, R, (eds), *Re-envisioning Sovereignty: The End of Westphalia?* (Farnham, Ashgate, 2008).
Jakovlijević, B, 'The Right to Humanitarian Assistance—Legal Aspects' (1987) 27 IRRC 469.
Jeannet, S, 'Non-Disclosure of Evidence before International Criminal Tribunals: Recent Developments Regarding the ICRC' (2001) 50 *ICLQ* 649.
Jenkins, R, *Peace Building: From Concept to Commission* (London, Routledge, 2013).
Jennings, R and Watts, A (eds), *Oppenheim's International Law*, 9th edn (London, Longman, 1992).
Jeong, H-W, *Peace Building in Post Conflict Societies: Strategy and Process* (Boulder, CO, Lynne Rienner, 2005).
Jessup, P, *A Modern Law of Nations* (New York, Macmillan, 1948).
Kaczorowska, A, *Public International Law* (London, Taylor & Francis, 2010).
Kamminga, MT, 'The Evolving Status of NGOs under International Law: A Threat to the Inter-State System?' in P Alston (ed), *Non-State Actors and Human Rights* (Oxford, Oxford University Press, 2005).
Katkin, K, 'Communication Breakdown? The Future of Global Connectivity after the Privatisation of INTELSAT' (2005) *International Journal of Communications Law and Policy* 1.
Kayode, SS, 'Intervention Brigade for the Congo: A Precedent for UN Peace Enforcement' (2014) 10 *Review of International Law and Politics* 88.
Keating, T and Knight, A, (eds), *Building Sustainable Peace* (UN University Press, 2004).
Kellenberger, J, President of the ICRC, Address: 'International Humanitarian Law and Other Legal Regimes: Interplay in Situations of Violence' (2003) 85 *IRRC* 645.
Kelsen, H, 'The Old and the New League: The Covenant and the Dumbarton Oaks Proposals' (1945) 39(1) *American Journal of International Law* 45.
Kelsen, H, *General Theory of Law and State* (Cambridge, MA, Harvard University Press, 1945).
Kennedy, D, 'International Law and the Nineteenth Century: History of an Illusion' (1996) 65 *Nordic J Intl L* 385.
Kennedy, D, 'The Move to Institutions' (1987) 8 *Cardozo Law Review* 840.
Klabbers, J and Wallendahl, Å (eds), *Research Handbook on the Law of International Organisations* (Cheltenham, Edward Elgar, 2011).
Klabbers, J, 'Presumptive Personality: The European Union in International Law' in M Koskenniemi (ed) *International Legal Aspects of the European Union* (The Hague, Kluwer, 1998).
Klabbers, J, *An Introduction to International Institutional Law*, 2nd edn (Cambridge, Cambridge University Press, 2009).
Klabbers, J, *Organisations: The Library of Essays in International Law* (Surrey, Ashgate/ Dartmouth Publishing Company, 2005).
Koenig, C, 'Observer Status for the International Committee of the Red Cross at the United Nations: A Legal Viewpoint' (1991) 280 *IRRC* 47.

Kolb, R, 'The Relationship between International Humanitarian Law and Human Rights Law: A Brief History of the 1948 Universal Declaration of Human Rights and the 1949 Geneva Conventions' (1998) 324 *IRRC* 409.

Kosirnik, R, 'The 1977 Protocols: A Landmark in the Development of International Humanitarian Law' (1997) 320 *IRRC* 483.

Koskenniemi, M, 'Hersch Lauterpacht and the Development of International Criminal Law' (2004) 2 *Journal of International Criminal Justice* 811.

Krahenbuhl, P, 'The ICRC's Approach to Contemporary Security Challenges: A Future for Independent and Neutral Humanitarian Action' (2004) 86 *IRRC* 505.

Krasner, SD, 'Sharing Sovereignty: New Institutions for Collapsed and Failing States' (2004) 29(2) *International Security* 85.

Krause, K, 'Is Human Security More Than Just a Good Idea?' in M Rzoska and PJ Croll (eds), *Promoting Security: But How and For Whom?* (Bonn, Bonn International Center for Conversion, 2004).

Krause, K, 'The Key to a Powerful Agenda, If Properly Delimited' (2004) 35 *Security Dialogue* 367.

Kreijen, G, *State Failure, Sovereignty and Effectiveness: Legal Lessons from the Decolonisation of Sub-Saharan Africa (Developments in International Law)* (Leiden, Martinus Nijhoff, 2004).

Krieger, H, 'A Conflict of Norms: The Relationship between Humanitarian Law and Human Rights Law in the ICRC Customary Law Study' (2006) 11(2) *Journal of Conflict and Security Law* 265.

Kunz, JL, 'The Chaotic Status of the Laws of War and the Urgent Necessity for their Revision' (1951) 45(1) *American Journal of International Law* 37.

Kunz, JL, 'The Laws of War' (1956) 50(2) *American Journal of International Law* 313.

Larrinaga, M De and Doucet, MC, 'Sovereign Power and the Bio Politics of Human Security' (2008) 39(5) *Security Dialogue* 517.

Lauterpacht, H (ed), *International Law: A Treatise by L Oppenheim*, vol II, 6th edn (London, Longmans, Green & Co, 1947).

Lauterpacht, H, 'The Grotian Tradition in International Law' (1946) 23 *British Yearbook of International Law* 31 in Teitel, RG, *Humanity's Law* (Oxford, Oxford University Press, 2011).

Lauterpacht, H, 'The Revision of the Laws of War' (1952) 29 *British Yearbook of International Law* 360.

Lauterpacht, H, *International Law: Being the Collected Papers of Hersch Lauterpacht*, vol 1: *The General Works*, ed E Lauterpacht (Cambridge, Cambridge University Press, 2009).

Lavoyer, J-P and Maresca, L, 'The Role of the ICRC in the Development of International Humanitarian Law' (1999) 4 *International Negotiation* 501.

Lederach, JP, 'Conflict Transformation in Protracted Internal Conflicts: The Case for a Comprehensive Framework' in K Rupesinghe (ed), *Conflict Transformation* (New York, Macmillan, 1995).

Lederach, JP, *Preparing for Peace: Conflict Transformation across Cultures* (New York, Syracuse University Press, 1995).

Lederach, JP, *Building Peace: Sustainable Reconciliation in Divided Societies* (Washington DC, US Institute of Peace Press, 1997).

Lederach, JP, 'Civil Society and Reconciliation' in Crocker, CA, Hampson, FO and P Aall, *Turbulent Peace, The Challenges of Managing International Conflict* (Washington DC, Institute of Peace, 2001).
Lemay-Hebert, N, 'The "Empty-Shell" Approach: The Setup Process of International Administrations in Timor-Leste and Kosovo, Its Consequences and Lessons' (2011) 12 *International Studies Perspectives* 190.
Lindblom, A-K, 'NGOs and Non-State Actors in International Law' in B Reinalda (ed), *Ashgate Research Companion to Non-State Actors* (Farnham, Ashgate, 2011).
Lindblom, A-K, *Non-Governmental Organizations in International Law* (Cambridge, Cambridge University Press, 2005).
Luard, E, *A History of the United Nations*, vol 1: *The Years of Western Domination, 1945–1955* (Hong Kong, Macmillan, 1982).
Martens, K, 'Examining the (Non-) Status of NGOs in International Law' (2003) 1 *Indiana Global Law Studies J* 1.
Martin, M and Owen, T, 'The Second Generation of Human Security: Lessons from the UN and EU Experience' (2010) 86 *International Affairs* 211.
McCorquodale, R, 'Beyond State Sovereignty: The International Legal System and Non-State Participants' (2006) *International Law: Revista colombiana de derecho internacional, junio-noviembre, número 008* Pontificia Universidad Javeriana Bogotá, Colombia 103.
McEvoy, C and Murray, R, 'Gauging Fear and Insecurity: Perspectives on Armed Violence in Eastern Equatoria and Turkana North' (Geneva, Small Arms Survey, Graduate Institute of International and Development Studies, 2008).
Meijknecht, A, *Towards International Legal Personality: The Position of Minorities and Indigenous Peoples in International Law* (London, Intersentia, 2001).
Meron, T, 'The Martens Clause, Principles of Humanity, and Dictates of Public Conscience' (2000) 94(1) *American Journal of International Law* 78.
Meron, T, 'Subjects of International Law: International Law in the Age of Human Rights' (2003) *Receuil des Cours de l'Academie de Droit International* 301.
Meyer, M, 'The Importance of the International Conference of the Red Cross and Red Crescent to National Societies: Fundamental in Theory and Practice' (2009) 91 *IRRC* 713.
Mgbeoji, I, 'The Civilised Self and the Barbaric Other: Imperial Delusions of Order and the Challenges of Human Security' (2006) 27(5) *Third World Quarterly* 855.
Milanovic, M, 'A Norm Conflict Perspective on the Relationship between International Humanitarian Law and Human Rights Law' (2010) 14 *Journal of Conflict and Security Law* 459.
Minkler, L (ed), *The State of Economic and Social Rights: A Global Overview* (Cambridge, Cambridge University Press, 2013).
Miyazaki, S, 'The Application of the New Humanitarian Law' (1980) 20 *IRRC* 184.
Moore, J, *Humanitarian Law in Action within Africa* (Oxford, Oxford University Press, 2012).
Moorehead, C, *Dunant's Dream: War, Switzerland and the History of the Red Cross* (New York, Carol & Graf, 1999).
Morgenthau, HJ, *Politics Among Nations* (New York, Knopf, 1948).
Morsink, J, 'World War Two and the Universal Declaration' (1993) 15 *Human Rights Quarterly* 357.

Muller, AS, *International Organisations and their Host States: Aspects of their Legal Relationship* (The Hague, Kluwer Law International, 1995).
Neff, S, 'A Short History of International Law' in M Evans, *International Law*, 4th edn (Oxford, Oxford University Press, 2014).
Neubert, D, 'The "Peacemakers" Dilemma: The Role of NGOs in Processes of Peace-building in Decentralised Conflicts' in M-C Foblets and T von Trotha, *Healing the Wounds: Essays on the Reconstruction of Societies after War* (Oxford, Hart Publishing, 2004).
Newman, E, 'Critical Human Security Studies' (2010) 36 *Review of International Studies* 77.
Noortman, M, 'Human Securities, International Laws and Non-State Actors: Bringing Complexity Back In' in C Ryngaert, and M Noortman, *Human Security and International Law: The Challenge of Non-State Actors* (Cambridge, Intersentia, 2014).
Nussbaum, A, *A Concise History of the Law of Nations*, rev edn (New York, Macmillan, 1954).
Oberleitner, G, 'Human Security: A Challenge to International Law?' (2005) 11 *Global Governance* 185.
Oberleitner, G, *Human Rights in Armed Conflict: Law, Practice, Policy* (Cambridge, Cambridge University Press, 2015).
Odello, M and Cavandoli, S, (eds), *Emerging Areas of Human Rights in the Twenty-first Century: The Role of the Universal Declaration on Human Rights* (London, Routledge, 2011).
Oeter, S, 'Methods and Means of Combat' in D Fleck, *The Handbook of International Humanitarian Law*, 3rd edn (Oxford, Oxford University Press, 2013).
Okimoto, K, *The Distinction and Relationship between* Jus ad Bellum *and* Jus in Bello (Oregon, Hart Publishing, 2011).
Orr, R, 'Governing When Chaos Rules: Enhancing Governance and Participation' (2002) 25(4) *Washington Quarterly* 140.
Owen, T, 'Human Security-Conflict, Critique and Consensus: Colloquium Remarks and a Proposal for a Threshold-Based Definition' (2004) 35(3) *Security Dialogue* 373.
Palmieri, D, 'An Institution Standing the Test of Time? A Review of 150 Years of the History of the International Committee of the Red Cross' (2012) 94 *IRRC* 1273.
Paris, R, 'Human Security: Paradigm Shift or Hot Air?' (2001) 26(2) *International Security* 93.
Paris, R, *At War's End: Building Peace after Civil Conflict* (Cambridge, Cambridge University Press, 2004).
Partlett, K, *The Individual and the International Legal System: Continuity and Change in International Law* (Cambridge, Cambridge University Press, 2011).
Peck, C, *Sustainable Peace: The Role of the United Nations and Regional Organizations in Preventing Conflict* (Oxford, Rowman & Little Publishers, 1998).
Perruchoud, R, *Les Résolutions des Conférences Internationales de la Croix-Rouge* (Henry Dunant Institute, Geneva, 1979).
Peters, A, 'Humanity as the A and Ω of Sovereignty' (2009) 20(3) *European Journal of International Law* 513.
Pictet, J, 'The Fundamental Principles of the Red Cross: Commentary' (Geneva, International Federation of Red Cross and Red Crescent Societies, 1979).

Pictet, J, *Development and Principles of International Humanitarian Law* (Geneva, Henry Dunant Institute and Dordrecht, Martinus Nijhoff, 1985).
Pictet, J, *Development and Principles of International Humanitarian Law* (The Hague, Martinus Nijhoff, 1985).
Pictet, JS, 'The New Geneva Conventions for the Protection of War Victims' (1951) 45(3) *American Journal of International Law* 462.
Pictet, J, *Red Cross Principles* (Geneva, ICRC, 1956).
Pilloud, C, Sandoz, Y, Swinarski, C and Zimmerman, B, *Commentary on the Additional Protocols of 8 June 1977 to the Geneva Conventions of 12 August 1949* (The Hague, Martinus Nijhoff, 1987).
Plattner, D, 'ICRC Neutrality and Neutrality in Humanitarian Assistance' (1996) 26(311) *IRRC* 161.
Portmann, R, *Legal Personality in International Law* (Cambridge, Cambridge University Press, 2010).
Pouligny, B, 'Civil Society and Post-Conflict Peace Building: Ambiguities of International Programmes Aimed at Building 'New Societies'' (2005) 36(4) *Security Dialogue* 495.
Pouligny, B, 'Local Ownership' in V Chetail (ed), *Post-conflict Peace Building: A Lexicon* (Oxford, Oxford University Press, 2009).
Provost, R, *International Human Rights and Humanitarian Law* (Cambridge, Cambridge University Press, 2002).
Prunier, G, *Africa's World War Congo, the Rwandan Genocide and the Making of a Continental Catastrophe* (Oxford, Oxford University Press, 2009).
Ramsbotham, O, 'The Analysis of Protracted Social Conflict: A tribute to Edward Azar' (2005) 31(1) *Review of International Studies* 109.
Ratner, SR, 'Law Promotion Beyond Law Talk: The Red Cross, Persuasion, and the Laws of War' (2011) 22(2) *European Journal of International Law* 459.
Reuter, P, *International Institutions* (trans JM Chapman from the French *Institutions Internationales* (Paris, Presses Universitaires de France, 1955)) (London, George Allen and Unwin, 1958).
Reyntjens, F, *The Great African War: Congo and Regional Geopolitics, 1996–2006* (Cambridge, Cambridge University Press, 2009).
Richmond, O, 'Resistance and Post-Liberal Peace' (2010) 38 *Millennium Journal of International Studies* 665.
Rieffer-Flanagan, BA, 'Is Neutral Humanitarianism Dead? Red Cross Neutrality: Walking the Tightrope of Neutral Humanitarianism' (2009) 31 *Human Rights Quarterly* 888.
Roberts, D, *Global Governance and Bio Politics: Regulating Human Security* (London, Zed Books, 2010).
Robertson, AH, 'Humanitarian Law and Human Rights' in C Swinarski (ed), *Studies and Essays on International Humanitarian Law and Red Cross Principles in Honour of Jean Pictet* (The Hague, Martinus Nijhoff, 1984).
Robson, C, *Real World Research: A Resource for Social Scientists and Practitioner-Researchers* (Oxford, Blackwell, 1993).
Rodenhäuser, T, 'Beyond State Crimes: Non-State Entities and Crimes Against Humanity' (2014) 27(4) *Leiden Journal of International Law* 913.
Rolandsen, OH, 'Land, Security and Peace Building in the Southern Sudan' (Oslo, PRIO Paper, International Peace Research Institute, December 2009).

Romero, GR, 'Voices Around Us: Memory and Community Empowerment in Reconstruction Efforts in Colombia' (2012) 6 *International Journal of Transitional Justice* 1.

Rossi, I, *Legal Status of Non-Governmental Organizations in International Law* (Cambridge, Intersentia, 2010).

Salter, M and Mason, J, *Writing Law Dissertations: An Introduction and Guide to the Conduct of Legal Research* (London, Longman, 2007).

Sandoz, Y, 'The Red Cross and Peace: Realities and Limits' (1987) 24(3) *Journal of Peace Research: Special Issue on Humanitarian Law of Armed Conflict* 287.

Sandoz, Y, 'Max Huber and the Red Cross' (2007) 18(1) *European Journal of International Law* 171.

Sands, P and Klein, P, *Bowett's Law of International Institutions*, 6th edn (London, Sweet & Maxwell, 2009).

Sayapin, S, 'The International Committee of the Red Cross and International Human Rights Law' (2009) 9(1) *Human Rights Law Review* 95.

Schabas, W, '*Lex Specialis*? Belts and Suspenders? The Parallel Operation of Human Rights Law and the Law of Armed Conflict, and the Conundrum of Jus ad Bellum' (2007) 40 *Israel Law Review* 592.

Schermers, H and Blokker, N, *International Institutional Law: Unity within Diversity*, 4th edn (Amsterdam, Martinus Nijhoff, 2003).

Schindler, D and Toman, J, *The Laws of Armed Conflict: A Collection of Conventions, Resolutions, and Other Documents* (Leiden, Brill, 1998).

Schindler, D, 'The International Committee of the Red Cross and Human Rights' (1979) 208 *IRRC* 3.

Schlesinger, S, *Act of Creation: The Founding of the United Nations: A Story of Superpowers, Secret Agents, Wartime Allies and Enemies, and their Quest for a Peaceful World* (New York, Basic Books, 2004).

Schlögel, A, 'International Red Cross' in R Wolfrum (ed), *United Nations: Law Policies and Practice* (Dordrecht, Martinus Nijhoff, 1995).

Scobbie, I, 'Principle or Pragmatics? The Relationship between Human Rights Law and the Law of Armed Conflict' (2010) 14(3) *Journal of Conflict and Security Law* 449.

Seyersted, F, 'International Personality of International Organizations: Do their capacities really depend upon their constitutions?' (1964) 4 *Indian Journal of International Law* 1.

Seyersted, F, 'Objective International Personality of Intergovernmental Organizations: Do their capacities really depend upon the conventions establishing them?' (1964) 34 *Nordisk Tidsskrift for International Ret* 3.

Shucksmith, C, 'Building Human Security through Humanitarian Protection and Assistance: The Potential of the International Committee of the Red Cross' (2017) *Journal of Conflict Transformation and Security*.

Silverman, D, *Interpreting Qualitative Data: Methods for Analysing Talk, Text and Interaction*, 3rd edn (London, Sage, 2006).

Sivakumaran, S, 'International Humanitarian Law' in D Moeckli, S Shah and S Sivakumaran (eds), *International Human Rights Law* (Oxford, Oxford University Press, 2010).

Sivakumaran, S, 'Re-envisioning the International Law of Armed Conflict' (2011) 22(1) *European Journal of International Law* 219.

Sivakumaran, S, *The Law of Non-International Armed Conflict* (Oxford, Oxford University Press, 2012) 36.
Slaughter, A-M, 'Security, Solidarity, and Sovereignty: The Grand Themes of UN Reform' (2005) 99(3) *American Journal of International Law* 619.
Smith, R, *Textbook on International Human Rights Law*, 6th edn (Oxford, Oxford University Press, 2013).
Stearns, JK, *Dancing in the Glory of Monsters: The Collapse of the Congo and the Great War of Africa* (New York, Public Affairs, 2011).
Stearns, J, Luff, J, Kiepe, T and Nash, J, *From CNDP to M23: The Evolution of an Armed Movement in Eastern Congo (Usalama Project)* (London, Rift Valley Institute, 2012).
Suter, K, *An International Law of Guerrilla Warfare: The Global Politics of Law-Making* (Basingstoke, Palgrave Macmillan, 1984).
Tadjbakhsh, S and Chenoy, AM, *Human Security: Concepts and Implications* (London, Routledge, 2007).
Taylor, P, *International Cooperation Today: The European and Universal Pattern* (London, Elek, 1971).
Teitel, RG, *Humanity's Law* (Oxford, Oxford University Press, 2011).
Thakur, R and Newman, E (eds), *Broadening Asia's Security and Discourse Agenda* (Tokyo, UN University Press, 2004).
Thakur, R, *The United Nations, Peace and Security: From Collective Security to the Responsibility to Protect* (Cambridge, Cambridge University Press, 2006).
Thurer, D, 'Dunant's Pyramid: Thoughts on the "Humanitarian Space"' (2007) 89 *IRRC* 47.
Torreblanca, G. 'The International Committee of the Red Cross and Human Rights Law' in R Kolb, and G Gaggioli, (eds), *Research Handbook on Human Rights and Humanitarian Law* (Cheltenham, Edward Elgar, 2013).
Torrente, N de, 'Humanitarian Action under Attack: Reflections on the Iraq War' (2004) 17(1) *Harvard Human Rights Journal* 2 in Abiew, KF, 'Humanitarian Action under Fire: Reflections on the Role of NGOs in Conflict and Post-Conflict Situations' (2012) 19(2) *International Peacekeeping* 203.
Trefon, T (ed), *Reinventing Order in the Congo: How People Respond to State Failure in Kinshasa* (London, Zed Books, 2004).
Trenholm, J, et al, 'The Global, the Ethic and the Gendered War: Women and rape in Eastern Democratic Republic of Congo' (2016) 23(4) *Gender, Place and Culture: A Journal of Feminist Geography* 484.
Truger, A, 'Operationalisation through Training: Human Security Training and Education for Peace Building' in W Benedek, MC Ketteman and M Möstl (eds), *Mainstreaming Human Security in Peace Operations and Crisis Management: Policies, Problems, Potential* (London, Routledge, 2011).
Tunamsifu, SP, 'The Right to Justice: A challenge for survivors of conflict-related sexual violence in the Eastern Congo' (2015) 15(2) *African Human Rights Law Journal* 473.
Turner, T, *The Congo Wars: Conflict, Myth and Reality* (New York, Zed Books, 2007).
Turns, D, 'Targets' in ND White and C Henderson (eds), *Research Handbook on International Conflict and Security Law: Jus ad Bellum, Jus in Bello and Jus Post Bellum* (Cheltenham, Edward, 2013).

UNDP, *Human Development Report 1994* (UNDP, Oxford, Oxford University Press, 1994).

Upadhyaya, P, 'Human Security, Humanitarian Intervention, and Third World Concerns' (2004–05) 33 *Denver Journal of International Law and Policy* 71.

Virally, M, 'Classification of International Organizations: A Legal Approach' in G Abi-Saab, *The Concept of International Organizations* (UNESCO, Paris 1981).

Visscher, C de, *Theory and Reality in Public International Law* (Princeton, Princeton University Press, 1968).

Vité, S, 'Typology of Armed Conflicts in International Humanitarian Law: Legal Concepts and Actual Situations' (2009) 91 *IRRC* 69.

Weber, C, *Simulating Sovereignty: Intervention, the State and Symbolic Exchange* (Cambridge, Cambridge University Press, 1995).

Weiss, TG, 'Humanitarian Action in War Zones' in J Nederveen Pieterse, *World Orders in the Making* (Basingstoke, Institute of Social Studies, Macmillan, 1998).

Weissbrodt, D, 'Humanitarian Law in Armed Conflict: The Role of International Nongovernmental Organizations' (1987) 24(3) *Journal of Peace Research* 297.

West, K, *Agents of Altruism: The Expansion of Humanitarian NGO's in Rwanda and Afghanistan* (Aldershot Ashgate, 2001).

Wemmers, J-A, *Reparation for Victims of Crimes Against Humanity: The Healing Role of Reparation'* (London, Routledge, 2014).

Werner, A-R, *La Croix-Rouge et Les Conventions de Genève* (Geneva, Georg & Cie, 1943).

Wessel, RA, 'Revisiting the International Legal Status of the EU' (2000) 5 *European Foreign Affairs Review* 507.

West, K, *Agents of Altruism: The Expansion of Humanitarian NGOs in Rwanda and Afghanistan* (Aldershot, Ashgate, 2001).

White, ND, *Keeping the Peace* (Manchester, Manchester University Press, 1993).

White, ND, *The Law of International Organisations* (Manchester, Manchester University Press, 2005).

White, ND, *The Law of International Organisations*, 3rd edn (Manchester, Manchester University Press, 2017).

Whittle, D, 'Peacekeeping in Conflict: The Intervention Brigade, MONUSCO, and the Application of International Humanitarian Law to United Nations Forces' (2015) 46 *Georgetown Journal of International Law* 837.

Wortel, E, 'Humanitarians and their Moral Stance in War: The Underlying Values' (2009) 91 *IRRC* 779.

Wright, Q, 'The Outlawry of War and the Law of War' (1953) 47(3) *American Journal of International Law* 365.

Yin, RK, *Case Study Research: Design and Methods*, 4th edn (London, Sage, 2009).

# Index


activities *see* interviews about activities
Afghanistan 136
agreements creating legal framework 43–4
Amerasinghe, CFR 31
*American Journal of International Law* 62
Anderson, M 136
Annan, Kofi 95–6, 100–1, 131, 183
Appia, Louis 25
Argentina 60
armed conflict and other situations of violence
  international human rights law (IHRL) 64–73, 175, 183
    development 67–8
    humanitarian core 66–7, 68–70, 73–4
    other situations of violence 67
    UN cooperation 71–3
  international humanitarian law 64–6
  *jus ad bellum* 58, 62, 177
  *jus in bello* (humanitarian) 58–9, 62, 78, 177
  key issues/conclusion xxiii, 57–8, 73–4
  laws of war 58–64
    development 59–64
    *jus ad bellum* 58, 62, 177
    *jus in bello* (humanitarian) 58–9, 62, 78, 177
    laws of war/law of peace, distinction 63–4
    pacifist ideology 60
    supranational organisation, ICRC as main 62–3
  non-international armed conflicts (NIACS) xvi–xvii, 12
    legal framework 70–3
  protected persons' protection 65
  *see also* Democratic Republic of Congo (DRC)
Armenian massacres 79
Assembly/Assembly Council 14
assured basic income *see under* economic security
Atlantic Charter (1941) 62
Autesserre, S 138, 162–3

Brandt Commission 98–9
Brazil 60
breach of mandate 53–4
Brownlie, I 40
Brussels Conference (1874) 59
budget 16
Bugnion, F 6, 9, 22, 80

Carlist War, Third 59
Casalin, D 4
Cassese, A 84, 85
Central African Republic 106
Charnovitz, S 31
Chimni, BS 95
civil capacity 65
civil society organisations 136–8
Cluster Munitions Convention 2008 109
post-Cold War 24
Collier, P 133
Colombia 139
Committee on Economic, Social and Cultural Rights (CESCR) 110, 130
Committee of Five (International Committee for Relief of the Wounded) 25–6
Common Understanding of Human Security 102–3
communities dialogue *see under* Democratic Republic of Congo (DRC)
Concert of Europe 23
Congo *see* Democratic Republic of Congo (DRC)
constituent treaty *see under* international legal personality
Convention against Transnational Organized Crime and its Protocols 2000 109
Convention for the Amelioration of the Condition of the Wounded in Armies in the Field (Geneva 1864) *see* Geneva Conventions
Convention on the Rights of the Child, Protocols to 2000 109
Corbett, PE 62
*Corfu Channel* case 81
Cornell, D 88–9
corporal punishment prohibition 65
Council of Delegates 6, 7–8
crimes against humanity 79
Cuba 101–2
customary law 45

Democratic Republic of Congo (DRC)
  armed forces' composition 153–4
  armed groups 170

communities dialogue 169–70, 172
First Congo War 149–50
Second Congo War 150–2
current situation 147–8
detention assistance 159
dissemination of IHL 158, 170
economic security 166–71, 173
food security 164–6, 173
healthcare assistance 158–62
core activities 158, 159–60
hospitals 161
training needs 161–2
ICRC involvement 155–9
Inter-Congolese Dialogue 150, 152–3
key issues/conclusion xxiv, 148–9, 172–3
Lusaka Ceasefire Agreement 151–2
microeconomic initiatives (MEIs) 168–9
MONUSCO (UN Stabilization Mission in the DRC) 154, 157, 158, 173
national society management 171
people displacement 168
perceptions of ICRC 157–8
protection and assistance involvement 156–7
sexual-violence-related counselling 162–4
socioeconomic development 167–8
state sovereignty 182–3
transitional period 153
UN involvement 154–5
wars/conflict 149–55, 172
water access 164–6, 173
*see also* armed conflict and other situations of violence
Deng, FM 9 *see*
detention assistance *see under* Democratic Republic of Congo (DRC)
Directorate 15
dissemination of IHL *see under* Democratic Republic of Congo (DRC)
Droege, C 69
Dufour, General 25
Dumbarton Oaks Conversations 24–5
Dunant, Henry 1, 25, 26, 57, 114, 127

early recovery 122–8, 144
elements 122–3
food, right to 125–7
health and well-being 125, 126
intersection of food, health, shelter and water needs 124–8
practical initiatives 123–4
water, right to 126
economic security 128–34
assured basic income 130
definition/practice 128–9
Democratic Republic of Congo (DRC) 166–71, 173
development/human development 130–2
local population inclusion 129
official policy 130
production interventions 129
socioeconomic activities 132–4
*The Economist* 95
EcoSec Unit 134
Enlightenment 67

Falk, R 95
*Financial Times* 131
First World War 60, 63, 64
food, right to *see under* early recovery
food security *see under* Democratic Republic of Congo (DRC)

Gaza 106
Geneva Conventions xvii–xix, xxi–xxii, xxiv, 175–6, 179–80, 183
armed conflict 57, 59, 64–5, 68–9, 72, 74
Convention for the Amelioration of the Condition of the Wounded in Armies in the Field (Geneva 1864) 59
Democratic Republic of Congo (DRC) 148–9, 160, 170, 172–3
governance of IRCRCM 3, 7, 10, 12
humanity, as core principle 76, 80, 85, 87, 89
international legal personality 26–7, 37, 43, 46–9, 55–6
interviews about activities 114–16, 119–22, 127, 143–4
neutrality definitions 85
new humanitarianism 97–8, 100
post-WWII 64, 68, 69–73
genocide 99
governance of IRCRCM
cooperation/coordination 16–17
Council of Delegates 6, 7–8
ICRC *see* International Committee of the Red Cross (ICRC)
International Conference *see* International Conference of IRCRCM
International Federation of the Red Cross 10–11
key issues/conclusion xxii, 1–2, 17–18
mission 1
national societies (Red Cross and Red Crescent) 9–10
Standing Commission *see* Standing Commission of IRCRCM
Grotius, H 23
*Grundnorm see under* new humanitarianism

Hague Convention (1907) 59, 78
Martens clause 77, 78
Hartwig, M 38
headquarters agreements
international legal personality 50, 52, 55
interviews about activities 117, 134
health and well-being *see under* early recovery
healthcare assistance *see under* Democratic Republic of Congo (DRC)
Henckaerts, J-M 87
Herzegovina insurrection 59
High-Level Panel on Threats, Challenges and Change (Secretary-General's) 96
Human Development Report (HDR) 100–1, 107, 109–10, 130
human security 92–3, 97–107, 179–81
broad threats 98–9, 104–6
civil society participation 103
criticism 101–2
defining process 98–107
economic, social, cultural rights as minimum core 108–10
elements 100–2
on the ground practice 110–11
holistic approach 109
human-centric challenges 97, 111–12, 179–80
ICRC application 107
and IHRL/IHL complementarity 107–11
international law as regulatory instrument 108–9
maximum of available resources 110
minimum essential levels 110
narrow threats 104, 105
neutrality balance 97–8
non-military threats 99
people-centred/context-specific/prevention responses 103
permeation of humanity principle 111
post-conflict reconstruction 106–7
state threats 98
transboundary violations 99
treaty law exemplars 109
post-Westphalian sovereignty 93–4, 103–4
human-centric challenges *see under* human security; humanity, as core principle
humanity, as core principle
crimes against humanity 79
definitions/meaning 76–8, 88–9, 178–9
history of 78–9
human-centric concepts and ideas, permeation 83–4, 89
impartiality/neutrality/independence 75–6
inherent understanding 77
inhumanity 77, 81
IRCRCM definition 80–1
judicial interpretations 81–4
*jus in bello* 58–9, 62, 78, 177
key issue/conclusions xxiii, 76, 88–9
neutrality *see* neutrality
*see also* new humanitarianism
*Humanity's Law* (Teitel) 66, 177
Hungary, Soviet invasion 70

Ignatieff, M 69
'In larger Freedom' (Annan) 100–1, 131
inalienability of rights 65
inhumanity *see under* humanity, as core principle
INTELSAT (International Telecommunications Satellite Organisations) 29–30
intergovernmental conferences 19
intergovernmental organisations *see under* organisation types
Internal Audit Unit 15
internal sovereignty *see under* sovereignty as responsibility
International Committee of the Red Cross (ICRC)
armed conflict impact on local people/communities xv–xix, 11–12
Assembly/Assembly Council 14
budget 16
Directorate 15
foundation 26–7
governance 13–15
humanitarian initiatives as neutral intermediaries xvii–xviii, 13
hybrid nature 13
infrastructure 12
Internal Audit Unit 15
international armed conflicts 12
as international organisation 13
non-international armed conflicts (NIACS) xvi–xvii, 12
as private association (Swiss domestic law) 13
protection and assistance role xv–xvi, xviii, 175
protracted armed conflict xv
research method/methodology
interview method xx–xxii
interviews with delegates 181–3
methodology of research xix–xxii
primary/meta question xviii–xix
structure of book xxii–xxiv
sub-questions xix
International Conference of IRCRCM
agenda 5
authority of decisions 5–7
concept note 5

crisis/disasters/health and social care issues 5
functions 4–5
guides to state parties' objectives 7
as humanitarian forum 3, 5
national societies and governments, equal footing/consensus 3–4
International Covenant on Civil and Political Rights (ICCPR) 108
International Covenant on Civil and Political Rights (ICESCR) obligations 110
International Federation of the Red Cross 10–11
international human rights law (IHRL) *see under* armed conflict
international humanitarian law (IHL)
dissemination *see under* Democratic Republic of Congo (DRC)
*see also under* armed conflict
International Law Association Committee on Non-State Actors 34
international legal personality
agreements creating legal framework 43–4
aims and objectives 46–7
autonomous actions 50–1, 54
breach of mandate 53–4
claims 42
constituent treaty 37–8
customary law 45
essential component 56
formal contexts 40–1
functions and rights 45–50
headquarters agreements *see* headquarters agreements
humanitarian initiatives 49–50, 54
impartial/neutral humanitarianism 47–9
independent activity 35
intention to be ILP 41–2
key issues/conclusion xxii, 21, 54–6
lead agency 48
legal process, immunity from 44–5
mandate interpretation 51–2
objective existence as organisation 38–40
organisations with 19–20
performance implying 39–40
privileges and immunities 44–5
recognition of 34–5
*Reparations Case* 35–7
separate will/will theory 39, 45–6, 55
sociological circumstances 37
Swiss Civil Code 21–2, 56
treaties 42–4
United Nations 20–1
*see also* organisation types
internees, complaints/petitions from 65
Interview Guide 2014 191 *Appendix 2*
Interview Guide 2016 185 *Appendix 1*
interviews about activities
delegate reflections 114–22, 181–2
early recovery *see* early recovery
economic security *see* economic security
flexibility of mandate 119–20
on the ground pragmatism 113–14, 118–19
headquarters agreements *see* headquarters agreements
as humanitarians 121, 144
initiative right 116–17
international humanitarian law (IHL) 117–18
interviewees 113–22
key issues/conclusion xxiii, 114, 143–4, 181–2
local ownership *see* local ownership
megatrends 142–3
overreach consequences 119
prevention of conflict 141–3
protracted armed conflicts 116, 120–2, 142
recovery from conflict 122
role changes 121–2
sui generis status 114
victims of conflicts 115

Jackson, Robert 79
*jus ad bellum* 58, 62, 177
*jus in bello* 58–9, 62, 78, 177

Kabila, Joseph 151–2
Kabila, Laurent 150, 151
Kagame, Paul 150
Kellenberger, J 69, 71
Kellog-Briand Pact (1928) 60
Kinshasa 166
Klabbers, J 39, 40
Korean War 70
Krähenbühl, Pierre 128
Krause, K 105
Kreijen, G 149
Kunz, JL 58, 60, 61, 64

Lamb, C 4
Lauterpacht, H 63, 79
laws of war *see* armed conflict and other situations of violence, laws of war
Lederach, JP 137, 143
legal personality *see* international legal personality
legal process, immunity from 44–5
Lieber Code (1863) 59

Lincoln, President Abraham 59
local ownership 134–41, 144–5
  Advisory Service access 134
  civil society organisations 136–8
  definition/approaches 135–6
  humanitarian diplomacy role 135
  national societies 9–10, 119, 139–41
  ongoing presence 134–5
  sustainability 138–9
Lusaka Ceasefire Agreement 151–2

Macedonia 60
Martens, Fyodor, clause 77, 78
Maunoir, Theodore 25
Maurer, Peter 158, 178
microeconomic initiatives (MEIs) 168–9
Milanovic, M 65–6
military occupation situations 65
Millennium Development Goals 101
Mobutu, President 149, 150, 167
MONUSCO (UN Stabilization Mission in the DRC) 154, 157, 158, 173
Morsink, J 69
Moynier, Gustave 25, 37

national societies (Red Cross and Red Crescent) 9–10, 119, 139–41
national society management *see under* Democratic Republic of Congo (DRC)
*Naulilaa* case 81–2
neutrality
  confidence of authorities/population 86
  definition/meaning 84
  elements 85
  expansion of roles 87
  on the ground challenges 88
  and humanisation of international law 85–6
  non-discrimination 86
  and non-state actors (NSAs) 87–8
  standing apart from contending parties 85
new humanitarianism
  *Grundnorm* 91
  human security *see* human security
  key issues xxiii, 91–3, 111–12
  practice changes 92, 178
  sovereignty *see* sovereignty as responsibility
  Statutes' definition 91
  *see also* humanity, as core principle
*Nicaragua* case 82
non-governmental organisations 31–3
  ICRC as 31–2, 32–3
  meaning 31
  recent international conferences 32
non-international armed conflicts (NIACS) *see under* armed conflict and other situations of violence
non-intervention principle *see under* sovereignty as responsibility
non-state actors (NSAs) *see under* neutrality
Noortmann, M 108–9

Oberleitner, G 91
Office of the President 14–15
Okimoto, K 69
Olivet, Georges 42
Olsen, L 136
Organisation for Security and Co-operation in Europe (OSCE) 35
organisation types
  intergovernmental conferences 19
  intergovernmental organisations
    associated by states 24–7
    definition components 24
    established by international agreement 27–8
    proliferation 23–4
  non-governmental organisations *see* non-governmental organisations
  private international organisations 29–30
  sui generis entities 33, 54, 114, 175–7
  *see also* international legal personality
Ottawa Treaty 1997 109
Owen, T 102
ownership *see* local ownership

pacifist ideology 60
Pact of Paris (1928) 60–1
Palme Commission 98, 99
penal procedure 65
people displacement *see under* Democratic Republic of Congo (DRC)
Peters, A 91
St Petersburg Declaration (1868) 59, 78
Petitpierre, Max 70
Pictet, JS 59, 63, 69, 80
Portmann, R 37
Pouligny, B 136, 138
President's Office 14–15
prevention of conflict *see under* interviews about activities
prisoners of war 61–2
private international organisations 29–30
privileges and immunities 44–5
protection and assistance
  Democratic Republic of Congo (DRC) 156–7
  ICRC role xv–xvi, xviii, 175
  protected persons' protection, armed conflict 65

Red Crescent, national societies 9–10
Red Cross
  International Federation of the Red Cross 10–11
  national societies 9–10, 119, 139–41
refugees 99
*Reparation for Injuries* advisory opinion 37, 39, 40, 55
*Reparations Case* 35–7, 39
research method/methodology *see under* International Committee of the Red Cross (ICRC)
revolutions/social disturbances 60
Roberts, D 102
Rome Statute of the ICC 1998 109
  Rome Statute on crimes against humanity 82–3
Rwandan genocide 150

St Petersburg Declaration (1868) 59, 78
Sandoz, Y 37
Schindler, D 60
Second World War 61–2, 64, 67, 93, 107, 177, 179
Security Council Summit Statement 99
sexual-violence-related counselling *see under* Democratic Republic of Congo (DRC)
Seyersted, F 39
Slaughter, A-M 96, 99
Smith, Rhona 86–7
social disturbances/revolutions 60
socioeconomic development *see* economic security; *under* Democratic Republic of Congo (DRC)
Solferino, battle of 12, 17, 25, 59, 114, 127
sovereignty as responsibility 92, 93–7
  as ICRC principle 96–7
  internal sovereignty 94–5
  non-intervention principle 94
  totalitarian states 94
  UN membership 94–5
  Westphalian sovereignty-94 93
Standing Commission of IRCRCM 8–9
  coordination role 8
  functions 8–9
  internal rules/structures 9
  and national societies 9
state sovereignty *see under* Democratic Republic of Congo (DRC)
statutes of IRCRCM 2–3
  comprehensive nature 2
  legal nature 2–3
Stearns, JK 149
Sudan 118
sui generis entities 33, 54, 114, 175–7
Swiss Civil Code 13, 17, 21–2, 54
Syria 106, 175

*Tadic* appeals decision 73
Teitel, RG 66, 83, 91–2, 152, 177
*Tharcisse Muvunyi* case 45
Thirty Years War 58
Torreblanca, G 66
Torture Convention, Protocol 2002 109
torture prohibition 65
totalitarian states *see under* sovereignty as responsibility
Trefon, T 166
Turns, D 78

Ukraine 175
United Nations 20–1
  *Reparations Case* 35–7
  war prevention policy 63–4
Universal Declaration of Human Rights (UDHR) 67–8, 70

Veale, FJP 61
Venezuela 60
victims of conflicts *see under* interviews about activities
Vienna Convention on the Law of Treaties 27
Vienna Declaration (1993) 108
Vienna Workshop on International Constitutional Law (2008) 96, 102

Wallendahl, A 39, 40
war, laws of *see* armed conflict and other situations of violence, laws of war
water access *see under* Democratic Republic of Congo (DRC)
water, right to *see under* early recovery
Westphalian sovereignty 93–4, 103–4
World Summit 100–1, 102

www.ingramcontent.com/pod-product-compliance
Ingram Content Group UK Ltd.
Pitfield, Milton Keynes, MK11 3LW, UK
UKHW021907150926
475560UK00003B/240

9 781509 908172